TO RIDE THE STORM

26/June
2ᵈ Jan '97

TO RIDE THE STORM
The 1980 Bristol 'Riot' and the State

Harris Joshua and
Tina Wallace
with the assistance of
Heather Booth

 Heinemann

Heinemann Educational Ltd
22 Bedford Square, London WC1B 3HH
LONDON EDINBURGH MELBOURNE AUCKLAND
HONG KONG SINGAPORE KUALA LUMPUR NEW DELHI
IBADAN NAIROBI JOHANNESBURG
EXETER (NH) KINGSTON PORT OF SPAIN

ISBN 0 435 82481 3 cased
ISBN 0 435 82482 1 paper

Phototypesetting by Inforum Ltd, Portsmouth
Printed in Great Britain by Biddles Ltd, Guildford, Surrey

Contents

Preface

The research for this book was started in September 1980, in direct response to the events in St Paul's, Bristol a few months earlier. We felt that there was an urgent need for an analysis and considered response to the issues and questions that April 2, 1980 had posed. In pursuit of this we had to become involved in a wide range of disciplines, methodologies and literatures, including history, sociology and law. These all had relevance, and in this book we have attempted to weld them together in order to try and produce a better understanding of the significance of the 'Bristol Riot' and the subsequent state and media responses to it. Specialists of each discipline are asked to bear with the inevitably, at times, cavalier treatment of their particular subject. A primary concern throughout this research had been to try and make the research accessible to a wide, interested readership, rather than to produce a too detailed, and possibly obscure academic tome.

A large number of people were involved in these events on 2 April 1980, and afterwards: all of them, with the exception of one group, appear in this book under their own names. For a number of reasons it was decided to make an exception of the police officers who were on the streets of St Paul's on that afternoon. The primary reason for this decision was that because of the number of different officers the text was difficult to follow, there were too many names and too many stories making the argument hard to find. So we decided to identify the police officers involved by describing them by their various characteristics, such as which force they were in, and hope that this makes the book clearer. A second reason was that while the activities of individual policemen were very important to the people on the streets, our concern was to focus more on the role of the police as a force rather than to highlight the behaviour of named individuals. To do this would have detracted from the wider significance of the argument. The 16 defendants are named in the book, because it was they who had their names in the newspapers, who had to undergo the ordeal of a lengthy trial and live for months with the prospect of possibly spending years in prison. They were pulled out of the crowd and were chosen to stand trial for the actions of the wider community; they were the people who experienced most sharply one of the main responses to the Bristol events.

We would like to thank several people who have offered practical help and encouragement during the course of this research, particularly

Annie Phizacklea and Steve Fenton of Bristol University who helped to get the project off the ground. We want to thank Francis Salandy of the St Paul's Advice Centre and the St Paul's Defence Committee, and Barbara Thompson of the Bristol CRE for their hospitality and invaluable help in St Paul's; and Carmen Beckford and Peter Courtier, also of the Bristol CRE who provided written and verbal information. Desmond Pierre helped us by making available a lot of court material collected by himself and other members of the defence committee. Our special thanks go to Graham Reid, of the Bristol Resource Centre, who made available a great deal of essential material which has been used throughout the book. Two lawyers, Ms Gareth Pierce and Mr Edward Rees provided us with a great deal of law material, and advice relating to the legal and court issues, and their comments were much appreciated. Annie Phizacklea and Robert Moore read the drafts of the manuscript at an early stage and their useful criticisms helped to improve the text. Finally we want to thank Christine Dunn and Rose Goodwin for all their very hard work on the word processor, for which we are very grateful.

This research was a response to the events in Bristol and while it was carried out within the Research Unit on Ethnic Relations, it was not a part of the main programme of that Unit. Ultimate responsibility for the book is ours and the views presented are not necessarily those of the Social Science Research Council, nor those of the SSRC's Research Unit on Ethnic Relations.

Acknowledgements

The authors and publishers would like to thank the following for permission to use their photographs in this book: Julio Etchart (photos 1–3); Bristol United Press Ltd (photos 4–5); David Hoffman (photos 6–8).

Introduction

'This was a preparation for the beginning'
(Resident of St Paul's, Bristol: *Guardian*, 5 April 1980)

Such were the prophetic sentiments expressed by one black woman in the wake of the crowd violence in St Paul's, Bristol on the afternoon and evening of 2 April, 1980. Not only were the remarks founded on the apparently accepted inevitability of violent confrontation between black citizens and the state, but they were proclaimed for all with ears to hear that this confrontation was only in its infancy. Confirming that warning, and indicating that Bristol was no freak occurrence but rather symptomatic and expressive of the crisis which racial contradictions in the United Kingdom have now reached, racial and race related violence have since occurred in almost every city with a black population. Taking only major instances, the list would include Brixton, Finsbury Park, Peckham, Southall, and Lewisham in London, Toxteth in Liverpool, Moss Side in Manchester; Birmingham, Leicester, Wolverhampton, and Bradford 1981, and Brixton in 1982.

The primary concern of this book is with the substance and implications of those events that came to be labelled the 'Bristol riot'. We shall be concerned with these events principally from a political perspective: that is to say, with the crowd violence as an expression of the political struggles and aspirations of black communities settled in Britain, and with the political processes by which that violence commanded and compelled the attentions of powerful institutions and agencies. Except for the media, the institutions and agencies in question are those located within the state. Thus we ask, how was the crowd violence in Bristol understood, explained and responded to, within and by the state?

Given this orientation, and given that we shall be involved in what is essentially an empirical study, some theoretical indication of what we mean by the state, and how that meaning informs our work, is necessary. It is not our intention to enter into a detailed theoretical analysis but rather to indicate the broad parameters within which our understanding of the state falls.

Let us make clear from the beginning that we do not subscribe to that liberal-democratic view of the state as essentially neutral. Rather in a class divided society, the state reflects and condenses class interests and conflicts (Poulantzas, 1973). The class interests referred to are primarily those of capital and labour. These, however, are not uniform,

St. Pauls, Bristol.

indivisible interests, and conflicts also occur between the interests of different sections of capital and different groupings of labour. The state is the principal *means* through which social classes and groupings exercise political power. What therefore is expressed in the content of state activities is the complex *relations* within and between capital and labour. As those relations are characterised by inequalities, so these inequalities, and the means by which they are reproduced, are also to be found within the state:

For the institutional structure of the state has unequal and asymetrical effects on the ability of different social forces to realise their interest through political struggle.
(Jessop, 1978, p. 12)

The argument here is not that the state simply acts in the interests of capital while negating the interests of labour; rather, both basic interests find expression within the state in the power relationships that exist between them. The same equally applies to dominant and sub-ordinate sections of capital, strong and weak groupings of labour.

Given this complex interaction of interests, in conjunction with changes and shifts in them over time, the state cannot be described as unified or monolithic. Nor, for the same reasons, can the content of its activities be said to be predetermined. Thus the purpose of this book is not simply to examine the state's responses to 'THE BRISTOL RIOT', but to trace how these responses came about at both the political and organisational levels of the state. Clearly to pursue such a project, our notion of the state must include race. This, it must be stressed, does not change the basic model outlined above, but adds to and extends it.

If the state as is argued reflects, condenses and is part of the relation between capital and labour, then it is the *specificity* of that relation that matters in respect of race. Patently, black labour is not just another category of labour, like skilled/unskilled, mental/manual. Within the labour force it occupies a distinctive and subordinated position that is first a product of those aspects of its relation to capital that is specific, and secondly a product of its relations with other groupings of workers. The exact nature of these relations and of black subordination will obviously differ from period to period and these differences are dealt with in Chapters 1 and 6. What is important here is the consideration that not only are the relations that produce black subordination ex-pressed within the state but the state is also part of the means through which that subordination is imposed and reproduced. It may not be deduced from this that black labour, the black population and its class allies are without some access to and influence upon the state. Indeed, in the post-war context these contradictory interests and influences are clearly to be seen in the objective form of the state with regards to race – i.e. immigration legislation based on race and its enforcement agencies on the one hand, and anti-discrimination legislation and its bureaucratic complex on the other. There is no doubt, however, which has been dominant, and on this issue we can find no reason to disagree with an observation made by Martin Luther King some eighteen years ago:

> Immigration laws based on colour . . . would eventually encourage all the vestiges of racism and endanger all the democratic principles which this great country held dear.
> (*The Times*, 7 December 1964)

It is within this context that we approach the state in relation to its understandings of, and reactions to, the crowd violence in Bristol. From a methodological point of view we shall be concerned firstly with individual institutions and agencies within the state, and the interrelations between them: particularly we focus on Parliament, various departments of national and local government, the Courts, the police, and that network of agencies whose exclusive purpose it is to manage race relations. The book thus builds up a case study of the way in which Bristol came to be understood and dealt with.

First, however, in Chapter 1, we contextualise the area of study. Bristol was not the first instance of collective racial violence in recent times as anyone familiar with the 1976 Notting Hill Carnival will be aware. In fact, Britain has had a history of collective racial violence spanning the present century. In seeking the historical antecedents of Bristol we therefore first looked at this violence, its causes and changing patterns. Our purpose here is not only to lay the framework for a wider understanding of the phenomenon, but to arrive at modern forms of collective racial violence from some other perspective than current circumstance. Only too easily can Bristol come to be 'explained' as purely an inevitable effect of the current economic crisis.

Then the book moves on to a specific case study of state and media responses to the violence in Bristol. The first question posed is how was the crowd violence in Bristol reconstructed as a public event? The process of reconstructing a coherent and comprehensible account of an event is the essential first stage in defining, understanding and explaining it. In Bristol, that process was largely the responsibility of the state on the one hand, and the media on the other. Both combined to produce what effectively became the 'public knowledge' of the event. In the absence of other sources of information, it was this knowledge with its official and media labels, ascriptions and representations that came to dominate the debate about the violence and in part to determine 'appropriate' responses. This knowledge was widely accepted and has structured analysis of the event for most people, including academics. In this book we go behind this common knowledge and understanding and assess its veracity and validity: if it is a flawed picture, then so too must be any subsequent analysis and policy initiatives that follow from it.

It is the ways in which 'what happened in St Paul's?' was reconstructed that form the subject of Chapters 2 and 3. Our objective in these chapters is to look at how official and media descriptions came about. Given the obvious difficulties inherent in accurately recording such events, how did officials and journalists come to their definitions and what functions did these serve both within individual institutions and within the larger state? It is only through an understanding of the processes by which highly complex and emotive disturbances like Bristol are transformed into simple, easily understood public events to which ready explanations and solutions suggest themselves, that the dominant accounts may be challenged. By analysing the way in which these accounts were structured we resist the easy acceptance of terms like 'riot' and challenge the dominant official perspective which defined the violence purely in criminal 'law and order' terms.

In Chapters 4 and 5 we explore in detail the political responses of the state. There could be little doubt that for the state the violence in Bristol would pose an immediate crisis of law and order. In scale and intensity, the violence was then without precedent in post-war Britain. But how would that law and order concern articulate and co-exist with other seemingly undeniable dimensions – in particular, race and the inner city? There is nothing new in this basic issue: the tensions between law and order and policing on the one hand, and race relations and urban deprivation on the other have been a definitive feature of the political climate of the 1970's and early 1980's.

In Chapter 4 we document the way in which race and inner city perspectives were squeezed out of Government responses, while preparations ensued to reorganise police procedures for the suppression of any future revolt. This is not as might be supposed simply an inevitable consequence of a Conservative Government elected on a law and order ticket, but is related directly to the management of race within the various departments and levels of the state, and in particular to the pre-eminence of the Home Office in any law and order situation. In Chapter 5 we concentrate exclusively on the courts and the law. It is here, in so far as the state was concerned, that the issues raised by Bristol were worked out. Rather than a public inquiry into these issues, they were effectively ignored and instead half a million pounds was spent on trying sixteen participants on the charge of riot. The intense conflict that focused around this charge, the composition of the jury, the nature of police evidence in court, and the legal definition of riot, highlighted some of the political issues involved.

In the final chapter, we attempt firstly to locate our understanding of the crowd violence and the responses of the state in the wider economic and political crisis of the 70's and early 80's. Secondly we seek to show the implications of the manner in which the state responded to Bristol, for the massive and almost nationwide violence of 1981. The central theme running throughout our analysis is that collective racial violence in all its forms is associated with and a product of racial subordination. The form the violence took in Bristol in 1980 and elsewhere in 1981 constituted a revolt against that subordination and in particular the role of the state in facilitating and perpetuating it. As such the violence was not incidental, and its meanings and significances are to be found in the political activities of black associational forms in the 1960's and 70's. This violence was not revolutionary violence but a reactive attempt to gain access to state power, and to change the stance and role of the state on race. Though the attempt had some limited success, our conclusion is that the response of the state was basically repressive. Repression may be a politically expedient 'solution' in the short term; in the longer term the problem returns again and again.

Part I Background

1 Race and Collective Violence – an Historical Overview

On the 2 April 1980, the St Paul's area of Bristol became the scene of a prolonged and violent confrontation between the police and a predominantly black crowd. That confrontation was significant not only because of the scale and intensity of the violence – which included the burning and looting of private property, but also because race and racial issues were clearly involved. Additionally, events in Bristol proved neither to be singular or isolated, little more than a year later the same basic pattern of violence was to be repeated in almost every major city with a black population, precipitating a crisis of race unprecedented in the post-war era, and a crisis of law and order unprecedented since the 1930s.

We are concerned in this book principally with those events that became labelled 'THE BRISTOL RIOT'. More specifically we are concerned with the impact of that 'riot' on the state: how was the 'riot' understood and explained within the state? What were the significances and implications of the political, legal and other policy responses to which those official understandings led? These questions will be the subject of later chapters. Our purpose here is to lay the essential groundwork for a wider understanding of the Bristol 'riot' and of the phenomenon of collective racial violence in Britain in general.

Though 'popular disturbances' and 'crowd violence' have in recent times become of increasing interest to historians and social scientists in Britain, the specific question of collective racial violence has been ignored. This omission cannot be accounted an oversight, or even the result of some mysterious form of selective historical amnesia. Quite simply it is based on the widely held – but mistaken – conviction that there is nothing of substance worthy of study. Thus one major contributor on the subject concluded:

Events of 1958 (the Notting Hill and Nottingham 'race riots')* notwithstanding, there have been no major outbreaks of racial violence in England.
(Grimshaw, 1969, p. 257)
* Our insertion.

This curious assertion of historical 'fact' is neither arbitrary nor accidental. It is founded upon, and consistent with, one of the basic underlying themes within the sociology of race relations. That theme emerges from the historical delimitation of developing metropolitan or domestic race relations to the onset of mass post-war black immigration. Thus, not only does it follow that Britain is thought to have no significant history of race and black settlement in the present century up to the second world war, but by implication the arrival of the first post-war black immigrants comes to represent the first line on an otherwise clean sheet.

In challenging post-war mass black migration as the supposed 'beginnings' of race relations in Britain, we intend to show that Britain has a prior history of race in the present century, and that this history includes major incidents of collective racial violence. Moreover, collective racial violence in Britain – like America – rather than static, has assumed different distinctive forms in different historical periods. Our purpose is more than simply to demonstrate that collective racial violence is not a 'recent arrival', it is to show that Bristol, and other recent instances of street violence, cannot be understood in abstraction from the evolving historical pattern of collective racial violence. Such an abstraction would not only falsely represent the phenomenon as 'new', but imprison the process of explanation within the straightjacket of current circumstances and concerns. As will become clear in later chapters, all too easily did official, media and even sociological understandings of 'The Bristol Riot' comes to focus on such concerns as 'immigrant numbers', 'immigrant urban concentrations', 'immigrant cultural differences', and 'immigrant pathologies'. But as Tilly et al have observed, there exists the danger that in looking at a long term pattern of collective racial violence we slip into the error of attempting to explain only that violence (Tilly et al, 1975). In this chapter violence is undoubtedly our particular window on history, but its significance lies in its relationship to social structure and structural change. It is upon this relationship and the broader conflicts and contradictions implied, that we shall be focusing in successive historical periods.

What then of the terminology we intend to use, and of our approach to collective racial violence and its changing distinctive characteristics?

In employing the term 'collective violence', we seek a more neutral approach than is afforded by such terms as 'riot', 'disorder', 'disturbance' or 'disruption', all of which incorporate definitions and formulations derived from the law, and therefore from the state. The exact legal definition of 'riot' will be addressed more fully in Chapter 5. What concerns us here is that both the legal and wider popular senses of the term constitute an inadequate and necessarily misleading basis from which to approach crowd violence. In its legal context 'riot' lies at the extreme end of a complex of laws dealing with 'public order' and by implication 'disorder'. More popularly riots are defined as a breach of the peace, a sudden outburst, uproar or eruption of violence. Even in law, notions of 'order' and 'disorder' are not as static as many would like to think. Historically both may be seen to change with changing social and political circumstances (Hay, 1975), raising questions concerning by whom, and through what processes, notions of order and disorder are defined and imposed (see Berger and Luckmann, 1966). But our concern with crowd violence is exactly the opposite of legalistic or commonsense notions of disorder. As a form of 'collective', i.e. mass behaviour, instances of crowd violence cannot come into existence unless some commonality of cause is assumed: nor can they continue without some shared rationale. It is often held that that rationale is no more than an agreement to pursue anarchy, violence and destruction. But it must be noted that the violent behaviour involved is rarely indiscriminate or arbitrary; it exhibits a 'social character' in that it is ordered, harnessed and directed at chosen and specific targets. Collective violence cannot be understood or treated as merely a form of rampant criminality. Further, it is only 'sudden' or an 'eruption', if a priori the violence is labelled as irrational and abstracted from the wider social conflicts of which it is a part.

To take a collective, rather than a legalistic or commonsense, approach to crowd violence is only to indicate a general direction. Indeed the approach to crowd violence as collective behaviour has a long history and numerous themes; though not all these themes are able to make a rigorous distinction between the collective and the legal or commonsense dimensions outlined above. Gustave Le Bon, for example – probably the originator of the collective approach in the context of violence – not infrequently represented the crowd as associated with, or composed of, the lower and criminal classes, easily led or manipulated, and exhibiting base, irrational and destructive instincts (Le Bon, 1896). Le Bon, however, was interested in the French crowd as a psychological rather than a social entity. Subsequently, the approach to collective violent behaviour as a consequence of the disintegrative processes within society has dominated the field. Within this rubric, the basic logic is of major social upheaval – i.e. mass population movements, economic recession or decline, industrialisation – subjecting society to inordinate stresses. These disproportionately affect certain individuals or groups who consequently resort to various categories of deviant, anti-social, criminal or violent behaviour. In many formulations a new if different status quo is eventually achieved, whether it is imposed by the state or comes from within the group itself. What is of interest to us here are the different processes by which disorganisation or disintegration are understood. One concept commonly used in this context is 'alienation', used so as to mean a sense of isolation, powerless or not-belonging (Ransford, 1969).

Elsewhere social disorganisation is seen in terms of 'anomie', in conjunction with the partial disruption of traditional norms, social mores and controls which normally act as restraints on anti-social behaviour (Smelser, 1962). Smelser, however, adds an important rider to this in that he sees in the process of re-integration itself a source of even greater potential conflict should displaced, alienated or anomic individuals or groups collectivise their anxieties and hostility into a social movement which comes into conflict with the established order (Smelser, 1966).

Disintegration theories have been powerfully influential in explanations of the specific types of collective violence with which we are concerned – collective racial violence. Fogelson observed of the interracial violence that plagued American cities up to the Second World War:

The riots were inter-racial, violent, reactionary, and ultimately unsuccessful attempts to maintain the racial status quo at times of rapid social change. They were inter-racial because whites, first- and second-generation European immigrants in Chicago and uprooted southerners in Detroit, were the aggressors, and blacks, newcomers themselves, the victims. They were violent because the Whites did not know how to achieve their goals through legitimate means. They were reactionary because the whites hoped to deprive the blacks of freedom of movement, equal access to public accommodation, and other rights which inhere in America whatever their colour.
(Fogelson, 1971, p. 8)

As the patterns of collective racial violence changed in America from communally inter-racial in character to black ghetto uprisings, similar explanatory theories sufficed. The McCone Commission, for example, in assessing the causes of the massive 1965 Watts riots in Los Angeles, held that:

Many (rural blacks) have moved to the city only in the last generation and are totally unprepared to meet the conditions of modern city life. At the core of the cities where they cluster, law and order have only a tenuous hold; the conditions of life itself are often marginal; idleness leads to despair and finally mass violence a momentary relief from this malaise.
(Governor's Commission, 1965, p. 3)

Whether in general, or as specifically applied to collective racial violence, perhaps the most telling criticism of those theories that stress social disorganisation is the question of how collective action comes to be mobilised by marginal, dislocated, socially maladjusted and isolated individuals or groups (Feagin and Hahn, 1973). While conceding that men often find migration, urbanisation, industrialisation, or other forms of major social upheaval bewildering, Tilly et al take the criticism one stage further and question whether these strains necessarily result in anomie (Tilly et al., 1975). To these criticisms might be added the tendency within these theories to conceptualise collective violent behaviour as 'involuntarily caused' by the action of broad impersonal social forces on the individual; in other words mass violence is not a deliberately chosen response, it is ultimately blind and meaningless. Only too frequently – like Le Bon – is a simple equation arrived at: violence is more likely to come from maladjusted marginalised people, such people are more violent.

In contrast, some more recent theories have posed the question of collective violence not as an incidental and mechanistic response to social upheaval and strains, but as part and parcel of the 'normal' repertoire of political strategies employed by groups and classes in all societies. Along with others Hahn and Feagin suggest that:

Historically, collective violence has been part of the regular and normal political life of all nations, part of the process by which competing interest groups maintain power, gain power, or lose power in the process of jockeying for influence and control over governmental and other social institutions. (Hahn and Feagin, 1973, p. 146)

It is not that social upheaval has no part to play in this approach, but as Tilly observes, collective violence cannot be seen as a mere 'side effect' of social strains, rather it is a consequence of the impact of structural changes on the arrangements of 'groups contending for power' or for 'established places in the structure of power' (Tilly, 1972). Thus, instead of the processes of disorganisation leading to meaningless violence, the stress is on group and class cohesion, and the mobilisation of violence to 'complement and extend organised, peaceful attempts . . . to accomplish . . . objectives' (ibid., 342–3).

Clearly, in a number of areas theories stressing group and class cohesion refute disorganisation theories. Further, it would not be inaccurate to describe the former as in many ways inspired by and growing out of the failed propositions of the latter. In this respect the findings of the National Advisory Commission on Civil Disorders (The Kerner Commission) are of interest. Applying the disorganisation approach to the 1967 ghetto uprisings, the Commission supposed that typical riot participants would be '. . . criminal types, over active social deviants, or riff-raff – recent migrant members of an uneducated underclass – alienated from responsible negroes and without broad social or political concern'. However, from the arrest records of twenty-two riot-torn cities, numerous interviews and eye witness accounts, the 'typical rioter' was found to be male, between the ages of 15 and 24, not a migrant but a life long resident of the city, likely to be of the same economic status as his neighbour who did not riot, but somewhat better educated, informed about politics, and more likely to have been a political activist (Kerner Commission, 1968, Part III, pp 73–77). Additionally, in the same report (Supplemental Studies, pp. 221–248) and drawing on a wide range of studies of the 1967 riots, Fogelson and Hill, draw attention to another important finding concerning black participation in, and support for, the riots:

First, that a substantial minority of the Negro population, ranging from roughly 10 to 20 per cent, actively participated in the riots. Second, that the rioters, far from being primarily the riff-raff and outside agitators, were fairly representative of the ghetto communities. And third, that a sizeable minority (or, in some cases a majority) of the negroes who did not riot sympathized with the rioters.

Curiously, it is in the work of E.J. Hobsbawm, G. Rude, and E.P. Thompson and their study of violent crowds in 18th Century England and France, that we find powerful support, both for the findings above, and for the approach to collective violence as political struggle and protest conducted by *ordinary* people in pursuit of identifiable and agreed goals. In his examination of participants in disturbances in 18th century Paris and London, Rude found a representative cross-section of the working classes, involved in what was often highly ordered and 'ritualised' protest informed by coherent, if not fully developed, ideologies. According to Rude these disturbances and the 'associational movements' interest groups, and political demands that inspired them, were an important part of the effective political opposition of the day (1970). Echoing these sentiments Hobsbawm sees his 'Primitive Rebels' as engaged in 'collective bargaining by riot' (Hobsbawm, 1968, 1971). Developing the theme, Hobsbawm indicated how riots impinged upon the political process, and why the phenomenon did not simply 'erupt' and 'disappear':

. . . there was the claim to be considered. The classical mob did not merely riot as protest, but because it expected to achieve something by its riots. It assumed that the authorities would be sensitive to its movements, and probably also that they would make some sort of immediate concession. For the mob was not simply a casual collection of people united for some ad hoc purpose, but in a recognised sense, a permanent entity, even though rarely permanently organised as such. (1971, p. 111)

Likewise in addressing the question concerning the ideas and beliefs underpinning the direct actions of the crowd, E.P. Thompson (1971, pp. 76–136) talks of a 'moral economy' based on traditional notions of rights, liberties and justice:

It is possible to detect in almost every 18th century crowd action some legitimising action. By the notion of legitimation I mean that the men and women in the crowd were informed by the belief that they were defending traditional rights and customs; and in general that they were supported by the wider consensus of the community.

To the extent that this approach focuses on collective violence as political protest, opposition, or dissent, it obviously has more direct application to instances of collective racial violence where black communities confront the coercive forces of the state. Indeed Rude himself saw in the American black rebellion of the 1960's a 'distinct flavour' of the 'pre-industrial riot' in 18th and 19th century Europe (Rude, 1970). But in that this approach to collective violence is based on social groupings competing for power, informed by identifiable ideologies, pursuing specific objectives, it also has application to instances of inter-racial communal violence. It is within this orientation that we intend to pursue the history of collective racial violence in Britain in the present century. This history we see as divided into two phases: the period from 1900 to 1948, when violence largely took the inter-racial communal form; and the period from 1948 to the 'Bristol Riot' in which violence increasingly resulted from confrontation between black communities and the police. As will be seen neither of these periods nor the categories of violence are discrete. Rather particular forms of violence predominate in particular periods, and the periods overlap, evolving one into another.

In the first period we intend to examine collective racial violence as *one* aspect of wider changing conflicts and contradictions between social groups and interests. The groups and interests in question are, and emanate from, early migrant colonial workers, sections of the white working class and sections of capital. The conflicts and contradictions which are racial, within class and between classes, all incorporate a power and political dimension; but in the formal sense this dimension is also evident in the role of the state. The state embodies in condensed form these primary conflicts and contradictions and the nature of its actions and interventions must be seen in terms of them. Earlier forms of inter-racial conflict cannot be seen in abstraction from the state: the state is relevant as the ultimate source of power to which white violence sought to appeal; it is relevant to the manner in which the local police respond to inter-racial violence; it is relevant to the nature of the black response to violent racial attack. When therefore we come to the second phase, our increasing and direct focus on the role of the state will not be a new departure. This is not to say that our examination of collective racial violence will not continue to be based on racialised inter-class and intra-class conflicts. But it is impossible to ignore that within this period race becomes more central in the political arena, and its embodiment within the state of greater complexity and significance. It is in the changing social circumstances of the post war era – particularly the nature of the states's disposition on race – that we expect to find an explanation of declining collective white racial violence, and growing confrontation between blacks and the state.

The History of Collective Racial Violence in Britain

1900–1948: White violence – black resistance

We begin our inquiry at the turn of the present century for two reasons: first, by this time the underlying pattern of 'modern' metropolitan race relations was sufficiently established to be discernible and secondly, the first major instance of violent racial conflict we wish to examine occurred in 1911. It must be stressed that this particular instance – an attack on Cardiff's Chinese community – was not the first case of collective racial violence in Britain. There are reports of clashes from as early as the 1870's (Daunton, 1978). But while these tended not to escalate beyond an initial incident, the 1911 attack, both in scale and in the deliberation and determination of the white crowd, took on more major proportions.

At the turn of the century, the presence of colonial peoples in Britain was largely a seafaring presence. It was a seafaring presence primarily because the essential condition underlying black settlement and domestic race relations, both then as now, was the combination of colonial labour and metropolitan capital in the metropolitan environment; in this period that condition was initially established through Britain's massive merchant shipping industry. Colonial labour had long been employed in the Mercantile Marine, but after 1880, the complement – composed mainly of West Indians, Arabs, Somalis, Indians, and Chinese – began to increase. From the point of view of shipowners, the rapidly expanding industry needed labour, and colonial labour was perceived and represented as 'plentiful', 'docile' and 'cheap'. The situation, however, was somewhat more complex. Racial and imperial ideologies apart, the incorporation of colonial labour was part and parcel of the structural and technological transformation of merchant shipping from the 1860's onwards. Between them, the introduction of the steamship and the telegraph radically changed the nature of seafaring. Noting the completely different skills subsequently required, one commentator observed that the steamship involved the creation of a new rating with no sea-going tradition, whose job was shovelling coal into a furnace (Thornton, 1959). As an occupation, the new rating – that of Fireman – was 'arduous, dirty and hot'; and it eventually came to account for nearly half the total number of seamen employed afloat. In addition, the steamship's speed and reliability, together with improved communications facilitated by the telegraph, brought into existence a new class of merchant-ship, the 'Tramp Steamer'. This category of ship did not ply regular routes, but went instead from port to port depending on the availability of cargo. Employment aboard such ships generally meant longer periods away from home and tended to be insecure and discontinuous, since it might begin and end at any port. Both the new rating of Fireman and the Tramp Steamer were shunned by white European labour, and it was with these that colonial labour quickly became identified.

If the expansion and transformation of the merchant marine was directly responsible for the increased use of colonial seafaring labour, then racial and imperial ideologies ordered the deployment of that labour within the industry. The impact of the Empire on structures within the British maritime labour market is too complex to explore in detail here. But that market could be likened to a pyramid, at the pinnacle of which stood white British and European seamen, with the various nationalities and races of the Empire occupying the middle and base layers.

Over and above occupation and class of ship, three factors further differentiated maritime labour: wages and conditions aboard ship; conditions of employment; and the right of domicile in, and employment out of, United Kingdom ports. White British seamen enjoyed the highest levels of wages, the best conditions aboard ship, and the least regulated conditions of employment. In general, colonial labour commanded the lower levels of wages applicable in the port of origin, except where the seamen concerned were domiciled in the United Kingdom and sailed under 'European Articles'. However only a small proportion of colonial seamen ever became permanently domiciled in United Kingdom ports. By far the largest section, Indian seamen – referred to as 'Lascars' – were legally prevented from remaining in Britain (despite their status as British subjects) under an 1823 Act amending the Charter of the East India Company, and later under Section 125 of the Merchant Shipping Act, 1894 (Lester and Bindman, 1972). Not only were Indian seamen paid anything up to 75% below 'European Standard Rates', but their conditions of service obliged them to 'accept' employment for a return voyage to an Indian port lest they be punished under the criminal provisions of the 1894 Act for desertion or indiscipline.

Except during boom conditions, when domicile regulations on Indian seamen were relaxed, it was West Indian, West African, Middle Eastern, and to a lesser extent Chinese seamen that tended to become established in United Kingdom ports. That this was the case demonstrated the importance of this section of colonial labour, particularly to the Tramp Steamer trade. But numbers were kept down first by the practice of shipowners returning these seamen to their ports of origin, thereby restricting them to lower levels of wages; and secondly by Section 185 of the 1894 Merchant Shipping Act which made it an offence for such seamen to be brought to the United Kingdom and awarded Public Assistance within six months. Establishment in United Kingdom ports, however, did not mean that this category of colonial labour could be equated with white British labour. For West African seamen sailing out of Liverpool, a special agreement resulted in their being paid wages 25% below European Standard Rates. In addition colonial seamen settled in the United Kingdom were restricted to the rating of Fireman whose conditions of work were amongst the last to be improved by legislation (Kirkaldy, 1914).

This then was the British maritime labour market. The racial practices by which it was structured first evolved unofficially amongst shipowners and masters, and later found formal expression in either legislation or official agreement. Section 5(2) of the Aliens' Restriction (Amendment) Act, 1919, for example, underlined the broad principle that British subjects of different races could be paid different wages. Additionally, the Shipmasters Manual legitimated the practice of racial and ethnic segregation both in the hiring of crews and in accommodation aboard ship. Within the industry such practices and structures laid the foundations for wider tensions and conflicts perceived in racial terms. From the 1880's onwards to the Second World War and even after, organised white maritime labour constantly agitated against the use of colonial labour to replace white seamen and undercut white wage levels. Predictably, this agitation had particular consequences for colonial seamen permanently domiciled in the United Kingdom. Though most received European Standard rates and were thus not in wage competition with white British labour, the fact that they were there, readily accessible, made them a target for organised white maritime labour in ways that other categories of colonial labour were not.

Clearly, the pattern of metropolitan race relations in the period was very much a consequence of structures and labour relations in the shipping industry. To this, however, one other important dimension must be added – the reactions of different sections of the white population to more extensive black settlement. After 1880, the small colonial seafaring communities already established in the Lime House Street and Canning Town areas of London began to grow, and colonial seamen began to settle in a number of other ports, most notably Cardiff, Liverpool, South Shields and Glasgow. In these cities, black settlement tended to be restricted to the port or dock areas, often becoming sufficiently geographically concentrated to form distinct communities. While this pattern of settlement reflected occupational specialisation and the need for community amongst colonial seamen in a strange environment, it also indicated the extent to which these communities were socially isolated and even ostracised within the city. There can be little doubting the importance of racial ideologies in this latter process. In Cardiff, the largest of these early communities, the black population was almost entirely concentrated in the Butetown area, an enclave that soon acquired the name 'Tiger Bay'. The comments of the socialist reformer, George R. Sims, visiting the city in 1907 are particularly illuminating on attitudes to this area and its people. Entitling his subsequent publication 'In Nigger Town', Sims wrote:

The conditions which prevail in this unpleasant quarter are responsible for a grave scandal. It is a scandal which would not be tolerated for one moment in – say America. . . . The district has, of course, a number of respectable inhabitants, honest and decent people, black and white, who toil and trade and are superior to their environment. But it has certain features which make it one of the most repellant places in which a Briton, blest with pride of race, can spend a morning, afternoon, or an evening.
(*Western Mail*, 19 July, *1907*)

Sims' visit was part of a wider investigation into working class housing conditions in South Wales towns. In relation to Butetown, however, it was the people that commanded his attentions, and the 'grave scandal' to which he referred was not poverty or squalor, but black seamen, their white wives, and most of all, their children.

The 1911 anti-Chinese attack
It was against this background that the Chinese community came under racial attack in Cardiff on 20 April 1911. The violence initially developed out of a national strike called by the National Seamen and Firemen's Union in pursuit of higher wages. In an industry where unionisation was intrinsically difficult, and where less than half of those employed were union members, the success of the strike depended crucially on solidarity, on the organisation of an efficient picket, and on the ability of the Seamen's Union to win sympathetic support from other trade unions. In Cardiff, then the Tramp Steamer capital of Britain and thus an arena in which the strike would be won or lost, all three strategies soon came to focus on one section of colonial labour employed in the industry – Chinese seamen.

Numerically a small group, Chinese seamen permanently domiciled in Cardiff represented no substantive threat to the strike. Though traditionally, Chinese seamen were restricted to ships bound for the Far-East, their numbers in the Bristol Channel began to increase after 1902, probably as a result of the exclusion of 'foreigners' (aliens, mostly Europeans) through the application of a language test. As British Hong Kong subjects, Chinese seamen were not subject to this test. Though those permanently domiciled in Great Britain did not receive full European Standard wages, they did receive substantially more than Chinese seamen sailing under Hong Kong articles, a number of whom were always present in British ports awaiting a return voyage. In Cardiff, the permanent Chinese community probably numbered less than two hundred at any one time. The majority were of course seamen, located in some four or five Chinese boarding houses in Butetown. The rest were occupied in running some twenty-two Chinese laundries and a number of small 'eat houses' scattered throughout the city. Ironically, there is little evidence to suggest that either of these two groups had any significant part to play in the strike (*Western Mail*, 5 July, 1911). And when the shipowners threatened to break the strike using Chinese labour, they intended to use Chinese seamen on Hong Kong articles, over whom they had more control and who could be brought in from other ports. The attack on the whole of Cardiff's Chinese community thus demonstrated the extent to which such communities were hostage to wider conflicts within the shipping industry. More significantly, it also demonstrated the extent to which racial hostility both integrated and amplified the conflicts originating within the shipping industry with those associated with colonial settlement.

Animosity against the Chinese in Cardiff was part of an ongoing process orchestrated in the main by the Seamen's Union and Christian middle class pressure groups concerned with the 'moral order' of the city. To the Union, the Chinese represented an uncontrollable source of non-union labour used by employers to undercut the wages and take the jobs of white seamen. The Union's ready resort to racism in its campaign against Chinese seamen was made all the more forceful by fancied parallels struck between their own situation and that of the Transvaal in South Africa, where indentured Chinese labour had been used to replace white labour in the mines. In the context of the 1911 strike, racial animosity against the Chinese quickly became an expedient and effective method of mobilising pickets and gaining the support of other trade unions including the influential local Trades and Labour Council. Nor did the Seamen's Union have to look far for its material. A typical anecdote from the autobiography of Captain Tupper, the strike leader in Cardiff at the time, serves to illustrate the types of characterisations with which the Chinese were likely to be generally labelled:

. . . the yellowman used to sell sweets to the white kids from the slums – there were dirty little sweet shops connected with some laundries – and the sweets were smeared with some sort of dope that fetched the eaters back like flies to a honey pot. But the Chinks were clever – they used to send the kids back to their houses at night, and with intimidation and corruption, prevent the police from ever getting evidence. (Tupper, 1938)

These, however, were by no means the most serious accusations levelled against the Chinese. By far the greatest hostility was reserved for the association of Chinese men with white women, either as wives or as laundry employees. In this respect the Chinese were likely to be accused of anything from organised prostitution to 'white slavery'.

The threat by shipowners to break the strike using Chinese labour, and the sight of Chinese seamen arriving in South Wales ports under police protection, effectively set the tone of the strike in Cardiff. By the third week of the strike, with tempers already inflamed through frequent clashes between pickets and the police, and with numerous other workers in the city also out, either in sympathy with the seamen or in pursuit of their own disputes, it was difficult to separate the Trade Union from the 'moral' case against the Chinese. Indicative of this, the Trades and Labour Council – having been initially reluctant to side with the seamen – passed a resolution condemning the Shipowners for the use of Chinese 'blacklegs', and calling upon the workers of Cardiff to 'refrain from patronising Chinese laundries in the City' (*Western Mail*, 7 April, 1911).

On the night of 20 April, matters came to a head. A white crowd estimated at over a thousand strong gathered in the Grangetown area of the city and began systematically sacking Chinese laundries, smashing equipment and starting fires. At the same time, smaller crowds were similarly dealing with laundries and other Chinese property in other parts of the city. Notwithstanding a reinforced police presence, which included a contingent of the then infamous Metropolitan Police, twenty-one of the twenty-two Chinese laundries in the city were either damaged or destroyed that night. A local reporter doing a tour of the city at 2.00 am found 'that damage had been done over a whole area' and even at that late hour the street still presented an animated appearance, with 'knots of boys and grown men, and even girls parading about, cheering and singing popular songs'. The violence eventually subsided when mounted police were brought out to disperse the roaming crowds.

According to press reports the Chinese made little effort to defend their property, preferring to depart quietly rather than confront hostile crowds. Further, the violence that night was represented as a popular and spontaneous outburst prompted by six weeks of frustration, rumour and agitation. Tupper, however, recalled the night's activities quite differently. Investing the mob's actions with all the significance of a religious crusade, he wrote in his autobiography:

I arranged for a great demonstration to take place outside Roath Dock Yard . . . All the available police mustered at what was to turn out to be a very orderly meeting. (Meanwhile) . . . I was leading my storm troops to the back alleys which house the Chinese Laundries and Boarding Houses . . . A good many of the dives caught fire that day; quite a lot of Chinamen got hurt. But there were little white girls, some no more than thirteen years old, running out of the places . . . We cleared the decks – and the Chinese Laundries shut up shop. We let go over this job, and I confess my conscience never suffered . . . England's conscience wasn't bothered anyway. I received thousands of letters – many from the Church – blessing us for this bit of riot. (Tupper, 1938)

The summer of 1919

1919 was a bad year for race relations. In the United States no less than twenty-six serious race riots occurred in what became known as the 'red summer'. Unlike earlier experiences, most of these riots were in the urban north with the worst in Chicago. According to one description:

White mobs seized control of whole cities for days on end, shooting and burning, assaulting and looting, and when Negroes displayed a sudden determination to defend themselves, the fury increased. (Segal, 1966, pp 229–30)

In Britain, between April and August of that year, almost every seaport city with a black population experienced violent racial upheaval. The violence, unlike that up until 1911, was not the product of trade dispute, nor was it directed at any one colonial group. In the commonly accepted sense of the term, these were 'race riots' characterised by white crowds attacking black localities, by blacks defending themselves and their property, and with the police in some instances capable of decisive intervention, at other times not.

Indicative of the racial climate in post-war Britain, from as early as February of that year, minor incidents began to show a marked tendency towards violent escalation. One brawl between blacks and whites at a cafe in Cable Street, London, overspilled into the streets as a fierce free-for-all in which it was alleged firearms were discharged. The incident could have developed into a major confrontation had not the police prevented a large white crowd from pursuing the blacks back to their boarding house (*Liverpool Daily Post and Mercury*, 17 April, 1919).

It was in Liverpool, however, that the pattern of street violence was established. On the night of the 4 June, a fight between a group of blacks and Norwegian seamen in Great George Square quickly developed into a siege of black boarding houses in the surrounding streets. According to one policeman observing the night's disturbance in the vicinity of Upper Stanhope Street, 'the place was in an uproar . . . every coloured man who was seen was followed by a hostile crowd, and in two instances negroes retaliated by pulling out knives' (*Liverpool Echo*, 9 June, 1919). Different white crowds, varying in number from two hundred to two thousand, proceeded to attack and destroy consecutive black boarding houses, removing furniture to the street for bonfires. There was little, the police claimed, they could do. Nor did some of their actions have the desired effect. One Inspector, having been informed that a West Indian by the name of Charles Wootten had been involved in the initial incident, decided to raid his boarding house and effect an arrest. The mob attended. On being confronted by the police and the crowd, Wootten chose to flee. From there the crowds took over. Anything and everything that came to hand was thrown at him. The police eventually caught up with Wootten near the Queen's

Dock, but he was wrested away by the crowd. At the Coroner's enquiry later, no one could remember how Wootten came to end up in the water. Eyewitnesses recalled only that he had swum around for some time before going down (*Liverpool Echo*, 10 June, 1919).

On a lower level of intensity, intermittent violence continued in Liverpool for over a week. The police, unable to protect the black community or control white crowds, adopted a strategy of taking whole black families into 'protective custody'. By 10 June over seven hundred blacks were so held (May and Cohen, 1974).

The example set by Liverpool was not long in communicating itself to South Wales ports, and violence broke out in Newport on the day following the initial flare up in Liverpool. Compared with Liverpool or Cardiff, the black community in Newport was tiny and made up mostly of seamen concentrated in a few streets in the Pillgwenlly area near the docks. Nevertheless, this community came under intense attack on two consecutive nights. Started by an incident in which two blacks were alleged to have insulted some 'respectable white women', a large white crowd gathered and began attacking boarding houses, cafes, a Chinese laundry, and several houses occupied by blacks living in the area. Heavily outnumbered, blacks fired warning revolver shots into the air, and defended themselves with whatever weapons came to hand. Eventually, the violence was brought under control by vigorous police action. On the following night the police saturated the area in an attempt to prevent further trouble. Initially this tactic appeared to work with only minor incidents reported. Later however, around 11 pm, a crowd estimated at five thousand and reportedly led by ex-soldiers launched an attack on boarding houses in George Street. Such was the ferocity of the fighting that even after repeated baton charges by the police, this crowd could not be dispersed. That night's activities ended with many casualties and the arrest of twenty blacks and two whites (Evans, 1980).

With racial violence already in South Wales, it was only a matter of time before Cardiff became involved. Racial tensions in Cardiff had been simmering throughout the War, and the extensive coverage given the events in Liverpool and Newport by the local media could not have alleviated an already tense situation. By and large, local newspapers took the view that blacks were responsible for the initial incidents elsewhere and had brought the wrath of the white crowds down on themselves by their excessive use of knives and firearms (*South Wales Echo*, 7 June, 1919). Certainly the police in Cardiff were anxious to avoid any incident likely to inflame racial feelings. Fifteen Chinese seamen signed-off at the port were immediately rounded up, served with deportation orders by the Aliens Department, and promptly placed under police escort on a train bound for Birkenhead where there was a ship awaiting them.

As to which incident eventually sparked the violence in Cardiff, no one is certain. According to the Chief Constable, two buses containing black men and their white wives arriving in the city centre after a day's excursion on the evening of the 11 June, caused a hostile crowd to gather. Any chance the few constables present had of maintaining order, according to this report, disappeared when 'the coloured men rushed towards the white men and fired several revolver shots'. A young constable, however, had different information. According to his account events started with a brawl in Canal Parade, Butetown:

A group of coloured men, some of whom had apparently been drinking, were coming towards St Mary Street. They were being followed by a crowd and suddenly one of the coloured men made a dash amongst them and started slashing about with a razor. There was then, of course a wild rush, and within a few moments hundreds of people had congregated. (*Western Mail*, 12 June, 1919)

With numbers escalating on both sides, continues the account, the blacks were obliged to fight a retreating action towards Butetown.

Whatever the immediate causes of the initial clash, the situation quickly became uncontrollable, and there followed what were probably two of the worst nights of racial violence that summer. White crowds gathered and headed for Butetown. There, initially unable to find anyone on the streets, they vented their anger on property. Houses were set on fire and boarding houses attacked. Anyone found within was hustled out and beaten. One report mentions two coloured men being beaten with frying pans. By midnight Bute Street and the upper part of Butetown was a confused melee with several different battles going on at the same time. The violence did not subside until much later that night.

At the end of the first day one man had died in Barry (Cardiff's sister port) and several blacks were under arrest in Cardiff charged with firearms offences. On the next day all indications were that tempers still ran high, and blacks were careful to keep off the streets. Those who did not were invariably chased by small bands of whites. One such incident received coverage in a local newspaper under the title 'Exciting Manhunt'. Incidents like these kept up the momentum for the serious confrontations that were to follow later that evening. Before this was over another two men were to lose their lives.

At around 9.00 pm, a large white crowd gathered in the vicinity of Hayes Bridge, the mutually accepted dividing line between black and white Cardiff. Their exploits that night are too numerous to recount, but undoubtedly the high point was the siege of a boarding house in Millicent Street. This incident typified much of the violence that night, and serves to highlight differences in police methods between Liverpool, Newport and Cardiff.

As in Newport, ex-soldiers were said to be prominent amongst the ringleaders besieging the boarding house (*Western Mail*, 13 June, 1919). Eyewitnesses described how the door was smashed in and men crowded into the narrow hall and crept upstairs. Outside the crowd howled encouragement with an enthusiasm that one newspaper likened to the French Revolution. Half way up the stairs a coloured man appeared on the landing and discharged several revolver shots into the attacking party, killing one and wounding another. The party retreated but were not to be denied. Grabbing a table as a shield, they gained the first floor landing where fierce hand to hand combat ensued with razors and bits of broken furniture used as weapons. One Somali occupant received severe injuries to the head in this fracas, of which he later died. Meanwhile, the people outside became impatient and set fire to the house. The attackers came tumbling out leaving the defenders behind, who apparently preferred to brave the fire than face the hostile crowd. Eventually a fire engine arrived, and on the instruction of the Chief Constable rained a torrent of water on the building, continuing even after the fire had been put out. The ploy did not satisfy the ringleaders who still expected the black seamen inside to come out. By this time, the Chief Constable had achieved what one newspaper described as 'a degree of control over the situtaion'. Arguing with the ringleaders, he pointed out that '. . . the coloured men had no chance of living under the torrent of water with which the house was flooded, and that they must either give themselves up or die' (*Western Mail*, 13 June, 1919).

In the following two days the violence slowly subsided. Though large white crowds continued to gather in anticipation of further trouble, a heavily reinforced police force effectively sealed off the dock area. According to the Chief Constable, priority was given to keeping the coloured men out of sight of the whites. This, he explained, was a difficult task as 'the Europeans were too exasperated by the free use by the coloured men of revolvers and razors'. White crowds contented themselves in the meantime with periodic rushes in response to sightings of blacks, or reported sightings of blacks. 'Negro Hunting', commented the South Wales Daily News, 'had developed into something like a fever'. As for the black community, on the day after the second night's rioting, as mounted police attempted to restrain white crowds, a meeting was called in Loudon Square to discuss how best to deal with the situation. They were reported to be in a determined mood, and prepared to defend their quarter of the city at all cost. One West African was quoted as saying:

It will be all hell let loose, as your people say, if the mob comes into our streets . . . We are ready to obey the white man's laws, but if we are unprotected from hooligan rioters who can blame us for protecting ourselves? (*South Wales Daily News*, 14 June, 1919)

By the end of that week the violence had entirely petered out, but the area continued to be heavily policed for some time afterwards.

As accounts of these events are taken largely from the press some attention is paid here to the nature of press coverage. Two basic themes dominated the approach of the local dailies in Cardiff: on the one hand there was the supposedly wild and unjustifiable violence perpetrated by blacks; and on the other, the apparent heroism of the police both individually and collectively in containing it. Having taken the initial stance that the disturbances had been sparked off by blacks, the behaviour of whites was presented as a justifiable reaction to excessive black violence – a reaction, backed up by long standing and 'legitimate' grievances. The following are typical of the many 'eye-witness' accounts of the rioting published in the *Western Mail*, illustrating these themes:

Everything was apparently quiet, and the crowd dispersed. However, a bunch of coloured men were seen coming along Canal Parade, and several Police Officers . . . went towards them. Immediately shots were fired at the Police and several had narrow escapes, a bullet actually piercing the tunic of Police Constable Clarke. The Constables drew their batons and the attackers fled, but two were secured and taken into custody. (*Western Mail*, 13 June, 1919)

Similarly:

A huge negro was attempting to rally his compatriots when Constable Badger pluckily charged him. A razor, which seemed to be the most popular weapon with the negroes was drawn by the man from his hip pocket and the Constable received a nasty gash across the neck. (*Western Mail*, 13 June, 1919)

One eyewitness even claimed to have seen 'a coloured man discharge three shots into the face of a Constable', adding, 'it was a miracle that he was not hit'.

On the basis of such reports the *South Wales Echo* could justifiably ask, 'WHY ARE POLICE NOT ARMED?' Consistent with this question, and the continual reference to the Butetown area as a WAR ZONE, it published, amongst others, a letter from a 'British Tommy', the text of which is informative:

Should not the police be armed with revolvers whilst on duty down Bute Road where there are men of different races? We all know that the coloured men carry firearms. If the Policemen were armed, it would save a lot of bother. (*South Wales Echo*, 13 June, 1919)

Media representations of the scale and ferocity of black violence, however, were not borne out in the courts. Notwithstanding the fact that it was black people and black areas that were attacked and invaded, the experience in Newport demonstrated that blacks were still more likely to be arrested than whites. Of thirty-one persons arrested and charged in Newport, twenty-one were black. In Cardiff, given the huge numerical imbalance between black and white participants, the situation was no more equitable. Nineteen blacks and eighteen whites were brought before the courts. Of the sixteen blacks charged with offences involving firearms, only four were found guilty. Firearms were used, but in the majority of cases where evidence was produced the Court took the view that the men involved had good reason to fear for their lives. In contrast, the eighteen whites were charged variously with wilful damage, arson, murder, and unlawful rioting. Of the ten charged with unlawful rioting, all were found guilty.

If the themes of 'black violence', 'white reaction', and 'police heroism' dominated media reconstructions of events in Cardiff, then they also structured media explanations. Represented as having an affinity for violence, the behaviour of blacks seemingly needed little explanation or justification. Where such was forthcoming unemployment was held to be the major source of black bitterness and disaffection. Many of these men, the argument ran, had been reduced to a state of poverty, 'often clad in rags'. They were thought not to be appeased by twenty six shillings per week 'out of work pay', having earned £15 per month during the War, and coming ashore with anything up to £100 in their pockets (*Western Mail*, 13 June, 1919).

Certainly black seamen, and by extension the black community, had good cause to be bitter about employment. During the War, the policy of the Seamen's Union reflecting critical labour shortages in the industry and its strategic relevance to Britain's survival, had converged about the slogan 'British and British Coloured Seamen First'. With the War at an end and shipping tonnages being laid up on a massive scale, both Union and shipowner 'patriotically' reverted to giving preference to white seamen. The result in Cardiff, according to a black delegation giving evidence to a visiting Parliamentary Committee after the violence, was something like '1,500 coloured men in and about Cardiff' out of work (*South Wales Daily News*, 18 June, 1919). Reports from Liverpool suggested that a similar situation existed there, with most of the additional two thousand or so West African and West Indian seamen employed during the War also unemployed (*Liverpool Courier*, 11 June, 1919). The media claims of excess violence were disproved by the courts, but clearly the sense of injustice implicit in the post-war treatment of black seamen in part explained the determination with which they resisted white violence.

Apart from this issue the major preoccupation of the media was to explain the causes of white resentment. One theme dominated to the almost total exclusion of all others, and that was the association, in any form, of black men and white women. Since the establishment of black settlements in British ports, sexual relations of this type had been a constant source of racial tension. Amongst the middle classes in particular, these relations were always likely to be imbued with the characteristics of lust, degeneracy, and vice. For the cities these issues were complexly interwoven with a number of different aspects related to black settlement. In 1918, for example, a campaign to cleanse Cardiff of its 'moral pollution' organised by an alliance of small middle class Christian, philanthropic organisations culminated in a famous slander trial at the Swansea Assizes. The trial was occasioned by remarks allegedly uttered by the Chairman of the Cardiff Citizen's Union where he described a fair-ground in Butetown as 'absolute hell. There are young girls here eighteen years of age mixing with coloured men . . . Every woman on this ground is a prostitute and the police are up-holding it' (Cardiff and District Citizens' Union, 1918). In the event these remarks were only incidental to the trial, which centred on an accusation by the Citizens' Union that the black district was being used by the authorities to 'centralise vice'. This the Chief Constable, heading a long list of official witnesses, denied. But as 'vice' tended to be defined throughout the trial in terms of any association between black men and white women, and as the attitudes of official witnesses to this were often as hostile as those of the Citizens' Union, the former experienced great difficulty in refuting the accusation.

Drawing many of these issues together, a letter published in the Liverpool Echo during the hostilities demonstrated that similar circumstances and considerations also existed there:

Few of our ports can show a tendency to the formation of distinct foreign colonies as Liverpool does. We have our China-town, Dark town, and other alien quarters all in more or less distinct areas of the City. In some respects this tendency is a safeguard. It enables our guardians of law and authority to more easily overlook the doings of foreigners. It is partly a check against the pollution of a healthy community by undesirables, other peoples, other manners . . . The system of foreign colonies nevertheless has disadvantages. The colonists are apt to look upon their particular quarters as their own. They take over, as it were the general amenities, to the exclusion of the English and other peoples, who may be regarded as intruders. Licensed houses and shops become the exclusive rendezvous of negroes and chinese, where whites become undesirable customers. The profound difficulty of the problem as it affects white women is obvious. This moral trouble is the principle cause of most of the racial conflicts. The feud which has led to the spilling of blood . . . cannot end here. It may have served a good purpose by leading to the elimination of a distinct menace. (*Liverpool Echo*, 6 June, 1919)

It was in the full throes of journalistic and editorial enquiry during and following the violence that white sexual indignation and outrage reached its maximum extension. Compared with the outpourings of newspapers closer to the scenes of major confrontations a caricature in *The Times* might almost be thought charitable:

The negro is almost pathetically loyal to the British Empire and he is always proud to be acclaimed a Briton. His chief failing is his fondness for white women, and American Naval Officers stationed at the American Naval base at Cardiff have often expressed their disgust at the laxity of British law in this connection. (*Times*, 13 June, 1919)

The links between the racial situation in British ports and that in America were commonly made. In an editorial entitled 'DEPORT OR COLONISE', the *Liverpool Courier* suggested that if blacks were to be allowed to remain in Britain, then like 'Montreal and other places', quarters should be found 'where they would not be able to mix with whites' (9 June 1919). However, in its censure of sexual relations between black men and white women an editorial in Cardiff's *Western Mail* was the most explicit. The main cause of white resentment, it argued, was the black seaman, who spent his earnings freely 'on the swankiest garb he could obtain' and paraded 'the streets and visiting houses of entertainment' with 'a flashily dressed white girl' on his arm. Any tolerance exhibited towards this, it continued,

is due not to far-fetched ideas of racial equality, but to slackness. Such consorting is necessarily an ill-assorting, it exhibits either a state of depravity or squalid infatuation . . . it is repugnant to all our finer instincts in which pride of race occupies a just and inevitable place. (*Western Mail*, 13 June 1919)

While the editors could not envisage dealing with the problem through legislation, they did point out that 'in the United States the force of public opinion, reinforced by *unofficial public action of a ruthless kind* is sufficient to prevent the mischief' (our emphasis). The 'evil', concluded the editors, would not have arisen in Britain had like in 'the United States – the public been more vigilant'.

The inter-war years and the 1948 Liverpool clashes

Despite the economic instability of the 1920's, and the recession of the 30's, this period was not marked by any major racial disturbances. This is not to imply that metropolitan race relations improved in the inter-war years. On the contrary, the period saw the fortunes of early black communities reduced to their lowest ebb. Colonial seamen domiciled in British ports experienced disproportionately high levels and long periods of unemployment compared with their white fellow workers (Richmond, 1950). If occupational specialisation had, in the pre-war era, been the bastion of the black community's relative prosperity, then in the inter-war years this proved the exact opposite. Not only did unemployed black seamen find it almost impossible to obtain alternative work, but such was the extent to which the emergent black second generation found themselves in the same trap, that one researcher concluded that it was almost impossible for these children to become part of Britain's industrial life. Further, the Seamen's Union, having abandoned in the early 1920's its strategy of agitation against colonial labour through rank and file militancy, was to win a number of important state interventions via robust Parliamentary lobbying. These had consequences not only for black employment, but also for the whole legal status of blacks as resident citizens of the United Kingdom.

Of the violent racial incidents that did occur during the inter-war years the most significant were in Cardiff in 1923 and 1929, and in South Shields in 1930 (Byrne, 1977). Those incidents in Cardiff were between different nationalities of colonial seamen and illustrated the degree to which the maritime labour market was structured by racial and ethnic division. The violence in South Shields however, took place between black pickets and the police. All were the direct product of industrial dispute and as such, were more akin to the 1911 disturbances than to the major rioting of 1919 and that which was to follow in Liverpool after the war. In 1948 Liverpool's South End experienced three nights of racial violence spread over the August Bank holiday. On the first two nights the pattern of violence seems to have been a repeat of events in 1919. Following a fight outside a cafe frequented by blacks, a large white crowd gathered, attacked the cafe, and then turned its attentions to a nearby seamen's hostel amongst other property owned or used by black colonials. On the second night, in addition to a series of running street battles, the same hostel was again attacked by white mobs, and much damage was done before the police arrived and arrested a number of blacks who had barricaded themselves inside for protection. On the third night the pattern changed. Though there was an initial encounter between a large group of blacks and whites outside a club in Upper Parliament Street, the whites were chased off, and the main confrontation took place between the blacks and the police.

Even more so than in 1919, the behaviour of the police was an issue in these clashes. In his account of events, Richmond noted that following clashes between blacks and the police on the first night:

the police appear to have retaliated with a singular lack of discrimination, with the result that a number of men who had not been involved in the affair received unwarranted injuries and were arrested. Some men claim that the police entered their homes and that they were beaten up without justification. Police appear to have entered premises in search of particular men and cases of mistaken identity certainly arose. On the second and third nights police reinforcements were called in from other districts who were not familiar with the coloured population . . . The general impression appears to be that the police took action which they thought would bring the disturbances to a close as quickly as possible – which, in their view, meant removing the coloured minority, rather than attempting to arrest the body of irresponsible whites who were involved. (Richmond, 1954, p. 103)

Police tactics during these violent confrontations and their use of excessive violence in arresting blacks, whether participants or not, became central to the solidarity of the black community and its responses after the violence. A defence fund was organised to help with the legal expenses of the sixty blacks (as opposed to only ten whites) arrested. One observer at the trial of six blacks charged with being in possession of offensive weapons, noted that:

The police case was rather thin and though they had all evidently been well-rehearsed, several slips were made and each constable was mauled in turn by the defending solicitor. Each witness persisted in his story that there was no violence during or before the arrests and 'could not say' how the defendants had received injuries described in picturesque detail by the defence. (Quoted in Richmond, 1954, p. 105)

Communal inter-racial violence – the responses of the state

The role of the state in confirming and legitimating racial practices and structures within the Merchant Shipping Industry will already be apparent, particularly through the attachment of 'immigration clauses' to those Acts of Parliament regulating maritime colonial labour. At the turn of the century, it would have been difficult to separate the ship-owning interest from the national interest; the shipowning interest was both powerfully influential in the 'city', and well represented in Parliament. When, therefore, violence against the Chinese community resulted in organised white labour demanding the exclusion of all forms of colonial labour from the European theatre of operations, predictably, neither shipowners nor the legislature were favourably impressed. Too much was at stake: the substantial economic benefits from operating ships with a whole or part of the crew on substandard wages, and the advantages of having in United Kingdom ports a variegated pool of colonial labour. Coming during boom conditions, the 1911 attack on the Chinese community resulted in no significant official intervention to limit Chinese labour. Indeed, particularly during the First World War, all forms of colonial labour employed in the industry continued to increase.

Things were somewhat different in 1919, and it is with local and national responses to these events that we are primarily concerned. The violence of 1919 demonstrated that the fate of Britain's black communities no longer depended exclusively on the outcome of the struggle between organised white maritime labour and the shipowning interest. While issues relating to black immigration and settlement were a significant factor in the 1911 disturbance, they had been considerably amplified in 1919 by the popular nationalism generated during the War. At its most basic level, this nationalism was expressed in terms of 'sacrifice' and 'right' – blacks had not sacrificed, suffered and died during the War, and therefore were not entitled to any post-war benefits. Thus at the height of the violence in Cardiff, as a lone constable attempted to arrest a soldier in uniform for interfering with a black man, people in the mob seeking to effect the soldier's release were heard to shout, 'he is one of us, and has fought for us, not like the blacks' (*Western Mail*, 14 June 1919). As *The Times* noted, this accusation was false and black seamen 'had faced the perils of the submarine campaign with all the gallantry of British seamen' (13 June, 1919), and many had died in the process. Nevertheless the sentiment was widespread, and often linked to other issues behind the violence such as 'numbers' and 'housing'. With the innuendo that blacks had somehow managed to 'do well' out of the War, an editorial in the *South Wales Daily News*, was typical:

There are no reliable statistics regarding the Arabs, but there are certainly three times as many here as was the case six years ago. The coloured men and the Chinese are also growing in number, and all appear to be prospering. The withdrawal of our men for the Army has provided foreigners with a good opening which they have promptly seized. (*South Wales Daily News*, 3 August, 1919)

Similarly, the Cardiff Citizen's Union talked of 'Arabs, Coloured men from the desert, from East and West Africa, Chinese and other Asiatics' all earning high wages and 'able to buy property for fancy prices and clear out the British residents' (Annual report, 1918).

Hardly had the violence subsided when the chorus demanding black repatriation began. The loudest and most sweeping demands emanated from elements within the press. Thus the *Western Mail* advised:

The Government ought to declare it to be part of National Policy that this country is not to be regarded as an immigration field, that no more immigrants can be admitted, and that immigrants must return whence they came. This must apply to black men from the British West Indies as well as from the United States. (*Western Mail*, 13 June, 1919)

The cry was taken up by trade unions and ex-soldiers' organisations, though not all demanded the sweeping measures outlined above. A local Cardiff Branch of the National Union of Railwaymen passed a resolution stating that 'they viewed with alarm the serious state of affairs prevailing in this and other seaport towns' and called upon the Government 'to do their duty by the coloured men in this country and send them back to their homelands' (*South Wales Echo*, 12 June, 1919). In response to a deputation from the Cardiff 'comrades of the Great War', the National Union of Seamen undertook to make representations to the Government about the repatriation of blacks who had entered the country since the War (*Western Mail*, 23 September, 1919). The Cardiff Maritime Board, of which the Seamen's Union was a part, took a similar stand adding, probably on the insistence of local shipowners, that after white seamen, preference should be given in employment to those black seamen in regular employment before the War (*Western Mail*, 13 June, 1919).

In Cardiff, a week after the disturbances, the Chief Constable submitted his report to the Watch Committee. 'The riots', he explained, 'were caused by strong feeling aroused amongst members of the white population against coloured men.' The Watch Committee listened to the Chief Constable's report, authorised extra expenditure incurred by the police, made arrangements for the assessment of damages, and then proceeded to any other business. 'A policy of masterly inactivity', observed the *Echo*, 'a Watch Committee which does not watch' (18 June, 1919). 'There was no demand for a full and searching inquiry', noted the *South Wales Daily News*, 'the affair is as good as closed' (18 June, 1919).

The affair however was not closed. If the city saw no need for a full and searching inquiry, it was because it considered that no useful purpose would be served by one. In three respects the attitudes of the city to black settlement had changed. In the first place, where formerly the city had accepted black settlement as a necessary by-product of an international port, with the post-war crash in British shipping this acceptance was no longer clear cut. Secondly, whatever the importance of colonial seamen to the local economy, as a result of the violence this now had to be balanced against the implications and consequences of settlement. Thirdly, in the city's estimation, the black colonial population and the problems thrown up by the violence were primarily the Government's responsibility, and not its own. The problem, therefore, was not what had caused violent racial conflict but, given that it had occurred, what the Government was going to do about it. On this issue, by the time of the Chief Constable's report, the Local Authority already had decided views. Privately, both the Local Authorities in Cardiff and Liverpool made representations to the Home Office, the Colonial Office, the Ministry of Shipping and the Ministry of Labour seeking the repatriation of blacks (*South Wales Echo*, 13 June, 1919). But the results were not decisive. The Home Office eventually replied, that although it could not forcibly deport British subjects, it would make as many berths as possible available for this purpose on ships bound for the West Indies and Africa (May and Cohen, 1974). Blacks would have to be 'persuaded' to make the fullest use of these berths, and at the local level this 'persuasion' was to be left to the police. In both Cardiff and Liverpool, the evidence suggests that though the police initially had some success in registering blacks for repatriation, they met increasing resistance as the immediate impact of the violence receded. In Liverpool, of the five hundred berths made available, and the two hundred black seamen and ex-soldiers registered to occupy them, only forty-three turned up on the day (*Liverpool Courier*, 19 June, 1919). Similarly in Cardiff, a ship eventually departed containing some four hundred coloured men, but only thirty were of local origin (*Western Mail*, 11 September, 1919).

The issues of immigration control and repatriation did not end with these limited departures. If a major constraint on Government action immediately after events in 1919 appeared to be the lack of suitable legislative means by which black British subjects could be deported, that means was created in 1925 using Article 11 of the Aliens Order, 1920. On the face of it, the 'Special Restriction (Coloured Alien Seamen) Order' appeared to be a response to the Seamen's Union and its demand 'British seamen for British ships'. The order was drawn up by the incoming Conservative Government in 1924, and being a ministerial edict, it required no parliamentary debate. According to the Home Office, its primary objective was to regulate the entry of those colonial seamen formerly entitled to seek discharge and domicile in British ports; if such seamen were not in possession of satisfactory documentation proving that they were British subjects, they would have to obtain the leave of an Immigration Officer before landing. This leave, the Home Office stipulated, would be granted only 'very sparingly', and those to whom it applied would be subject to repatriation or removal from the United Kingdom. The Order, however, was not to apply to colonial seamen already domiciled in Britain, or to those signing on in United Kingdom ports for a round trip (Hansard, Vol. 196, 8 June, 1926).

To those familiar with seafaring, it quickly became apparent that the 1925 Order had very little to do with the seamen's demand 'British seamen for British ships'. Hardly had it been imposed when seaport MP's, on behalf of angry white seamen, were bitterly complaining that coloured seamen registered under the Order were being employed on British ships in exactly the same way (Hansard, Vol. 197, 6 July, 1926). In terms of its application, the Order reflected more the new concerns of Local Authorities and the police in ports like Liverpool and Cardiff. In other words, like current immigration legislation, the Order was specifically designed to restrict the entry and settlement of black colonial British citizens. But, because the Conservative Government did not wish to undermine the notion of a British subject which was at the very heart of the Empire, the Order could only achieve its ends through a series of legalistic contortions and double standards.

To begin with, the category 'Coloured Alien Seamen' was literally an invention. If a seaman was an Alien, then whatever his racial category, he would come within the terms of Section 5(3) of the Alien Restriction (Amendment) Act, 1919, and Article 6a(2) of the Aliens Order, 1920. Further, though the 1925 Order in its title referred to 'seamen', in practice it applied to all black colonials wishing to enter the United Kingdom. Within the terms of the Order, a black seaman wishing to enter the United Kingdom could do so without let or hindrance, provided he was in possession of 'reasonable proof' of his British status. The Order, however, did not specify what documentation constituted 'reasonable proof'. That was left to Immigration Officers and the police at local ports; nor did they receive much guidance on the question from above. The following Parliamentary exchange on the issue of documentation between a Cardiff MP, Captain Evans, and Sir W. Joynson-Hicks, Principal Secretary of State for the Home Office, is reproduced here, not only because it demonstrates in practice that 'reasonable proof' could be made to mean anything, but also because it clearly foreshadows many of the controversies over documentation that surround the 1971 Immigration Act.

Evans: if it is necessary for a British West Indian subject to report to the police and to take out a card of identification on his arrival in this country if he is in a position to produce a birth certificate proving his claim to British citizenship?

Hicks: A person who is in a position to prove that he is a British subject does not come within the scope of the Aliens Order, 1920, or the Special Restriction (Coloured Alien Seamen) Order, 1925, made thereunder. The production of a birth certificate, however, is not sufficient to establish British Nationality without proof of the identity of the holder with the person named in the certificate. An impression of the left thumb is one of the prescribed particulars to be taken in the case of every person registered under the Order relating to Coloured Alien Seamen.

Evans: . . . whether it is necessary for British West Indian subjects who can read and write to have their finger prints taken like criminals?

Hicks: . . . it is adopted as affording the best means of identification. The mere production by a coloured seaman of a birth certificate is no proof at all that he is the person named in that certificate, and, therefore, a British subject.

Evans: May I ask what proof my right honourable friend would be prepared to accept as showing that a British West Indian subject is a British subject?

Hicks: I am prepared to accept any reasonable proof that will convince any one of my officers at the port that he is a British subject. I have to be particularly careful, as my honourable and gallant friend would be among the first to complain if I let in any doubtful cases.

Col. Wedgewood: I presume that in every case a passport is a proof?

Hicks: These men do not need passports, and we want to avoid the necessity of burdening them with passports. If they can identify themselves with the birth certificates, we will admit it.

(Hansard, Vol. 210, pp. 335–336, 10 November, 1927)

Consistent with the view that the 1925 Order was more to do with immigration and settlement than with the shipping industry, despite Home Office assurances that the Order did not apply to black British colonial subjects already resident in the United Kingdom, the police, local Alien Departments, and Immigration Officers were able to take an entirely different view with total immunity. The League of Coloured People, a London based organisation led by black professionals, conducting an investigation into the application of the Order found that men in possession of passports, birth certificates, British Mercantile Identification Certificates, Seamen's Continuous Certificates of Discharge, Records of Military Service and Discharge, had all been made to register under the Order (*The Keys*, Vol. 3, No. 2, 1935). In Cardiff this registration process took the form of a 'campaign' by the police:

> One section of the coloured seamen, the West Indians, were told that the Acts were not aimed at them at all, but rather at the Arabs, and being thus placed in a false position of security, the West Indians submitted to registration, without protest. Others were led to think that registration was a mere formality which every seaman had to undergo, and as a result they fell victims to the snares cunningly devised for them by the Police. So convinced were these men that this procedure did not affect their status as British Subjects, that a few who had hitherto escaped the irksome vigilance of the Police, voluntarily registered as aliens so as to observe what they considered to be the requirements of the law. (*The Keys*, Vol. 3, No. 2, 1935)

Where 'persuasion' failed, the report further noted, threats of arrest and imprisonment were not uncommon.

Those registered under the Order ceased to be British subjects and became aliens. As such they were subject to the formidable powers laid down under the Aliens Order, 1920, and the Alien Restriction (Amendment) Act, 1919. Aliens were obliged to inform the police of any intended change of address; they could be arrested and detained without warrant for contravening, or being suspected of having contravened, or being about to contravene, any part of that Order. They also could be deported by any court as part of, or in lieu of, sentence for any crime, or directly by the Home Secretary if he deemed it 'conducive to the public good'.

Colonial seamen finding themselves suddenly deprived of British status immediately attempted to gain some form of redress through their MP's. The least the Home Office could concede, they argued, was that with some documentary claim to British citizenship, they were not aliens in the sense of e.g. Europeans registered under the 1920 Aliens Order. The argument must have posed the Home Office with something of a dilemma. Any concession that the possession of some form of documentary evidence made a difference would be tantamount to admitting that persons registered under the 1925 Order were British subjects, and had been falsely deprived of their status. In any case where could 'alien' West Indians or West Africans be deported to? The solution in the end was as absurd as so many other things relating to this Order. On the Card used to register Coloured Aliens, beside the heading 'Nationality' was stamped in red ink the word SEAMAN (Hansard, Vol. 193 (42), 15 March, 1926).

Only in 1932, and largely through the political agitation of the black community, was a procedure laid down by the Home Office whereby registration under the 1925 Order could be reversed. Made deliberately difficult, this procedure was not greatly used until 1935 when a provision made under the Shipping Assistance Act, 1935, virtually debarred aliens from employment on British ships eligible for Government financial aid within the terms of the Act (Hansard, Vol. 296 (1408–1512), 20 December, 1934). Overnight, the Act threw hundreds of 'Coloured Alien Seamen' out of work. Even then, most registered seamen preferred to use the process of 'naturalisation' rather than the 1932 procedure (Hansard, Vol. 300 (525), 4 April, 1935). Understandably, the 1925 Order dominated the lives and political struggles of Britain's black population during the inter-war years. For the seaport city, it provided the means through which black settlements could be more intensively policed and the numerical size controlled. The issues of immigration, settlement and repatriation having been brought to the fore by the 1919 disturbances, subsequent periodic panics over numbers, unemployment, Public Assistance, and the 'moral' question, led to further demands for tighter restrictions or the removal of sections of the black population. The Order was not repealed until shortly before the Second World War, when again Britain was in need of the services of colonial seamen.

From 'race riot' to 'black revolt'?
Commonly, the kinds of violent racial confrontation we have been describing are referred to as 'race riots', and as such they are supposedly distinguished from the modern phase of black revolts. However, our contention is that these categories of collective racial violence may not be distinguished simply by the use or non-use of the term race. Race, meaning racial ideologies, structures and practices, and not simply racial categories, is an integral part of both types of violence. When therefore we come to look at the 'Bristol Riot' it shall be as no more or no less a 'race riot' than the 1919 confrontations. Racism – though differently – is involved in both. In black revolt there is an aspect of the violence that is inter-racial; and in violent inter-racial communal conflict there is more than simple black resistance, there are elements of an emergent black revolt.

As a form of collective racial violence, the distinctive characteristics of violent inter-racial confrontation are addressed by three basic questions – Who mobilises and initiates the violence? In what context or circumstance? And to what ends? In 1911, 1919 and 1948 clearly whites were responsible for the initial and protracted attack. While it is tempting to dismiss these attacks as purely racist and reactionary, and in many senses they are, it is to be noted that the violence in question is not a product or extension of individual racial attacks organised by racist organisations; nor do such organisations have a role to play in the larger conflict. Instead of the circumstances that shape the concerns of white crowds we must look to the nature of race, class and power in the seaport city.

To organised white maritime labour – and their concerns in large part underpin the actions of the white crowds – colonial seamen signified both an economic and a political threat. The economic threat stemmed directly from shipowners' employment of the major part of colonial labour on discriminatory wage levels, and from the tendency, given the substantial and direct benefits to capital, of the complement of colonial seamen to rise. Though on the face of it that discrimination is against the interests of organised white labour, it is neither challenged nor contested. Instead, organised white labour collaborates with capital in the elaboration of racial structures within the industry. Having rejected the strategy of equal pay irrespective of race and nationality, in other words putting all within the industry on an equal competitive wage footing, organised white labour – in defence of its sectional interest – brings its collective bargaining power to bear on the task of restricting colonial labour. This applies particularly to non-domiciled colonial seamen on substandard wages, and marginally less so to those colonial seamen permanently settled in United Kingdom ports. Indeed, in the rhetoric of the seamen's union, the two groups of colonial labour are often indistinguishable. Attempting to restrict colonial labour added an additional and bitter dimension to conflict between organised white labour and capital.

The political threat followed from the economic. The majority of colonial labour, though outside the union, was yet very much within the industry. This labour significantly structured power relations between capital and organised labour, it limited the ability of the union to pursue better wages and conditions for its members, and enabled capital to resist union demands. In the eyes of organised white labour resident colonial seamen not only represented a threat to jobs and wage levels, they were also perceived as an unwitting tool in the hands of capital through which the union could be contained, even undermined. Thus there were sufficient reasons to oppose colonial labour in its own right, but additionally, to oppose colonial labour was also to oppose capital.

The actions of the Cardiff Trades Council preceding the attack on the Chinese community during the 1911 strike demonstrated the extent to which the concerns and understandings of organised white maritime labour were generalised amongst organised labour in the seaport city. This process of generalisation, however, was not simply a product of sympathy or class solidarity with white seamen. It was, in no small part, facilitated by residential and settlement concerns based on competition between sections of the white working class and colonial workers over housing and residential space. The form which that competition took was also shaped by inter-class considerations. Clearly the employment of colonial labour was most advantageous to maritime and maritime-related capital, and in Cardiff the majority of this labour was to be found living in rented accommodation in Butetown, a part of the Bute estate with its massive investments in the docks. In a city which owed its very existence to shipping, the interests of maritime capital were likely to be those of the city, though these were not identical. Whereas the city recognised the necessity of black settlement, it sought to contain and restrict that settlement to one area. These were the issues at the centre of the 1918 Slander Trial. The same issues were even more clearly present in an earlier controversy in which a city councillor claimed that houses outside the Butetown area were being used as black boarding houses, and that black seamen were being allowed '. . . to spread all over the city' (*South Wales Daily News*, 19 July, 1917). The fact was that wider black settlement depended on the siting of boarding houses, and boarding houses had to be licensed by the city authorities. The segregation and isolation of black settlement in Cardiff was thus, in part, a consequence of local official policies. It was this residential divide that invested housing and spatial competition with much of its essential force; for it was to this divide that wider and more coherent racial and imperialist ideologies were directly related and amplified. We cannot comment on the extent to which these formal ideologies, particularly the themes of cultural and biological contamination, informed the concerns of white working class crowds. They were undoubtedly part of the ideological terrain. But specifically they emanated most vociferously from the middle classes, from the local media, small Christian and philanthropic associations, senior police-men and other officials within the local administration.

These then were the circumstances that shaped the concerns of white crowds. In this context collective violence represented an extension of conflicts and antagonisms constantly in progress, not a sudden, new, or exceptional development. Given the proximity of major instances of collective racial violence to the two world wars, certainly social up-heaval cannot be discounted as a factor. The relationship, however, is neither direct nor pre-determined. During the world wars both the complement of colonial seamen and black settlements expanded with corresponding effect on the concerns of these groups and interests involved. Yet even in the depths of the great depression with all its social upheaval there were no major instances of collective racial violence.

Finally, the goals and objectives of the white crowds were consistent with their concerns, and confirmed by the activities of working class organisations and associations subsequent to the violence. After the 1911 strike the seamen's union returned with renewed vigor to its project of restricting colonial labour with special reference to the Chinese. This they first pursued through stricter enforcement of the 'language test' under section 12 of the 1906 Merchant Shipping Act. When this strategy failed however, the union stance changed from restriction to outright prohibition of Chinese labour (*South Wales Daily News*, 26 November, 1917). Similarly, after the violence of 1919, in addition to widespread and partially successful demands from working class organisation for various degrees of repatriation, the seamen's union managed to win the 1925 Coloured Alien Seamen's Order through Parliamentary lobby.

In concentrating on the mobilisation of white collective violence, there is a danger of falling into the error of representing blacks only as victims. Victims the Chinese in 1911 certainly were; small in numbers and scattered throughout the city they were in no position to offer collective opposition to white crowds. In 1919 black resistance tended to be most determined where the black community occupied a distinct residential space, whether a few streets as in Newport, or a whole area as in Cardiff. In Liverpool where black settlement was more widely scattered around a central nucleus, outlying black families had little alternative but to allow themselves to be interned by the police. If an identifiable territorial space made black collective resistance possible, it was not the source of that resistance. For that source most immediately we must look at the wholesale involvement of the resident black population in the war. A large part of the black population in seaport cities in 1919 would have been seamen employed during the war specifically to meet the severe shortage of labour in the Merchant Marine, in addition to demobbed colonial soldiers. In both Cardiff and Liverpool, the majority of these men were unemployed, not only because of the post war slump in shipping tonnage and freight prices, but also because the shipping federation had adopted a policy of giving first preference to white seamen in United Kingdom ports. For black seamen there were no alternative forms of employment, and the deep sense of injustice felt at the dramatic turnabout in attitudes after the war would only have been compounded by violent white racial attack. To make the point black servicemen took to wearing their uniforms during the hostilities. There is some evidence that this ploy had some sway with white crowds in Cardiff (*Western Mail*, 14 June 1919), but in Liverpool according to one local newspaper, uniforms and service medals were worn to no avail (*Courier*, 11 June 1919).

There is one final and important dimension to the source and nature of black resistance during the 1919 and 1945 confrontations that is not communicated by such terms as 'race riot' or 'inter-racial communal violence'. Misleadingly such terms imply a 'balance' or 'equality' of collective violence on both sides; they do not indicate who initially mobilises the violence or the disposition of the forces involved. Yet characteristic of this form of collective racial violence is not only the huge numerical imbalance between black and white crowds, but the often less than impartial intervention of the forces of law and order. Waskow, in relation to 'race riots' in America, makes two important points:

the unneutral actions of the police on behalf of the white community had much to do with turning incidents into full scale riots . . . To whites, unneutral behaviour by the police meant that it was 'open season' on Negroes, and that the usual protections offered by the law were temporarily in abeyance. (Waskow, 1966, p. 210)

The unneutral behaviour of the police 'legitimated' and 'reinforced' the actions of the white crowds; it was thus germaine to the way in which particular instances of violent confrontation developed. In 1919 there is ample direct and circumstantial evidence to suggest that the local police were not impartial. There was, in the first place, the publicly stated convictions of senior policemen that blacks were responsible for initial incidents and had brought the violence of white crowds on themselves by their 'free use . . . of revolvers and razors' (*Western Mail*, 18 June, 1919). There were the disproportionate numbers of black arrests. There was the strategy of attempting to contain the violence by – as the Chief Constable of Cardiff put it – 'keeping the coloured men out of sight of the whites'; the effect on white crowds in Liverpool of seeing blacks interned in camps as a direct result of their actions may only be supposed. There was the unwillingness on the part of the police (Newport clearly excepted) to confront and disperse white crowds; instead crowds were manoeuvred, even pleaded with. Finally, there was that aspect of the violence most readily seized upon by the press, fighting between the police and black crowds both in 1919, and even more so in 1948. Why it might be asked should these crowds take on the police, supposedly their only protection from white violence?

The actions of the police were, as Waskow suggests, 'on behalf of the white community', shaped and structured by local white concerns. We cannot explore in depth the nature of police/black relations over the period in question, so a few insights will have to suffice. During the

1918 Slander Trial for example, the attitudes of senior policemen to blacks and black settlement came very much into question. Pressed on the issue of blacks being allowed to use a cricket field outside Butetown the Chief Constable replied, 'you must bear in mind the class of people you have there are little better than cattle'. He went on to express his '. . . disapproval of black men being put in flannels and young girls being allowed to admire such beasts' (Citizen's Union, 1918). Subject to pressure from the black community, the Chief Constable was obliged to apologise for these remarks, but on the issue at the core of the statement even in apology he was intractable: 'I am against the temptation of co-mingling of white women with black men from the racial stand-point, and equally, of course, of the association of white men with black women.' The tendency of senior policemen to see themselves as the guardians of the city's 'morals' constituted a continuing theme in police/black relations. For example, in 1929, it led to a call by the Chief Constable for the implementation of the 1927 South African Immorality Act (prohibiting sexual relations between black and white) in Britain (*Western Mail*, 11 April 1929). The attitudes of the police were also evident from their actions in other spheres; in their determination to suppress black cafes (Council Minutes: Special Watch Committee, 1929), and in their enforcement of the Special Restriction (Coloured Alien Seamen's) Order 1925. If these attitudes informed police be-haviour during the 1919 and 1948 violent confrontations, then they may well have been good reason for black crowds to resist the police, and thus white racism in one of its institutional forms. Significantly it was that resistance, through supra-national black associations – the Coloured Seamen's Unions and the League for Colonial Freedom in Cardiff and the League of Coloured People in London that domin-ated black political activism in the inter-war years.

In looking at long term changes in the patterns of collective racial violence in Britain and America, there are notable similarities. Like Britain, the phase of inter-racial communal violence in America came to an end after the Second World War with the massive Detroit riot of 1948. And where after the relative calm of the 1950's the phase of collective black violent revolt was in full swing in America by the 1960s, in Britain it was not long in following. We have, by and large, resisted the temptation to draw significances from these similarities because the phenomenon of collective racial violence in both societies is not freely interchangeable. In relation to the transition from 'race riot' to 'black revolt' however, the American experience supports the arguments above. That is in both form and period the two types of crowd violence are not discrete, and though black revolt did not emerge in America until the 1960's its antecedents are clearly discernible in the preceding phase. From as early as 1935 in Harlem, 'new style' rioting involving direct confrontation with the police and the destruction of white property had already begun to emerge (Meier and Rudwick, 1971).

1948–1980: Black Revolt

We begin this section with a number of general understandings: that the racial differentiation of the black labour force, the residential segregation of black communities, and the involvement of the state in reinforcing racial structures and practices are all already distinctive features of British domestic race relations. The conflicts and contradictions implicit in these arrangements have already led to violent collective racial conflict which also involved violent conflict between blacks and the police. Lastly, the principal response of the state to the most serious instance of this conflict was an attempt to deport blacks, followed by an imposition of legal controls designed to restrict the entry of black workers to the UK, notwithstanding the fact that it was black communities that were attacked.

To those who would reduce all problems of race relations to numbers, it is important to realise that at no stage in this first period did the permanently settled black population in Great Britain exceed 100,000 (Richmond, 1954). What is of importance as we come to look at the modern phase, is that the broad distinctive and defining features of British domestic race relations are not creations of the post-war; they do not somehow spring into life with the onset of mass black migration. Rather the post-war era is a new phase in which these features are extended, developed and elaborated. This is not to adopt some crude form of historical determinism, for we recognise that race in the post-war is shaped by circumstances specific to the period, circumstances which include the changing political relationship of Britain to her colonies – in particular the movement of colonial peoples towards de-colonialisation; the changing labour demands of metropolitan capital and its relationship to peripheral colonial labour; the creation and development of the welfare state; and changes in the make-up of racial ideologies. Nevertheless, our assertion is that along with these historically specific factors, race in the post-war era was also powerfully shaped by the pre-1948 history of black settlement in Great Britain.

As in the preceding section we could not hope to cover the history of black settlement and race relations in this period as a continuous historical progression. Therefore we intend to continue our method of concentrating in detail on those areas determined by the issue in question, collective racial violence, within a broad outline sensitive to major developments. In the patterns of racial violence in this period there are a number of trends. There was, in the first place, a decline in collective white violence. Nottingham and Notting Hill in 1958 and

Dudley in 1962 were the most noteworthy instances in this period; but not only are these small scale in comparison to 1919 and 1948, they display features that render them atypical of the earlier phase. Secondly, there was the growth of individualised white racist attacks from the late 1960s. Highlighted by the media label 'paki-bashing', it is not restricted to any one racial group, further it is both incidental and organised by white racist/fascist organisations which began to make their presence felt on the racial and political scene in the period. Thirdly, dating from the middle 70's, there was the growth of 'race-related' collective political violence. As in Lewisham in 1976 and Southall in 1979, the venue was public protest by the anti-racist movement, and the violence occurred between the crowd and the police. Finally, dating most notably from the early 1970's there was an increasing incidence of violent collective conflict between blacks and the police. This took two forms: clashes occasioned by black political demonstrations and other kinds of black street assembly, for example the Mangrove demonstration 1971, the carnivals in Chapeltown – Leeds, 1975, and in Notting Hill, 1976; and clashes resulting from specific police actions within the black community, such as the Metro Youth Club incident in 1971, or the Four Aces club – Dalston, 1975. It is to this last aspect that the massive collective violence that occurred in Bristol 1980, and elsewhere in 1981, can most directly be traced.

As the most significant development in the pattern of collective racial violence in the post-war era, it is on the explanation of the increasing incidence of violent conflict between blacks and the police culminating in the 'Bristol Riot' that we concentrate, though other trends are not ignored, for they are all inter-related. But we cannot proceed to concentrate on those conflicts and contradictions between blacks and the state simply because we already know these to be central in the structuring of race in the post-war era. Rather, from the point of view of inquiry, we must first ask the questions why and how this comes to be so? How does inter-communal collective violence come to be replaced by the mobilisation of black violence against the state? We have already located the seeds of this modern form of confrontation in the earlier pre-war period; and we have also shown how in America the black ghetto revolt of the 1960's had both antecedents and occurrences in the 1930's and 40's. The question here is how does this distinctive feature become the dominant form of collective racial violence? What is different about the involvement of the state in structuring race in the post-war era? And how did black political struggles come to be more and more concerned with the state? In responding to these questions we intend to situate race in the post-war era within two parallel but related processes: the distinctive subordination of black workers in the new phase of immigration; and the nature of the state's involvement in that subordinating process, with special reference to the politicisation of race within the state.

Post-war migration and the social location of black workers

In 1951 Britain's black population numbered less than 200,000. By 1971 that number had risen to 1.2 million, and by 1977 to 1.87 million – an estimated 3.4% of the total population (Runnymede Trust and Radical Statistics Race Group, 1980). Nor was this inward migration of colonial labour a phenomenon peculiar to Great Britain. It applied to most of Western Europe where the 'immigrant' population numbered some 11 million or 5% of the total population (Castles and Kosack, 1973). Unlike the earlier pattern of colonial migration which tended to be restricted to the needs of maritime shipping, particularly during wartime, post-war immigration was stimulated by a more generalised demand for labour in Britain, founded initially on post-war reconstruction and later on the economic expansion of the 1950's and earlier 1960's. This demand was met in the first place by an intake of displaced European labour and the Irish. Subsequently it was to the New Commonwealth that Britain turned. That there was this labour available was not simply a matter of coincidence. Indeed the issues involved, the nature and performance of British capital in colonial territories; unemployment and under-employment; labour unrest; the 'colour-bar'; and the emerging political revolt were all constituent parts of the discourse within the metropolitan state on what was then termed the 'Colour-question'. One suggested solution to these colonial problems was a massive programme of British investment in the colonies. But, this having failed to materialise, the alternative was the import of colonial labour into the metropolitan environment.

The influx of colonial labour – in the first phase from the West Indies but later from Pakistan and India – corresponded closely in the 1950's to the demand for labour within the British economy (Peach, 1968). Between different sectors of capital (both public and private) however, that demand was uneven; thus black workers were not drawn equally into all sectors of British industry. They were drawn into those sectors of the economy which, in an era of full-employment, were unable to attract upwardly mobile white workers without a substantial increase in wages. The public sector, i.e. health and transport, figured prominently here, but the same applied to the lower end of the service industry and industries like textiles and clothing, foundries, forges and rolling mills. Many of these industries were then in decline and in need of a 'breathing space' in which to accumulate sufficient capital to reorganise the production process. But black workers were also drawn into the more dynamic sectors of the economy, into the engineering, chemical and motor industries. Where this happened it tended to involve those plants using assembly line techniques, demanding fewer skills, routine and repetitive work and shift systems.

Clearly, the initial economic incorporation of black workers was highly germaine to their overall social location within British economy. But that location was also powerfully determined by the impact of widespread racial discrimination in the field of employment. That discrimination was most manifest at the level of recruitment, with the effect of restricting black workers to certain industries and occupations (Smith, 1974; Smith and McIntosh, 1974). It was also evident in the organisation of labour on the shop floor, with some shifts and shops being entirely manned by 'immigrants', and even in the organisation of the work process through the regrading of occupations and skills as black workers are incorporated (C.I.S., 1976).

Black workers thus formed a distinctive element in the labour force. The nature of that distinctiveness is complex, but may to some extent be indicated through macroeconomic statistics. Black workers tend to be concentrated in unskilled and semi-skilled occupations involving unsocial hours, shift work, and unpleasant working conditions. Though they are twice as likely to be doing shift work as white workers, their earnings as a group are lower (Henriques et al, 1980). That they are well represented in skilled occupations is subject to the observations concerning mechanisation noted above. They are substantially under-represented in managerial and supervisory posts. To these factors must be added, particularly in the period from 1970 onwards, the question of unemployment. Between 1973 and 1980, whereas total unemployment doubled, black unemployment quadrupled (Dept. of Employment, Gazette, 1980, Vol. 88(3)). That rise in black unemployment has been disproportionately concentrated among the 16 to 24 age group, but the larger suggestion is that black workers as a whole have been especially vulnerable to economic recession (Smith, 1977).

The distinctive location of black workers within the economy has led some theorists to surmise the operation of a dual or segmented labour market (Bosanquet and Doeringer, 1973; Edwards, Reich and Gordon, 1973) comprised of 'advantaged' workers in the primary or dynamic sector of industry, and of 'disadvantaged' workers in the secondary sector. According to Bosanquet and Doeringer:

'Disadvantaged' workers are employed in enterprises where wages are low, working conditions are poor, employment is often unstable, and opportunities for on-the-job training and advancement are severely limited: by contrast, 'advantaged' workers tend to receive higher pay, relatively secure employment and on-the-job training that leads to higher wages.
(Bosanquet and Doeringer, 1973, p. 422)

Other theorists have suggested that blacks have come to form part of a new 'reserve army of labour'. Sucked into the British economy as 'surplus labour' from the colonies in the first instance, they form a low-wage sector within the economy, drawn into and out of employment as a function of the changing needs of capital (Gorz, 1970; Castles and Kosack, 1973; Castells, 1975). Neither 'dual' and 'segmented' labour markets, nor 'reserve army of labour' theories sufficiently explain the economic and wider social location of black workers, but they do attempt to come to grips with the issues in structural terms of black workers comprising one of the most intensely exploited sectors of the labour force.

The economic incorporation of black workers is reflected directly in their residential distribution. Drawn to the public sector and the service industries in Greater London and the South; to manufacturing, engineering and foundries in the West Midlands; and to textiles and clothing in the North-East, in these areas they form a far greater proportion of the active labour force than the 2.2% national average (Runnymede Trust and Radical Statistics Race Group, 1980). It is however the deprived and decaying inner areas of these large conurbations that provide the residential setting. Whereas it is true that for early migrants these were the only areas where a cheap and ready supply of housing could be found, the impact of discrimination soon began to manifest itself in multi-tenancy and overcrowding (Rex and Moore, 1967). Though the phase of the lodging house and the rented room has largely passed, continued migration has acted so as to reinforce initial patterns of residential concentration, and that concentration is increasingly 'forced' (Sivanandan, 1976) with black families finding it increasingly difficult to escape the inner city. The Afro-Caribbean and Asian 'colony' in the inner city is stark. If it once provided the means through which black workers and their families became socialised within the metropolitan environment, more and more it has become a territorial space increasingly isolated in a social setting marked by racial hostility. Both in labour and housing markets the black workers are distinctively and differentially located and that location though achieved through a variety of mechanisms, is organised and experienced through race.

The absence of major instances of violent inter-racial communal conflict between black and white workers in the 1950's and 60's – the period of maximum inward migration – should not lead us to suppose the absence of conflicts. Clearly, however, those conflicts are different from those which applied in the pre-war era. Rather than black workers representing – as was the case with domiciled colonial seamen – the ability of capital to directly undercut white wages, they came to occupy the low-wage sector. Castle and Kosack argued that black workers came into competition only with a limited section of the indigenous labour force. Thus in the period of full employment up to the middle

1960's, (and that itself must be reckoned a factor in the relative absence of inter-racial collective violence) black labour in part facilitated the upward mobility of unskilled and semi-skilled white labour. But as Rubery (1978) suggests they also directly benefited skilled labour by facilitating the creating and maintenance of new categories of skill in an era where the process of de-skilling was weakening the collective bargaining position of skilled white workers. White workers then have had a role to play both in racial discrimination and in the racialisation of the work process, i.e. 'black shifts' and 'black shops'. And though black workers have joined the Trade Union movement in disproportionate numbers, they have not received the support of the movement generally, or in crucial disputes such as the Wolf plant – Southall, Mansfield Hosiery, Imperial Typewriter – Leicester, Fords, Courtaulds, ICI and Standard Telephones.

Conflicts then are implicit given the relative dispositions of black and different sections of white labour. Castles and Kosack, however, tend to minimise the degree to which black and white workers come into direct competition. While that competition is likely to be at its most intense at the unskilled and semi-skilled occupational level, it is nevertheless present at the skilled level where blacks are also well represented. Nor is the residential dimension – with blacks' settlement expanding in the inner areas of the city – to be ignored. It is in this context that we must locate the 1958 Notting Hill and Nottingham 'race riots'. Hall identifies three elements in the Notting Hill confrontation: '. . ①the structured antagonism between "colony" blacks and sections of the indigenous white working class and petty-bourgoisie of this decaying "Royal" suburb②the 'white teenagers' symbolising an emergent youth culture, and the 'active element' in that it is they that are most likely to be directly in economic competition with black workers; ③ and the involvement of a 'fascist political element', seizing on racism and the presence of blacks as the first opportunity for effective political organisation since the 1940's (Hall/CRE, 1978). It is these last two elements that render Notting Hill unlike 1919 and 1948, and more an indication of things yet to come. The Dudley 'riots' of 1962, however, do not exhibit this fascist element. The fighting – spread over four nights – occurred mainly between small white crowds bent on storming the black area, and the police. And prominent amongst those arrested were labourers and semi-skilled white workers (*Dudley Herald*, 21 August, 1962). A conscientious reporter interviewing some forty persons after the clashes found that in addition to suspicions with regards to blacks and crime, some whites

. . . were aggrieved that West Indians should still be in jobs no matter how long they had held them, when . . . whites were on short time. Others recalled with resentment occasions when they had had to queue on equal terms with coloured people in applying for jobs and did not think it quite right
(*Observer*, 5 August, 1962)

These two instances of violent collective action mobilised by whites demonstrate the range of concerns and tendencies within the working class. At the fore in Dudley is economic competition structured by both racial and 'common-sense' class ideologies; its context is the growing upward trend in unemployment and the gathering industrial recession. Within the wider organised labour movement, it reflects what Miles and Phizacklea describe as a 'negative and defensive reaction to immigration' (1977). In the political domain, it resonates with the politicisation of race within the state as indicated by the emergence of the Birmingham Immigration Control Association from 1960 (Foot, 1965) and confirmed in the 1962 Commonwealth Immigration Act. These are also considerations in the 1958 Notting Hill 'race riots', but there another important tendency was indicated, the connection between organised fascism and certain elements of white youth culture. This in the 1970's comes to be associated not only with the growth of incidental and organised individualised racial attacks, but also with the over-spill of race-related collective violence into the streets in the political struggles between fascism and black and anti-racist organisations.

Race and the State – *the primacy of black immigration*
If, on the face of it labour hungry post-war capital cared little about where it obtained labour power from, from the beginning the debate within the state on the issue of black labour was ideological. Where race and colonial considerations did not enter the picture the state acted decisively. Notwithstanding reservations about the possible impact on industrial relations, it identified both the extent and areas of labour shortages, and recommended an extension in the recruitment of Irish and European labour (White Paper, 1947; Cmnd 7046). By contrast, that continuing labour demand might be met by 'surplus colonial labour' was seen by, for example, a Colonial Office Working Party commissioned by the 1948 Labour Government, as 'extremely complicated' (PRO, 1948, CO/006/2). The complications were several. First, on the general level, there was a desire to keep the Empire's 'colour problems' in the colonies. Voiced most clearly in a report by the Royal Commission on Population in 1949, the argument was that immigration could only be welcomed 'without reserve' if

the migrants were of good human stock and were not prevented by their religion or race from inter-marrying with the host population and becoming merged in it.
(Cmnd 7695. 1949. para 329)

Second, there were official understandings of the experience of earlier black settlement. The 1947 Colonial Office Report described these settlements as a 'social problem', as 'coloured ghettos' associated with lawlessness and violence. That new black migrants might be attracted to these areas was considered 'the most undesirable thing' that could happen. Thirdly, there was the consideration that colonial workers were British subjects; unlike Europeans or other aliens, they could not be formally directed and restricted to specific industries, they could not be controlled in terms of where they settled, and most of all they could not be deported in the event of industrial recession.

The post-war state is the site of two basic and contradictory interests: the demand for labour by certain sections of capital, which is dominant, and the subordinate tendency towards the restriction and control of that labour, based upon those 'complications' outlined above and by the concerns within both major political parties. In an effort to mediate or rationalise this basic contradiction the state variously allowed its public sector to participate directly in the process of recruitment – i.e. to recruit immigrants with specific skills, for specific jobs, in specific places. There is an informal but nevertheless concerted attempt to direct incoming migrants to particular areas where their labour is in demand (Duffield, 1981); and there are attempts to regulate the overall flow of black immigration at source. Even as the 'Empire Windrush' arrives, questions prompted by this last aspect are already on the Parliamentary table (Hansard, 27 July, 1949). By 1955 restrictive legislation already existed in draft form (House of Lords Debates, Vol. 200 (420) 20 November, 1956). Subsequently the Conservative Government of the late 1950's resorted to bilateral agreements with colonial administrations to keep immigrant numbers down (Rose et al: 1969).

When therefore the 1962 Commonwealth Immigration Act was passed, it hardly represented – as is often implied – a new and un-principled departure within the state. What it did represent was the growing ascendancy within the state of that coalition of political forces that had argued for the prevention and/or the restriction of 'black immigration', as opposed to immigration itself. It is this ascendancy that marks the beginnings of the larger process of the politicisation of 'race' within the state. Not only does black immigration become an election issue (e.g. Smethwick, 1964) in this process, and therefore the subject of competition between political parties, but also the issues are widened from immigration to encompass all aspects related to black settlement. Additionally, there is an elaboration within the state of legal structures and agencies dealing specifically with race, and not only do these affect the body politic, they themselves become sites of con-tention between opposing political forces.

In the movement towards the greater involvement of the state in race, the Labour Party White Paper on 'Immigration from the Common-wealth' in 1965 marked a crucial watershed. Moore observed that the paper:

came at the end of a period of increasingly strident debate about black immigration. There were public incidents involving petitions against black residents in particular areas or burning crosses being fixed to black citizen's doors, and there was a rising tide of hysterical anti-black letters in the national and local press. (1975, pp. 24–25)

The paper signified the complete dominance of the 'immigration control' lobby, which may no longer even be termed a lobby because the restrictive principle now informed the policies of both major political parties. From this moment on, in what Patterson (1969) describes as a 'Dutch auction of illiberalism', the competition between political parties is over the severity of restrictive controls, and the back-drop is periodic 'panics' in the media over illegal immigrants and immigrant numbers (see Chapter 3), 'increasing organized fascist political activity', and Powellism. The result is the 1968 Immigration Act which removes the right of entry of British passport holders and links immigration to patriality, and the 1971 Act which further formalises and extends the principles of the 1968 Act. On the surface the logic binding these different legislative measures together is 'immigrant numbers'. But beneath that logic there are two other trends: the control and regulation of those black immigrants who are allowed in on a par with 'aliens'; and in the longer term, a complete end to primary black 'settler' immigration.

Moore, however, identified another important feature in the 1965 White Paper. In addition to labelling 'black immigration' as 'a problem' the solution to which was 'numbers', the Paper went on to suggest that restricting black immigration was itself good for wider race relations (1975, p. 25). Reducible to the simple argument that fewer blacks makes better race relations, this became received wisdom for both major political parties. In the words of Roy Hattersley, 'integration without control is impossible, control without integration is indefensible'. The structured link between immigration control and race relations, such that the former dominates (and is indeed the policy cornerstone of the latter), is hardly accidental. It not only reflected the principal means by which race had become politicised within the state, but the concern which shaped race relations thinking in the early 60's. Certainly it is true that there existed within Parliament from an early period a small anti-discrimination liberal race relations lobby; the M.P. Reginald Sorenson proposed such a measure in 1951, and Fenner Brockway again in 1956. In the early 1960's however, part of the argument mobilised in justification of restrictive immigration control was that blacks constituted a social problem in that they concentrated in particular areas in the city, put pressure on scarce housing resources, and overloaded local educational and social services. Thus ironically the very structural problems blacks had met, and the discrimination that determined their location within the city, were now being used to justify keeping them out – or at least restricting their numbers to the ability of the social services to cope. But at the same time a realisation that these 'social problems' also had to be tackled was generated. Two policy strands emerged – anti-discrimination and the inner-city – and on both, events across the Atlantic were powerully influential. Thus the mover of the 1965 Race Relations (Amendment) Bill argued:

If the Bill is not accepted what is the alternative? The danger is that the 2 per cent of our population of other origin, of other colour, in our midst, . . . will feel a special sense of isolation. The danger is that the futility which they feel will become corrosive. There will be a negation of hope, a loss of nerve and finally a descent to despair and violence. (Hansard, Vol. 738 (904), 16 December, 1966)

Similarly, writing about the period one sociologist recalled:

Dark forebodings that we too would have our American future in race relations if we didn't take action, led eventually to the notion that there were areas of multiple deprivation in the inner-city and that Inner-City Policy must be a focus of major government action. (Rex, 1978, p. 9)

Notwithstanding the direct link between race relations, the inner-city and potential social violence, given a political environment dominated by successive panics over black immigration, the political commitment to anti-discrimination and the inner-city has been weak. Though anti-discrimination legislation has become progressively stronger on paper, no government has been prepared to risk its popularity by granting such executive powers and funds as would make the Act effective. Inner-city policy in its broad conception has studiously avoided the ethnic dimension, formulating its provisions in strictly non-racial terms. Instead, the state has increasingly responded to the 'American Future' of which sociologists so eloquently warned, with a cost-effective, politically expedient means. Exercised through the law, the courts, the police, and a complex of agencies supposedly specifically concerned with race and ethnic relations, that means is social control.

Black resistance – black revolt

In the larger sense the stance of the state on race may simply be thought an expression, at the political level, of the changing needs of different combinations of dominant capitals in the post-war era. Thus broadly, as overall demand for labour contracted after the long expansion of the 1950's, the state moved both to restrict and link incoming labour to specific demands. Later towards the end of the 1960's as economic recession and mass unemployment loomed, primary black immigration was completely stopped, and moves made to restrict even the entry of dependants. But the expression of race within the state cannot be unproblematically reduced to changing labour demand. Thus some theorists have argued that over and above this, the state has acted so as to reproduce in changing economic circumstances the primary function for which black labour was initially imported – i.e. a reserve of highly adaptable 'low-waged' labour responsive to both swings and trends in the economy. (Gorz, 1970; Nikolinakos, 1975; Castells, 1975) These theories necessarily adopt a deterministic and conspiratorial view of the state to which we do not subscribe. Nevertheless, as an outcome of various political struggles within the institutions of the state, there is certainly substance in the conclusions of this theoretical approach. Notwithstanding, for example, Roy Jenkins's proclamation of a 'promised land' in which 'equal opportunity would accompany cultural diversity in an atmosphere of mutual tolerance', or Robert Carr's identification of the second generation as the 'real challenge of race relations', the same second generation has failed to advance significantly beyond the first. Instead, that second generation has come most violently into conflict with the state.

This then is the context within which race in the 1970's was situated: the consciousness and political resistance of black communities being shaped by their distinctive social location within the social structure, and by the role of the state in facilitating that location from period to period. It is against the 1971 Immigration Act – the cornerstone of the state's stance on race – that resistance has been most determined and protracted. The intent of this Act we have already referenced, but the true extent of its racial hostility may only be perceived through a description of the powers granted to immigration officers and the police. These include strip searches, vaginal examinations of Asian women, the right to stop and search blacks on the streets on 'suspicion' of being in the country illegally, and the right to search premises, without warrant, on the same suspicion. The enforcement of these powers, at times, takes the form of 'fishing' expeditions or 'passport' raids in the black community. Here:

substantial numbers of people who were not in breach of immigration laws, who may have lived long periods in the U.K., and who have not committed any offence were asked to prove their innocence by establishing their right to be in the U.K. simply because of their colour. (Moore and Wallace, 1975, p. 37)

Through such practices, the policing of immigration laws became an integral part of the policing of black communities. Contrasting sharply with standard legal procedures, anyone wrongfully arrested during one of these raids has no legal right of redress (Downing, 1980).

Routine and official, this racism is nonetheless very, very real. And the political environment within which it thrived was delineated not only by central political figures actively exciting public fears of 'swamping', but by the increasing intervention of far right racist and fascist organisations in the political process on the platform of total re-patriation (Fielding, 1981; Taylor, 1982). Opposition to the political interventions and other activities of these organisations by the black community in conjunction with the Anti-Racist Movement, took to the streets in 1975 when the National Front organised a march on London's East End. On this occasion no violence occurred, but it certainly did elsewhere, most notably in Lewisham and Ladywood, Birmingham, 1977, and in Southall 1979. In Southall, it was less the aggressive tactics of the National Front that led to violence, than the determination by the police that the local Asian and Afro-Caribbean community should not demonstrate against the National Front's meeting in the Town Hall. Equipped with riot shields and backed up by dogs, horses, and units of the Special Patrol Group, some 2,700 policemen bottled up the demonstration between crash barriers and police cordons in streets away from a 'sterile' area created around the Town Hall. In the violence that followed 345 people were arrested, 97 police officers and 64 members of the public injured, and Blair Peach lost his life (NCCL, 1980).

We have already argued that the politics and policies of anti-immi-gration have to be seen as the first constraint on anti-discrimination and inner-city initiatives. To that constraint may be added in the 1970's, a deteriorating economy and mass unemployment. As a consequence the enforcement of anti-discrimination legislation has at no time enjoyed high political priority. Additionally, inner-city policy, designed under the Urban Partnership and Programme Authorities to tackle the physical decay and social disadvantage in inner areas, have signif-icantly failed to achieve their own objectives (Demuth, 1977; Edwards and Batley, 1978). It is in this failure, in the unwillingness of govern-ment to respond in policy terms to the recognised differential impact of the inner-city on black communities (Meacher, 1974), and in the deepening economic crisis of the 1970's that we locate the second major area of confrontation between blacks and the state. That confrontation has brought race into almost every area of national political concern. It revolves in the first instance around those very agencies and structures erected within the state (e.g. CRE and CRC structures and the admin-istration of Section 11 funds under 1966 Local Government Act) to 'manage' race relations. Indeed some observers have seen these struc-tures – given their high visibility and negligible social impact – as performing a 'buffer' role between black political aspirations and the state (Hill and Issacheroff, 1971; Katznelson, 1970; Kirby, 1975). Secondly, race has become an integral part of the debate on housing, homelessness, education, crime, unemployment etc. In these areas the objectives of black self-help groups and other black organisations have been to modify, extend and challenge local and national policies on behalf of black communities. But it is in the third respect, between black communities and the coercive institutions of the state, that confrontation has been most intense.

A reflection of the larger stance of the state on race, from the middle 1960's onwards, is that black communities began to be officially perceived as presenting society with different – if not unique – problems of policing. Annual Reports of the Metropolitan Police during this period for example, often included a sub-section entitled 'Public Order and Racial Integration'. The juxtaposition of these two seemingly disrelated schemes captured at an early stage an official concern that was later to become increasingly pronounced in the 1970's: and that was the public order implications of black political demonstration and public protest. While this concern was part and parcel of wider anxieties within the state on the question of trade union and student militancy (Hall et al, 1978), it nevertheless exhibited distinctive features of its own. Crucial in this respect was the inordinate hostility with which the police reacted to early black associational forms – particularly those to which the emotive and often misunderstood 'Black Power' label could be tagged (see, for example the written and oral evidence of senior policemen in the 1972 Report of the Select Committee on Race Relations and Immigration). The Mangrove episode in the early 1970's demonstrates the kind of collective confrontation to which this hostility could lead. A restaurant in Notting Hill, and a well known meeting place for black radicals, the Mangrove was subjected to repeated police raids on a variety of pretexts. According to one police officer giving evidence at a trial later, the restaurant so far as he was concerned was the headquarters of the Black Power organisation (Humphry, 1972). When eventually a demonstration was organised to protest against these raids, some 150 protesters found themselves confronted by 500 policemen. A bitter clash occurred as the demonstration came to an end, and 18 persons later appeared before the courts, some charged with riotous assembly.

In addition to highlighting the attitudes of the police to black political organisation and protest, the Mangrove episode also indicated the way black public street assemblies – demonstrations or otherwise – were policed. The 1976 and 1977 Notting Hill carnivals need no extensive recounting here, but certainly the extent to which they were over-policed must be accounted as important factors in the violence that occurred. What these instances of collective black violence revealed was not so much that the black community presented the state with different problems of policing, but that these communities were being differently policed. Given that many areas of black settlement in the inner-city overlap with 'high crime' areas, certainly black communities were likely to experience the sharper end of standard police practices. The differential policing of black communities, however, was not based on standard police practices, but on ideologies, laws and methods of policing that applied exclusively or disproportionately to them.

The police have long since admitted that 'individual' officers reflect racial attitudes present in society (Select Committee on Race Relations and Immigration, 1972, Vol. 3, p. 493). That of itself – given the key role of the police in the community – would be a matter for concern. But what became increasingly evident in the 1970's was that the police did not simply reflect racial attitudes in society, they actively extended, reproduced and acted on those attitudes. The first indication of this on an institutional, rather than on an individual basis, came in the early 1970's when the metropolitan police 'produced' statistics to show that certain types of inner-city crime (formerly indistinguishable in terms of race) was black crime, committed by black youths against white people (Select Committee, 1977, Vol. II, pp. 177–187). These statistics were vigorously contested (ibid., Vol. III, pp. 548–554), nonetheless the practice has continued (Annual Report Metropolitan Police, 1982) and the dubious connections between black youth and crime reinforced. Acting on such assertions as black West Indian youth were 'estranged from their families', 'rejected approach by the police or West Indians' and comprised a 'sub-culture' which had a 'substantial criminal fringe' (Memo, Birmingham City Police, Select Committee 1972, Vol. III, p. 446), certain laws and police methods have become particularly applicable to whole black communities. First in some cities the 'sus' law has become a definitive feature of policing black areas (Demuth, 1978; NCCL, 1981). In these and other areas not only is policing blacks denoted by frequent police over-reactions, but by road blocks, saturation policing and the use of the Special Patrol Group (State Research, Vol. 3, No. 19).

These police methods led to a state of relations between the police and black communities such that in 1971 a Liverpool Labour Councillor and local magistrate said:

the coloured community is fed up with being hounded. No one is safe on the streets after 10 p.m. One gang we know has given the police an ultimatum to lay off within two weeks or they fight back. It could lead to civil war in the city. (Mrs Margaret Symey. Quoted in Humphry, 1972, p. 13).

From the middle 1970's onwards the police themselves began to note the increasing incidence of spontaneous collective black resistance.

Recently there has been a growth in the tendency for members of London's West Indian communities to combine against the police by interfering with police officers who are effecting the arrest of a black person . . . In the last 12

months forty such incidents have been recorded. Each carries a potential for
large scale disorder.
(Select Committee, 1977, Vol. II, p. 178)

Against this background, the events that occurred in Bristol on 2
April, 1980 could have occurred anytime during the last decade. We
have attempted in this chapter to demonstrate the changing patterns of
collective racial violence in Britain. We have argued that that violence
cannot be abstracted from the political struggles of the groups concerned, and that those struggles must be seen as shaped by the specific
articulation of race and class in British society in different historic
periods. We have concentrated particularly on the distinctive social
location of black labour within the economy in both pre- and post-war
eras, since this is foremost in our understanding of the collective
violence in Bristol in 1980 and elsewhere in 1981. Supposedly, given
the proportions that 'the Bristol Riot' assumed, and the public shock
and trauma that followed, the state would be forced into a critical
re-examination of race and racism in British society. We turn therefore
to state understandings of and responses to the 1980 'BRISTOL
RIOT', as a case study in itself, and as an important precursor of how
the state reacted to the more general violence of 1981.

Part II   Understanding Events

2   What Happened in St Paul's? The Construction of Official Accounts

On the afternoon of 2 April 1980 violence broke out on the streets of a city in England, Bristol. While historically this was not a unique event, it was apparently totally unexpected in Britain in the eighties; surprise and shock ran through many sectors of society. The questions that people wanted immediate answers to were how did it happen, what actually did happen, who was responsible and how could such an event be prevented from ever happening again? In order to answer these questions it was essential to have a very clear understanding of the event. Only after it was described and lines of responsibility drawn, could decisions be made about how to react in the short and the long term.

The Home Secretary was acutely aware of this need for a description of what happened which would provide the cornerstone on which explanations and understandings of the key features of the afternoon could be constructed. Indeed, so central was this need for an account of the events that at the same time as he called for a detailed report from the Chief Constable on the day after the trouble, he said that he would not outline government responses to the situation until he had received the necessary information, excepting of course general statements of concern and condemnation of the violence. Only when he held the Chief Constable's document in his hand was he able to speak about the causes of the event and the suitable responses. This was accepted without question by the Home Secretary and then Parliament, and it became the core 'knowledge' about what happened on the streets of St Paul's. The media, and the prosecution in the Crown Court a year later during the trial for riotous assembly, relied heavily on this knowledge. The Judge followed the essential features of this version in his summing up, though his account was far more detailed.

Indeed there has been little dispute about the 'facts' of what happened in Bristol in public. Even most academics have essentially accepted as uncontroversial the facts as given by the Chief Constable, facts endorsed and repeated so many times and in so many places subsequently that they have become common knowledge. These facts formed the basis for analysis, explanation and understanding of the

Bristol 'riot'. But how far are these facts straight-forward and incontrovertible? The afternoon of the 2nd was very confused and confusing; it is crucial to realise that a multitude of people and police were involved, that several things were happening at once, in different streets at different times, and that the mass of evidence available about the afternoon was provided by different people who experienced different things. So the Chief Constable had to be selective. What did he choose to emphasize and what did he ignore? Which issues were highlighted and which were never raised in his report? This process of selection, which has so far remained widely unchallenged, meant that his original account was inevitably a very partial view, but because this formed the basis for further accounts the question of what was omitted and what was highlighted becomes crucial.

In presenting his report, one of the major pressures on the Chief Constable was to explain and justify the police withdrawal from the streets of St Paul's for four hours, between 7.30 and 11.30 p.m. on the evening of the 2nd. A great deal of public criticism had been directed at the police for leaving the streets, there was much concern with the creation of what was emotively labelled a 'no-go' area, the use of that term inevitably evoking images of guerilla warfare and terrorism as they are represented in relation to Northern Ireland. His account had to address itself to that issue and he was inevitably concerned to illustrate the absolute necessity for the police to withdraw. He needed to demonstrate convincingly that the police were not to blame, either for the outbreak of violence or for the withdrawal. The Home Secretary was also concerned to show that the police had, by and large, done their job and that it was the violence of the crowd that had forced them to withdraw. The Director of Public Prosecutions presumably understood the events in the same way when he decided to bring the charge of riotous assembly three months later. The Judge, almost a year later, was also concerned with the violence of the crowd, but he was less concerned with the policing which was largely immaterial to the central fact of concern in the courts, that young people had committed grave public order offences on the streets. The different versions were used for slightly different purposes and there were some differences between these accounts, but these were sufficiently marginal to make it possible to talk about the construction and evolution of an 'official account'. The way in which this account affected the media reporting and analysis of the event will be dealt with in the following chapter.

There are certain key similarities in all the accounts with regards to both the sequence of events and the underlying assumptions about those events. They describe the afternoon as following a clear pattern which started with a legitimate police raid on the Black and White cafe in St Paul's. This raid was suddenly confronted by an outburst of

!/? violence when some drug squad officers were stoned. Later the violence escalated and led to the overturning and burning of a police car. The violence intensified thereafter, so that eventually the police were forced to withdraw by 7.30 p.m. because of the ferocity of the crowd. In each of the accounts no explanation is attempted; the violence is simply presented, and in some accounts there is a feeling that it was a totally inexplicable outburst. It is interesting that so little concern was shown for why a good-humoured crowd became violent. Apparently it was felt to be adequate to simply assert that it did. This official lack of concern with trying to understand why such eruptions occur is a thread that runs through the treatment of previous outbursts, such as the Notting Hill riots and the Mangrove violence. Perhaps one of the reasons for this persistent lack of concern about why such events occur can be found in a set of beliefs about West Indians. These can be found in police reports, parliamentary debates and in sociological analyses and suggest that West Indians are either biologically or culturally prone to violence, e.g. 'we are certainly not suggesting that blacks are naturally aggressive but that, because of their cultural background, they will react in a certain way' (Cashmore, *Birmingham Evening Mail*, October 26, 1982). There is a growing sociological body of thought which endorses a view of alienated West Indians who have a culture of violence due to their heritage of slavery. Also, because such violence was seen in the USA in the sixties this prepared people to believe that black people can be violent; it is something that potentially can always happen. This aspect and its effect on Government thinking were examined in Chapter 1.

Because all the accounts share this understanding of an unprovoked, inexplicable outbreak of violence, they all condemn it outright as unjustified and criminal. This has always been the state's perception of civil disturbances, and clearly continued to be so in 1981. Even Scarman, who documented a multiplicity of reasons for the Brixton riots, nevertheless said:

these young people, by their *criminal* behaviour – for such, whatever their grievances and frustrations, it was – brought about a temporary collapse of law and order in the centre of an inner suburb in London.
(Scarman, 1981, p. 14, our emphasis)

The official version must be assessed both in terms of the questions it was concerned to answer, and the understandings and interests of those who were asked to present the accounts. Looking briefly at the recent history of such understandings we will document the limited framework within which all conflicts between police and blacks have been understood before Bristol 1980.

To date, all recent outbreaks of violence between police and black people have essentially been interpreted and handled as unprovoked attacks by black people on the police. No official inquiries were undertaken prior to 1981, and the problems and issues raised by the troubles were dealt with solely in the courts, where the young people involved faced major criminal charges. The behaviour of the police was never seriously raised as an issue, even though in most cases the accused were found 'not guilty'. This continued to be the way in which the disturbances were handled, although juries often rejected the police versions and did not convict. Questions were not raised about why juries kept refusing to accept the prosecution case, based on police evidence; instead criticism was made of the jury system which was failing to support the police.

In 1970 there was the *Mangrove* trial. Police had carried out three drug raids on the Mangrove cafe in a period of six months and many black people were angry about these repeated raids. They planned a demonstration to call for just treatment of black people by both the police and the courts. The police response was to monitor the demonstration with several hundred police, and during the course of the day street violence erupted, and there was a pitched battle between the police and the demonstrators. The event caused great alarm; the media predictably accused outside agitators of coming into the area and causing trouble, and the police sent the papers of some of those arrested to the Director of Public Prosecutions to consider whether serious charges should be brought. Eleven weeks after the trouble nine people were charged with inciting the public to kill police, incitement to riot and causing an affray. No inquiry was set up to look into why the police repeatedly raided the Mangrove, nor why the demonstration was so heavily policed. The nine charged formed a strong defence committee and during the eleven week trial at the Old Bailey they challenged the veracity of the police evidence. The jury found five defendants not guilty on all counts and four were found guilty of lesser offences. No one was sent to prison. The fact that the jury did not convict did not however lead to any further official investigation into what had happened, or why.

In 1971 a similar case (the *Metro 4*) arose out of a police raid on the Metro Club, again in Notting Hill. One evening police filled the club saying that they were looking for a 'wanted' man, who was not found. The blacks resented this intrusion and resisted the police, who sent for reinforcements and fighting ensued. In the aftermath, sixteen blacks were arrested; four were subsequently charged with affray though no-one was found guilty. In 1974 the *Swan Disco 7* were charged with affray in Stockwell, London. This case also arose out of a police entry into a disco which led to a running battle between black youth and the police. In October 1974 a similar event occurred in a disco in Cricklewood, North London. On 12 October a police raid on the *Carib Club* led to a battle between them and the youth inside, and forty people were arrested as a result. During the fighting one policeman was stabbed and several black youths were injured. The *Evening Standard* stressed the ferocity of the fight against the police and reported that twelve of the seventy police involved had been injured. The Police Chief Superintendent in charge described the incident 'as most unfortunate' but that his officers had behaved well and that no complaints of police brutality had been received, the police had simply been trying to defend themselves following a virulent attack on them by black youths in the club.

When the *Cricklewood 12* came to trial charged with affray a different picture of events emerged from the police version that had been reported in the media. It transpired that the police had been to the club four times in the previous fortnight, each time looking for 'wanted' persons. On this occasion twelve policemen had entered for the same reason, and as soon as the young people started to express their hostility to this police presence, the police radioed for help and within minutes over one hundred police arrived on the scene, complete with three police vans containing dogs. The police had their truncheons out and at least two were equipped with riot shields, and at the trial the defendants said that they had been attacked by police and were trying to protect themselves. Much of the police evidence was found to be contradictory and unreliable during the eighty-three days of the hearing and the Judge dismissed one of the cases himself. The jury did not accept the police evidence, eight people were found 'not guilty' and there was a hung jury on the last three. Again, no police officers were asked after the trial to explain how their evidence had been collected nor how, in one case, an innocent youth had made a signed confession.

In a trial following trouble on bonfire night in *Chapeltown* Leeds in 1975, the jury found the ten young people charged with affray not guilty of twenty one of the twenty four charges against them. In this case it emerged in court that the fighting between the crowd and the police had started when a police car had driven into the crowd celebrating Guy Fawkes. Even though the police had been instructed to keep a low profile because of the recognised tension, they were in fact standing by and appeared instantly in large numbers to handle the 'mob': a crowd made up largely of West Indian, Asian and white school children.

Then in 1976 there was the trouble at the *Notting Hill Carnival*. Hundreds of police were present at the Carnival causing a lot of upset and aggravation to the participants. *The Times* (1.9.76) reported that the carnival was swamped with police, every few yards there were groups of two or three policemen, and police in lines shepherded the steel bands. As one local person told the reporter afterwards 'when the

protestors received criminal convictions in the courts, while the National Front and those police who had used illegal and excessive violence against the community were ignored both by the law and by the Government which had relegated the problem to the courts. The majority of cases were heard in the Magistrate's courts where there was no jury to convince of the validity of the prosecution, which led defence barristers to make several conclusions. First, that 'the inference is unavoidable that the prosecution manipulated the charges so as to avoid jury trial in as many cases as possible' (Lewis, 1980, p. 14). Secondly, that the Magistrates accepted police evidence uncritically, 'we are appalled (by) . . . the apparent ability of the Magistrates there to consistently and unconditionally accept evidence of police officers in the face of credible defence evidence' (NCCL, 1980, p. 109). And thirdly that many of the Magistrates appeared to conceive of 'themselves as engaged in teaching a lesson to some group' (NCCL, 1980, p. 10).

In each of these cases, particularly that of Southall 1979, the official response was to highlight the violence of the crowd and deal with it in the law courts. The reason for the eruption of the violence and the part played by the police were not legitimate issues in the courts and so they were glossed over. In none of these cases was there an official questioning of the police accounts, nor an inquiry into the wider issues involved. This is what also happened in Bristol, 1980. The submission of a report by the Chief Constable, and the Home Secretary's endorsement of that view of what happened, was the first stage in the process in Bristol which led to the law courts, and ostensibly pre-empted the need for a public enquiry.

The Methodology

The riot occurred in Bristol on 2 April. The Home Secretary immediately requested a detailed report from the Chief Constable which was submitted by 28 April and immediately reported on to Parliament. In June the Director of Public Prosecutions took his decision to prosecute sixteen young people on a charge of riotous assembly and in September 1980 their committal took place. The Crown Court trial took place over a six week period in February and March 1981. By looking at two of the key accounts, those of the Chief Constable, upheld by the Home Secretary, and the Crown Court Judge, in relation to the available evidence about the afternoon, the uniform, clear picture of events as presented starts to fracture and fragment. By looking at this in some detail it is possible to show which issues were highlighted and which ignored in these accounts, and how these excluded certain kinds of responses and facilitated others. The evidence to be used in this analysis comes from the police themselves, because the police evidence was the only body of

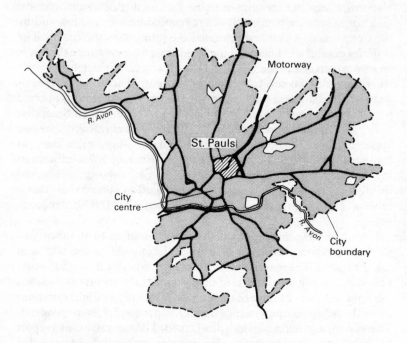

Figure 1   Bristol, showing St Paul's area

information available about the afternoon, consisting of the eye-witness accounts of a large number of police officers, and because the Chief Constable would have relied heavily on police evidence to make his report.

At some stage following the disturbance most of the police officers who were on the streets of St Paul's were required to write a formal statement describing what they saw. These statements were dated and signed as true accounts of what happened, who was seen, where and at what time. A police statement is always critical evidence in a court of law and is therefore expected to be an accurate record of what the police officer saw and heard. Police involved in St Paul's wrote their statements in the days that followed the trouble and these were ultimately sent to the Director of Public Prosecutions (DPP) in connection with charging some offenders with serious offences in court. The DPP accepted these statements as valid and admissible evidence and eventually over ninety statements (some officers submitted several statements) were used in evidence against those charged with riotous assembly in the Crown Court.

The bulk of these statements, plus some from civilian witnesses in support of the police cases, were submitted to senior police officers before 28 April 1980. Even if the Chief Constable did not have all these statements before him when he wrote his report, his account must have derived from some of the evidence of police who were involved in the events, as he himself was only present later in the afternoon. It is important to stress here that these police statements cover over six hundred pages of typescript. The accounts vary enormously at times, and some discrepancies are irreconcilable, and the disparities between these accounts have made it impossible for us to draw out one coherent, certain picture of the afternoon, even from a police point of view. Rather, by referring to only the significant police witnesses and using evidence relating only to the most important moments during the afternoon, we want to highlight the major conflicts that arise between the police accounts on the one hand and the official versions on the other.

The Setting

St Paul's is a very small area of Bristol, literally a few streets located beside the M32 motorway and close to the central shopping area of the city, Broadmeads. It is an inner city area of decaying housing, narrow streets, few facilities, and limited play areas. It no longer has a secondary school. Many people in the population of West Indian, Asian, Irish and English are unemployed.

There are few places for young people to go. For young black males there are some cafes and one or two community halls. The Black and White and the Shady Grove cafes are popular meeting places. The Black and White cafe is a converted front room of a terraced house located in Grosvenor Road in the heart of St Paul's. The room is about fifteen feet square with a small counter to one side, some tables and chairs for customers. The cafe is set back a little from the road and there is often a group of young men gathered in the small forecourt outside the cafe; the adjoining houses have low front-garden walls where others sometimes sit and chat. Across the narrow road – where cars have to slow down and manoeuvre to pass each other – there is a grass area in front of a block of council flats, another place to gather and talk.

The Shady Grove cafe was raided a few weeks prior to the 2 April raid on the Black and White, and both cafes had previously been raided by the police searching for drugs and unlicensed alcohol; neither cafe is licensed to sell alcoholic drinks.

The Chief Constable's Account

In a memorandum placed in the Library of the House of Commons by the Secretary of State for the Home Department on 28 April 1980, the

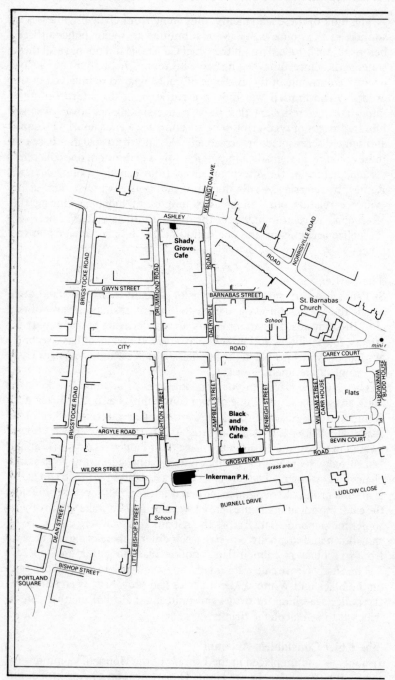

Figure 2   St Paul's in detail

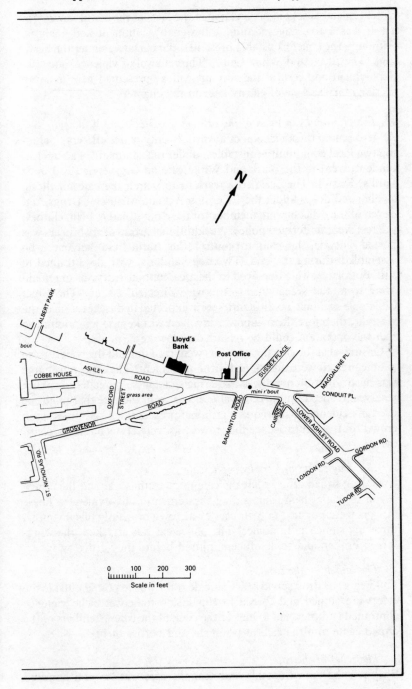

Chief Constable set out 'a narrative of the facts of the disturbances' (p. 1). It was a five page account followed by comment and analysis. Although the Chief Constable presented the narrative under the headings 'The Black and White Cafe', 'The renewal of violence' and 'Redeployment and return' the account will be presented here in seven sections for the sake of clarity later in the chapter.

1　The plan and execution of the raid on the Black and White cafe

At 3.30 pm on the afternoon of 2 April, twenty police officers, including two local community constables, under the command of a Superintendent, went to the Black and White cafe on Grosvenor Road in St Paul's, Bristol. They carried a warrant to search the cafe for illegal alcohol and drugs under the Licensing Act and Misuse of Drugs Act. Seven of the officers were members of the drug squad in plain clothes, the rest were uniformed police. An additional group of six officers was posted outside the cafe to control the traffic and 'anyone who assembled' during the raid. Two dog handlers, with dogs trained to sniff out drugs, were deployed in the area 'with instructions to remain away from the scene unless otherwise directed' (p. 1). The Chief Constable said that 'no difficulties were expected in the execution of the warrant, therefore the manpower involved was kept to a minimum so that the operation could be regarded as low key' (p. 1).

On arrival at the cafe the warrants were read out and the twenty or so people present were questioned without incident. The officer in charge was aware that a crowd was gathering outside so he called in police reserves to speed up the removal of items from the cafe that might be used in evidence in subsequent criminal prosecutions, and to assist in crowd control. At this stage the crowd was 'vociferous but not violent' (p. 2).

2　The drug squad officers leave the cafe

Two drug squad officers left the cafe to go to their car and the crowd began to jostle them, demanding the return of any evidence. These officers were pursued to their cars by a crowd of mainly black youths, throwing stones and missiles. The police car was attacked, the windscreen broken and some officers injured before they drove away.

3　The attack on the cafe

Following the drug squad officer incident the police posted outside the cafe were stoned and forced to run inside for cover. The violence continued and they had to hide at the back of the cafe. Members of the crowd came into the cafe to take cans and bottles of beer.

4　The relief of the cafe

By 5 pm the crowd outside and near the cafe was 'several hundred

(above) Black and White cafe   (below) Shady Grove cafe

(above) Grosvenor Road and 'The Green'   (below) The removal of the panda
car shortly before the renewal of
violence

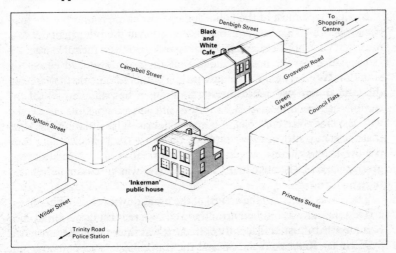

Figure 3   The Grosvenor Road area

strong' and about one hundred and fifty black and white youths were actively throwing stones and other missiles at the police. A further twenty police were called into the area and having mustered at the Inkerman pub (fifty yards along Grosvenor Road from the cafe), they set off under 'a rain of stones' to rescue their fellow officers trapped in the cafe.

5   The burning of the police car and the police march to guard it

Assistance was now being sought from other police divisions. One car which came into the area and stopped at the cafe to get instructions, came under attack from missiles thrown by the crowd there. The police officers sought cover round the corner in William Street, where they saw about twelve black youths turn over the police vehicles and set fire to one. The group of officers who had previously been in the cafe rescue march went to the scene of the burning car, recovered one of the vehicles, and stayed there until the fire in the second one had been extinguished.

6   The removal of the burnt-out panda car

Around 5.15 pm a Chief Superintendent arrived on the scene and soon afterwards the Chief Constable and his Deputy arrived. At this time there was a period of uneasy calm. On the one hand there were thirty officers waiting by the burnt-out car along with four dog handlers and their dogs, on the other hand there were a large number of people in the crowd, people watching from their houses and people going home in the rush hour. There was no violence at this time.

By this stage most of the police, apart from those round the car, had been withdrawn to a less conspicuous position at the Inkerman pub. As the Chief Constable believed that 'the police had been the sole targets of the violence' (p. 3) he concluded that their removal had eased the situation. While there were many people gathered outside the cafe and the atmosphere was tense there was no open hostility. So far all the trouble had been located close to the cafe and now people connected with the cafe were busy clearing up the debris. The situation was such that the senior officers were satisfied that once the police car had been removed the situation would revert to normal. This information was given to the Assistant Chief Constable who was in command at this time.

There was a delay in the arrival of the breakdown vehicle, but once it arrived the car was hitched up and towed by a rear lift down Grosvenor Road towards Sussex Place. By 6.30 pm it was under tow. As it reached St Nicholas Road both the car and the thirty officers accompanying it came under attack from missiles thrown by the crowd. The vehicle left the area and the police 'fell back' into Ashley Road.

7   *Events in City Road, Ashley Road and the police withdrawal*
'Simultaneously, some thirty riot shields had arrived in City Road' (p. 4) and the Superintendent in command authorised their use by his officers and others arriving from the Inkerman pub. There were about fifty to sixty police present including the Chief Constable and his Deputy. A crowd of several hundred, containing within it a mob of two hundred young blacks hurling missiles, was in open confrontation with the police.

The police formed a cordon and moved forward to try to establish a position across City Road, but they came under such a barrage of missiles from all sides that they were forced to retreat. Many police were injured, as were some pressmen.

As the police 'fell back' a pall of smoke was seen in Ashley Road where a police car had been set on fire and the bank (Lloyds) had been broken into. A separate crowd was involved, again with a hardcore of about two hundred trouble makers, and unsuccessful efforts were made by a Superintendent and some West Indian women to calm the crowd. The Superintendent was kicked and had to be protected by the women.

A Superintendent ordered a transit van loaded with officers and riot shields and a Landrover containing more men to try and reach the bank. The rest came on foot but came under such severe attack that they had to retreat. Other police vehicles coming into the area also came under fierce attack and were forced into Ashley Road where 'one hundred violent youths, predominantly black' (p. 5) subjected them to such violence, that they had to withdraw.

By this stage twenty-two police had been injured, twenty-seven more had minor injuries and twenty-one police cars had been damaged, of which six were totally destroyed. The police

> were clearly overwhelmed. The decision was therefore taken to withdraw to regroup, to gather strength and to obtain sufficient reinforcement to ensure a speedy return to law and order with a minimum of bloodshed . . . It was hoped that the removal of the police – the object of the violence – would quieten the crowd and itself help the return to order. (p. 5)

The police withdrew at 7.26 pm. They returned to St Paul's in force at 11 pm after much strategic reorganisation and 'by midnight the police were in control'. By this time over six hundred police had been involved.

The Chief Constable's Comments and Conclusions
From this brief account of the facts the Chief Constable made several deductions. He concluded that the police should learn some lessons with the benefit of hindsight. The first lesson was that any decisions concerning a raid should be made by the Assistant Chief Constable and not by an officer of lower rank. Secondly that the day and time chosen for the raid had been unwise because it was a school holiday. Thirdly, 'the use of drug dogs in a multi-racial area requires very careful consideration' (p. 8). The fourth lesson was that the local police Community Relations Officer should have been consulted. And finally, given that vehicles are an obvious target for damage it would have been preferable to abandon the vehicle in Grosvenor Road rather than attempt to tow it away.

Having conceded these errors the Chief Constable stressed the ferocity of the attack on the police, the extent of damage to vehicles and officers and concluded in no uncertain terms that 'without withdrawing, and adequate preparation, serious injury or loss of life was inevitable' (p. 8). He emphasised the unexpected nature of the violence and its extent, which served to highlight the organisational and logistical problems facing the police force when violence erupts unexpectedly. The Chief Constable ended with a paragraph showing his awareness that police/black relations require understanding 'coupled with reasonable firmness' and said that plans were underway to improve these relations through community units, liaison officers and instruction in 'background and culture' for police officers.

The Chief Constable's report presented an account which, although it is not clearly signposted and is somewhat vague in places, is a relatively straightforward account of a confusing afternoon, starting off with a 'low profile' raid on a cafe similar to others carried out before. He coherently ordered the events through the afternoon which culminated in the police withdrawal at 7.26 pm.

The account stressed the severity of the violence which forced the police to leave the area in order to save lives, it also emphasised the inexplicable nature of the attack and portrayed the violence of the crowd as without cause. While conceding that some tactical mistakes had been made, the Chief Constable essentially conveyed a picture of a police largely aware of, and sympathetic to, the needs of the community, coming under a massive and unprovoked attack which was so fierce that a police withdrawal was justified. Such a situation must be prevented in the future by the immediate improvement of police call-out procedures.

The Home Secretary's Statement

Having read and carefully considered this report the Home Secretary endorsed it. He told Parliament that there would be no dispute about the facts in the light of this 'full and clear report' (p. 1, Home Secretary's statement on the disturbances in Bristol, 2 April 1980). He accepted the account as factually correct and, condensing it, reported to Parliament that 'what began as a normal operation into possible criminal offences, turned sharply and unexpectedly into a serious public disorder'. He noted the lessons learned by the Chief Constable, but stressed the absolute necessity of the withdrawal of the police 'in the face of the great violence and extensive injuries to the police' (p. 2).

The Chief Constable's report, and the precis by the Home Secretary which further stressed the unprovoked nature of the violence and the need for better police handling of public disorder were the basis for most Government and public knowledge about what happened – and where the blame lay – in St Paul's.

The Judge's Summing Up

Almost a year later, in 1981, twelve youths stood in the dock in the Bristol Crown Court charged with 'riotous assembly'. In the case argued over seven weeks the prosecution had followed the sequence of events and the main assumptions about the nature of those events given briefly by the Chief Constable, endorsed by the Home Secretary and echoed subsequently in many Government discussions about the disturbance. While the defence lawyers challenged strongly the assumptions on which the account was based they did not systematically challenge the way the sequence of events was presented. In his final speech to the jury, the Judge summed up the events under ten headings: the plan and execution of the raid; the drug squad officers leaving the cafe; the drug squad car under attack; events in Denbigh and Campbell Streets; the siege of the cafe; the relief of the cafe; the police rescue mission of the cars; the burning and removal of the panda car; events leading to the police withdrawal; and the aftermath of looting.

The essential shape of this account bore a close resemblance to the much briefer report of the Chief Constable a year previously, though there were some notable differences due to the fact that he had heard very detailed evidence being presented and challenged in court. A few general points of difference must be discussed here (the specific detailed differences relating to the cases of individual defendants are discussed in Chapter 5) showing where the official versions diverged.

The Judge said that thirty-nine police – not twenty as the Chief Constable had said – attended a briefing at the police station at about 2.20 pm on 2 April, prior to the raid. He put the briefing an hour earlier than the Chief Constable. In addition to the traffic police on duty outside mentioned by the Chief Constable, Task Force 'A' police officers (SPG equivalent officers) were to wait in reserve at the Inkerman public house. Clearly a larger number of police were present on this raid than had been indicated in the earlier report where it was described as low key, using minimum manpower.

The raid went according to plan and quantities of illegal drinks and drugs were found on the premises. There was no trouble at this stage though undoubtedly the searching and questioning caused the customers some resentment. Outside the cafe a crowd was building up, unruly but friendly. At this stage the Judge referred to an incident not mentioned by the Chief Constable, there was an altercation between a police officer and a West Indian man who accused the officer of ripping his trousers. This caused some agitation in the crowd, and the whole affair escalated when four drug squad officers (not two, as the Chief Constable had said) left the cafe together. The Judge labelled this moment the turning point. A group of fifty to seventy people detached themselves from the crowd and ran after the officers; serious violence erupted and 'there was open riot'. The crowd bombarded the drug squad officers seemingly with the intention of retrieving the drugs the officers had removed from the cafe.

At this stage Superintendent Arkell decided to order the police van loaded with the illegal alcohol to leave the area; he told some of the police to stay and guard the cafe and the rest to disperse. Subsequently the action divided into two, and the Judge detailed a series of events that had been omitted by the Chief Constable. Rioting was underway in nearby streets, Denbigh Street and Campbell Street, between 4.30 and 5.00 pm and by 4.47 pm a police dog handler was lying unconscious in the road and other police had been attacked by the crowd. At the same time the Black and White cafe was under siege and twenty to thirty police officers armed with dustbin lids had to march in and rescue the police trapped inside. The same group of police then went to rescue the burnt-out car.

This was followed by the period of 'uneasy calm'. In stark contrast to the Chief Constable, the Judge concluded that some of the crowd had in fact engaged in collecting missiles during this period and so this was a period of re-arming, not a prelude to normality. The escalation of violence leading to the police withdrawal was then graphically recounted to the jury.

In court this account was very detailed; times, places and individuals were identified in a way that they certainly had not been in previous accounts. Disputes about these were discussed by the Judge in his summing up, but the overall shape of the events remained similar to that given by the Chief Constable. The Judge again laid emphasis on the lawlessness and criminality of the crowd behaviour, the unprovoked nature of that violent behaviour and the essential continuity of the troubles, unbroken by the short period referred to as the 'uneasy calm'.

But What Did Happen?

But how far do these accounts in fact reflect what happened on the streets of St Paul's? Taking only the police evidence as a yardstick, the first issue to emerge is that because the written police statements and their evidence at the committal proceedings and in the Bristol Crown Court produced a massive amount of confusing and often contradictory information, a simple reconstruction of the afternoon based on this evidence was not possible. The evidence is particularly problematic in relation to the accurate timing (and so to the sequence) of events. Every major incident in the afternoon had various times attached to it by different officers which meant that it is not possible to say conclusively which events happened first and which happened later. So the sequence of events is not actually clear. Secondly, as well as the timing, the numbers of police involved, the size and mood of the crowd, and the sequence and causes of different incidents are described quite differently in different police accounts, raising fundamental questions about the validity of the official versions.

The police evidence presented here is condensed and to some extent simplified because only major points are highlighted. However this account is drawn from a detailed reading and analysis of all the written police statements that were submitted as evidence for the Crown Court trial, plus the transcript of the committal proceedings where many of these police were cross-examined in detail, and written notes taken by us during the six weeks of Crown Court proceedings in Bristol.

The Police Evidence

1   The setting up and execution of the raid

The Chief Constable described this raid as one where no difficulties were expected and manpower was kept to a minimum, the operation was 'low key'. Twenty officers were briefed, plus a handful of traffic police and two dog handlers. Superintendent Arkell agreed in court that this was a routine and low-profile raid, but other police evidence suggested that a lot of police were used because trouble was at least expected, and there was an awareness that such a raid could become a public order problem.

Thirty-nine police officers were in fact briefed at 2.30 or 3 pm (even this time is not clear from the evidence) by Superintendent Arkell. Twenty-four of them were to enter the cafe looking for illegal drugs and alcohol, six were to be posted outside to keep the traffic and pedestrians moving during the raid (indicating a concern with crowd control), others were to be on stand-by at the Inkerman public house, about a hundred yards from the cafe. The reserve included six Task Force 'A' officers (SPG equivalent), two police dog handlers and dogs, only one of which was a drug-sniffing dog, the other was an ordinary police dog. In addition, a team of police were placed on stand-by at the police station to process offenders who would be arrested as a result of the raid. Given the small size of the cafe ($15' \times 15'$), the police outnumbered the customers. The size of the raid indicated that the police knew that this operation was potentially a threat to public order, and several police officers referred in court to the hostility of people in St Paul's to the police. The use of police dogs (which were used on the crowd and not for drug detection) further suggests that the police went prepared for trouble.

In spite of the known potential for public disorder, the raid was carried out without any consultation with the community liaison police officer, and without the presence of the local home beat officer who had his day off on 2 April. There was dispute in court about whether Arkell had talked to community leaders about police/black relations recently. No advice was given to the police at the briefing that there was need for caution or tact, nor were they warned that it was a school holiday so the streets would be full of children.

The Chief Constable reported that the legitimate search of the cafe, carried out under the Misuse of Drugs Act and the Licensing Act, was effected without trouble. This is largely borne out by the police evidence. Sometime between 3 and 3.30 pm the raid began (it is not possible to give a more precise time because even this clear-cut event had different times put on it by different police officers). The drug squad officers in plain clothes entered the cafe, walked to the counter and ordered hot drinks, two minutes later the uniformed police entered and the customers' reactions were closely watched by the drug squad. The police who entered the cafe found a quiet scene; one woman police sergeant described it as entirely peaceful, with young black men sitting around playing dominoes, drinking soft drinks and chatting. There were not many customers (police statements put the number between twelve and thirty), with a similar number gathered outside on the pavement. Everyone in the cafe had his particulars taken so it is unclear why the police cannot say exactly how many people there were inside.

During the raid everyone in the cafe was searched. Although there were several twists of 'ganja' lying on the floor, no evidence was found to connect the drugs with any individual, and only one customer was charged subsequently with possession of drugs. One person was arrested immediately for drinking beer. The proprietor was found to be in possession of both illegal alcohol and drugs but everyone else in the cafe was searched, found to be 'clean' and sent to wait outside the cafe. Personal details were taken from all of them, including place of birth and which car they had come in; one man from Southampton had his car number and particulars subsequently checked on the police computer.

The police said that the customers were cooperative at this stage, but defence lawyers pointed out at the trial that they had had no legal right to document innocent people nor to ask them to wait outside the cafe. The Judge agreed that such procedures would undoubtedly cause bad feeling among the customers, and the searching and documenting of everyone in the cafe rather undermined the Superintendent's statement that he respected the fact that many in the cafe were law-abiding customers and their rights had to be respected. The customers, however, offered no resistance and were in all probability greatly outnumbered by the police in the cafe, so the next move of Superintendent Arkell is difficult to understand. Five minutes after the start of the raid he sent for the six Task Force 'A' officers waiting at the Inkerman pub. They drove their van to the cafe, parked and entered, bringing the number of police involved inside up to thirty. They searched some people and then the premises for stolen property – although they had no warrant to do so and no stolen property was found.

The raid continued in this potentially provocative way. A corridor of police was formed through the crowd standing outside the cafe and crates of alcohol were passed along this corridor to a waiting police van, but as the alcohol had already been photographed by the police it need not have been removed at this stage at all. A man was placed under arrest for drinking beer, and was kept in a police vehicle, in view of the crowd, for half an hour before being taken to the police station; this caused agitation. About the same time the proprietor of the cafe was also placed under arrest and held handcuffed in the cafe. This was quite unnecessary as he was known to the police and the community and there was little fear of his disappearing or using violence. He could have been summonsed to appear at the police station rather than arrested and police awareness of this led every senior officer in court to deny ordering his arrest, and ordering him to be handcuffed.

Thirty to forty police officers were used to search and make arrests in a small cafe for crimes which carry limited sentences and are not even suggested by the police to be serious crimes. As a result of this massive exercise only two people were arrested, one for illegal drinking, who was subsequently not charged. The proprietor received a suspended sentence, and a third man who was charged later with possessing drugs had his case dismissed.

Outside the cafe

The Chief Constable said that as the alcohol was being removed from the cafe a vociferous – but not violent – crowd built up outside. But police accounts of what was happening outside the cafe during the raid are contradictory; different descriptions exist concerning the size, composition and mood of the crowd, and what it was doing. These accounts can be grouped into three versions, though it must be stressed that within each grouping there was great variation.

Most of the police officers subscribed to an overall view of a crowd ranging in number between fifty and three hundred (a significant variation), standing outside the cafe between the start and finish of the raid. This crowd was variously described as curious, jesting, bantering and good humoured on the one hand, and jeering, hostile, aggressive and even violent on the other. The crowd was contradictorily described as being made up of school children (who were on holiday); of young people; of blacks; of blacks and whites; of males; of men and women. While many police said they carried the crates of alcohol to the police van through the crowd for about twenty to thirty minutes without serious incident, others said there was an altercation between a police officer and a West Indian male who accused the officer of tearing his trousers. While this incident generated a lot of hostility the anger was quickly defused and a serious situation was averted. The crowd was portrayed as orderly and in good spirits by a female drug squad officer; as vocal, aggressive and out of hand by a traffic policeman; and as a mere group of observers by others. There was a general picture of a restive, but not violent, crowd present from the start of the raid around 3.20 until over an hour later. It was when the male drug squad officers left the cafe at 4.30 pm that violence erupted, and a 10:9 emergency call was put out for extra police help. The first hour of the raid, according to many officers, had been quiet.

A very different picture was presented by three detective constables driving in an unmarked police car. They were at the Inkerman public house as part of the reserve force and were called to the cafe by a radio message. They drove there, went inside, searched for stolen property and left, and as the situation was calm they left the area and went to town for a coffee. They returned to Grosvenor Road at 4 pm and found things dramatically changed. One to two hundred youths were throwing stones at the cafe, and a police car was stoned as it drove past it. When questioned at the committal about the timing, one officer maintained that it was around 4 pm, but he stressed that times were only approximate. When asked why he had not made a note about the precise time and the nature of the stone throwing he replied, 'because I did not think it would be significant'.

A third version was given by two other detective constables who arrived at the cafe at about 3.20 pm. They said in their statements, and repeated at the committal and in the Crown Court, that they came by car to St Paul's at 3.30 pm in response to a 10:9 call for 'assistance required at Black and White'. This was the 10:9 call that Arkell said was not put out until one hour later. These two detective constables admitted to being very surprised at this call, because when they arrived in Grosvenor Road they found no trouble at all. They saw a crowd of between fifty and sixty white and black youths just milling about, so they stood around on the grass opposite the cafe chatting to some white prostitutes and four black men. There was no trouble at all until the crowd suddenly ran off into a nearby street, Campbell Street, after the drug squad officers had left the cafe (at around 4.30 pm).

The issue of when the first call for assistance was put out was never resolved, though the official versions implied that this call followed, rather than preceded, the trouble. Arkell maintained that it was not put out until 4.30 pm, after trouble had broken out but these two officers, and another police constable – who said that he heard a 10:9 call at 3.35 pm when he was waiting in Brigstock Road – and a civilian witness (a woman taxi driver) all suggested that the first 10:9 call had gone out by 3.35 pm. If this was the case this would have been well before any disturbance at all. The taxi driver, who gave evidence for the prosecution, said she saw cars speeding into St Paul's with their lights flashing and sirens going at 3.30 pm and agreed with a defence suggestion that this had been early in the afternoon. It was dangerous and had been inflammatory to the crowd. When police started to pour into St Paul's is a crucial question. If the police started to arrive prior to any trouble this would have been very provocative to the crowd, especially if, as some of the evidence suggests, the raid had been underway for an hour with a large number of police.

2 The exodus of the drug squad officers from the cafe

Taking the majority view, about an hour to an hour and a half after the raid had started, and some time after the police had started removing crates of alcohol through the crowd, male drug squad officers left the Black and White cafe to return to their car. Two women officers left a few minutes before them and were, by their own accounts cheered by the crowd. The men however, fared less well and it is at this point that the Chief Constable and the Judge said that real violence, 'open riot', erupted. They said it broke out because the crowd wanted to retrieve the drugs that these police officers had removed from the cafe.

Four drug squad officers said that they left the cafe together (not two as the Chief Constable said) and they all described the events in broadly similar terms. They left the cafe, turned left and started to walk through a crowd of two hundred to two hundred and fifty black males towards their car parked in Ludlow Close. After they had gone fifty or a hundred yards a group of forty to sixty youths separated from the main crowd and started to chase them. They got cut off from their car so they turned and headed for an unmarked police car, a red Avenger parked in Denbigh Street. As they retreated to Denbigh Street they were jostled, kicked, punched and subjected to verbal abuse and only one of them managed to reach the car, and catching the keys thrown to him by another officer, got in. The other three failed to reach the car because of the attack so they returned to the cafe and got a lift out of the area in another police car. The crowd stayed in Denbigh Street throwing bricks, tiles and rubble at the red Avenger. The windscreen was smashed and one of the women officers already inside was injured as were several uniformed police outside who had recently arrived on the scene. The drug squad officer managed to start the car and left at speed. It was at this point, faced with such violence, that the Superintendent said he sent out a 10:9 call for assistance.

The reason given for this sudden attack by the crowd on the drug squad officers, and in the official versions, was that the crowd wanted to retrieve the confiscated drugs. It was never made clear how the people in the crowd knew that they had the drugs, which were hidden in a small packet inside a coat pocket of one of them. Not is it possible to clarify why the Chief Constable reported only two drug squad officers, when four officers said they left the cafe together, and all the police witnesses only saw three. There is also a problem concerning the size of the crowd. One officer put it at only twelve young men chasing the officers, others said forty, others said a large crowd all moving together chased the officers. Whether it was a few or many, the whole crowd or a section of the crowd the question still remains about *why* they suddenly moved. The police loading the alcohol van, those on traffic duty, and the two women drug squad officers were untouched by the same crowd, which had been observing events for some time by now.

There is a different account given by a handful of police officers which contrasts starkly with the majority version, and offers a more cogent reason for the running of the crowd. But it is only present in very few police statements and it does not really explain why violence broke out initially. One police sergeant in the Dog Section said that he received a call at 4.25 pm to go the cafe; as he was not on duty till 5 pm he was dressed in jeans. He left the police station with another dog handler and they drove to St Paul's where they parked. Leaving the dogs in the van he walked to Grosvenor Road with a third police constable also from the Dog Section. There they saw a large crowd of mainly coloured people throwing bricks and bottles at the police near the cafe, 'we returned to our vans and brought our dogs into Grosvenor Road where we moved this crowd away from the flats allowing the police to move away from the cafe'. His fellow police constable said in court that they used their dogs to clear the crowd at 4 pm, half an hour earlier but thought he might have got the times wrong. The third dog handler disagreed and said they had not used the dogs until *after* the drug squad came under attack. However, this evidence at least poses the question, was it the dogs chasing the crowd rather than the crowd chasing the drug squad that started the crowd running? Many police witnesses apparently did not see either the dogs or the drug squad officers, but just saw the crowd shout and start to move, so this question remains.

It was at this point that Arkell said he ordered the majority of police in the area to leave because they were the focus of the crowd hostility; simultaneously he sent out a 10:9 call asking for police assistance at the cafe. Many police statements show that from then on during the afternoon the police were ordered out of the area several times, but just as they were leaving a 10:9 emergency call summoned them back. This aspect of the afternoon was not referred to in the Chief Constable's report.

3   Events in Denbigh Street and Campbell Street
The next set of incidents described in the evidence did not appear in the Chief Constable's report at all, although they do throw a lot of light on the nature of the disturbance. During and following the exit of the drug squad and the stoning of the red Avenger, action was taking place both outside the cafe and in two nearby streets, Campbell Street and Denbigh Street. Although some police suggested that the whole crowd left the cafe for a time, the predominant picture that emerges from the evidence is of several small crowds in different places. Several police officers gave graphic details concerning the events in the two streets.

First there were descriptions of the stoning of the unmarked police car and its escape from Denbigh Street. Some police said there was a small crowd throwing bricks; others described a massive crowd; yet others said there were two crowds, one at the top and the other at the bottom of the street sandwiching the police and the car between them. By this stage the dog handlers and the dogs were certainly not on the street and two dog handlers described in detail their chases of different individuals in the crowd, others said they saw dogs loose in the streets at this stage.

While much of the evidence suggested that the street was full of people with crowds blocking the top and bottom of the street, two police officers gave evidence that there was no crowd at the City Road end of the street when they drove into Denbigh Street. Further down the street they did find a crowd blocking their way, so they reversed back up the street, their lights flashing and sirens on. By doing this they said that they diverted the attention of the crowd and so allowed the red Avenger to drive out of the area. After the drug squad in that car left the street, the crowd, variously put at twelve, twenty or one hundred strong, moved off into City Road and down into Campbell Street.

The overall picture to be gleaned from the evidence of the Task Force 'A' officers, the dog handlers and other police officers present at the time, was of a crowd dispersing after the red car left. Some ran off into their houses, others stood around in small groups, a few threw stones. Later a man was arrested in City Road causing some more stonethrowing and the arrest of a woman. The crowd that gathered round that incident was said to be about six to twelve people, mainly women. Subsequently there was a police chase on foot in Campbell Street involving at least one police dog, and a doghandler was knocked unconscious. The crowd in Campbell Street prior to the policeman being hit was put at about twenty people; afterwards the scene was described as quiet but uneasy with twelve police officers standing round the hurt man and a large number of coloured people standing in their doorways and milling about on the road, hostile but not violent. An ambulance came shortly after it was sent for at 4.47 pm and when the injured officer was driven away, the crowd dispersed.

The police were again ordered to leave the area quickly and quietly, but as they were leaving a 10:9 call went out calling them to go to the rescue of some police officers trapped in the Black and White cafe. This call was put out at about 5 to 5.15 pm. The clearest picture that emerged from the police statements and evidence in the courts of this period was of small groups of youths moving around, hostile and aggrieved. Some were throwing stones, many certainly were not. The youths drifted off after the drug squad car left, and again after the ambulance left. Groups formed but appeared to break up after a few minutes of expressed aggression. The police were moving together in small groups, some with dogs, some behind dustbin lids and at least one with a truncheon drawn. Police cars were coming in and out of the area. The police evidence at this stage does not justify the official accounts of serious violence involving a large crowd. The notion of 'an open riot' does not fit easily with the picture of individual police chasing individual young people through the streets while small groups stood and watched. The Chief Constable did not in fact mention any of these incidents at all but proceeded directly from the description of the stoning of the drug squad to the siege of the cafe.

4   The siege of the Black and White cafe

While some police described the whole crowd leaving the cafe and running into Denbigh Street (either chasing the drug squad or perhaps being chased by dogs), others suggested that throughout this time there was a crowd outside the cafe. Whether a crowd was indeed outside all the time or whether it returned, running, from Campbell Street was never clarified. Be that as it may, there were incidents at the cafe that became known as the 'siege' of the Black and White, a siege that the Chief Constable described as involving a crowd several hundred strong, one hundred and fifty of whom were stoning the cafe. The police inside had to be rescued by a contingent of police marching from the Inker-man public house.

(i) *Inside the cafe.* Several police were inside the cafe when the drug squad left and though some were ordered to disperse others were told to remain, close the cafe and guard the drinks. It is these officers who were 'trapped' and had to be rescued.

In the first statements made by several of these police inside the cafe there was no mention at all of this stoning of the cafe or the police rescue. The woman police sergeant in charge of four officers did not describe these frightening incidents until her second statement on 7 April: her first statement ended with an account of the police entering the cafe. The same was true for the Inspector who also made his second statement on 7 April. The Chief Inspector also made no reference to the attack on the cafe until 9 April, in his second statement. These were the three senior police officers present inside the cafe. From their second statements it is clear that there was confusion surrounding this exercise, and who was in command. The woman police sergeant said that she was instructed by the Superintendent to stay in the cafe with four police officers under her command, the male Inspector said he had requested to be in charge, and neither of them were apparently aware that a Chief Inspector was in command, standing outside the cafe.

Once the cafe door was closed the curtains were drawn and those inside could not see out, though they said they could hear a lot of noise. About fifteen minutes after the cafe door was closed the woman police sergeant said that bottles, bricks and stones crashed through the windows. The police officers from outside came into the cafe seeking refuge, one of them – a traffic policeman – was injured, having been hit on the head by a stone. According to her the stone-throwing stopped again, and the police continued to carry the alcohol up from the cellar. Five minutes later the missiles started being thrown again – bricks, bottles and stones: 'I noticed the front door of the premises was open but could not be secured because of the missiles coming through it and front windows. Bricks, bottles, stones and cans rained into the cafe striking the walls and floor around us.' The police were forced to take refuge at the back of the cafe, hiding behind barricades of tables, chairs and crates. At this stage she said the Inspector telephoned to the police station for help and sometime later the relief march arrived to rescue them.

The accounts of the police officers involved inside the cafe were fairly consistent. Although they could not see out, one police constable estimated the crowd to be about two hundred strong and in a very ugly mood, he was 'afraid for his life'. The police inside the cafe refused to put a time on the siege, though it must have been around 4.30 pm (if, as the Chief Inspector said, stoning began immediately the cafe was closed) or at 5 pm, if there was a lull following the exit of the drug squad, before the stoning began, as others said.

Police outside the cafe gave many different times for this siege. The two officers returning from having coffee in town put it at 4 pm, as did one civilian witness. A dog handler put the stoning of the cafe *before* the incidents in Campbell Street but most put it after at between 5 and 5.30 pm.

Four crucial pieces of evidence raise questions about the accuracy of the above accounts, which were reflected in the Chief Constable's account, and further questions will emerge when recounting the police evidence of those involved in the 'rescue march'. The first major problem was thrown up by the police photographs taken of the cafe after the trouble. The cafe window was certainly cracked, but being reinforced the glass was intact and nothing could have passed through the window. Secondly, several police said that the cafe door was closed and locked, in which case no missiles could have come through the door either. Thirdly, several witnesses, civilian and police, said that the door was open and they saw young people going in and out of the cafe during this period taking bottles of alcohol from the crates to drink; people could not possibly have wandered safely in and out of the cafe picking up beer if the bombardment was as fierce as has been suggested. Fourthly, while many police who described the siege said that there were no cars in Grosvenor Road at that time, others said there were – in which case were stones being thrown by the crowd at the cafe over the car roofs? These points throw doubt on the notion that these officers were under siege and needed a military-style rescue.

(ii) The rescue march. There were three very different pictures of the scene outside the cafe, and the nature and success of the rescue march. One given by the Superintendent in charge of the raid who said that he saw the cafe being stoned and a group of police, led by another Superintendent, try to march to the cafe. The police, however, were dispersed by severe attack from the crowd and were forced to take cover, and 'the Superintendent said the crowd was forced back when eight dog handlers moved forward' (*Western Daily Press*, 5 February 1981). This version of course fits with the accounts of the two dog handlers who described clearing the crowd with their dogs, although they put the incident at an earlier time. Some of the police officers on the rescue march confirmed this version and said that the severity of the attack on them did cause them to withdraw and they never reached the cafe.

This directly contradicts the account given by the majority of the police and the Chief Constable. According to them the police assembled at the Inkerman public house and under the command of a Superintendent who had just arrived in the area, they were formed up into columns of five (some said three) and marched, military style, down Grosvenor Road to the cafe. They went into the cafe (some said they had to force the door as it was locked) and rescued the officers trapped inside. The Superintendent in charge of this march did not mention this 'military' episode in his first statement at all, but described it graphically in a statement he made from memory four weeks later on 30 April. He agreed under cross-examination in court that, in spite of his statement about the ferocity of the attack and the fact that he had said in his statement that the cafe door was closed, young people were going in and out of the cafe during the siege. Nevertheless he insisted that he saw enough violence to justify his rescue march.

Although the marchers were ordered to be unarmed, some carried dustbin lids or crates and at least one had his truncheon drawn. Most of those in the march estimated the crowd to be about one to two hundred strong, though one put the figure at five to six hundred and another described it as composed of 'several hundred negroes'. But there was another view of the violence and the march which was voiced by some officers. One gave evidence on oath that the stoning did not seriously begin until the police started to march five abreast down the narrow Grosvenor Road. By almost all accounts, when the march stopped and the police left the cafe the stoning ceased, and the police who had hidden in nearby houses were able to walk safely back to the Inkerman pub. Things certainly went quiet quickly, so much so that the Chief Inspector from the cafe sent a police constable back to the Black and White to guard the drinks – this return to the cafe is inexplicable if the attack had been really dangerous and sustained.

During this time another police officer, posted on the corner of

Denbigh Street and Grosvenor Road, came under attack from the crowd. He took cover behind a police transit van (belying the statement that all cars were by this time clear of the immediate vicinity), but when a civilian asked the crowd to stop throwing stones at the officer, they did so. Again this jars with the projected image of a large, violent crowd. While there was undoubtedly violence on the street it was not sustained, it ceased when the military march ended and some of the evidence suggests that it only began when the police marched, army style, into the crowd.

From the police accounts it is clear that by this stage in the afternoon many police had no idea who was in command. Many were sending out their own 10:9 calls, cars were being ordered out of the area by one officer, and back by another. Different senior police gave very different accounts of how the cafe was cleared of the crowd and many of the police, when asked in court what they were trying to achieve by marching into a hostile crowd, said that they did not know. This confusion was not reflected in the official reports.

5 The burning of the panda car and the uneasy calm

The events at the cafe were followed by the burning of a police car. As the police rescue marchers returned to the Inkerman pub they saw a pall of smoke in the air further down Grosvenor Road. They were re-formed into a second military-style formation and set off towards the burning police car, ostensibly to rescue anyone who might be trapped in the car; in the event the car was empty. Many police said that the crowd fell back as the police advanced and an Inspector said that the crowd was pliable. On reaching the burnt car the police surrounded it, and using dogs, cleared a space for themselves. People were advised to stand clear for their own safety, and they did so. According to many police officers, the crowd and police held this position for up to one hour, no stones were thrown, there was no violence. Things were so quiet that the Chief Constable had cause to note in his report that the officer-in-charge thought that the trouble was over. Consequently, several police were again ordered out of the area to reduce tension and one officer was told to remove all the parked police cars from St Paul's. Many of the young people from the crowd started to clear up the debris from the cafe, while others stood around watching. Most officers agree that there was no stone throwing or any kind of trouble between 5.30 and 6.30 pm. Only one or two policemen said they saw anything sinister during this time, and it was their evidence that caused the Judge to deny the importance of this period of calm. Nevertheless it is significant that the senior police officers on the spot had thought it signalled the end of the trouble. Up to now one police officer had been badly hurt, others had been hit by stones; one police car was burnt out and two had been stoned; the street outside the cafe was full of debris but some people had already started to clear up. There had undoubtedly been some trouble in St Paul's and hostility had been shown to the police during and after the cafe raid; but the trouble had been limited and it did not signify a major incident.

6   The removal of the panda car

Some time between 5.30 and 6.30 pm (again the evidence on timing varies) a towing vehicle came to tow the burnt-out car away. The Chief Constable acknowledged that this might have been a mistaken tactic and certainly heralded the start of the serious trouble.

The police officer who was connecting the car to the towing vehicle was ordered to do the job quickly. He said that he explained to the Superintendent in charge that it was important that he should first break the steering lock on the car, because to tow the vehicle without doing so would be very dangerous. The Superintendent agreed to that, but just as he was trying to break the steering lock another order came from elsewhere countermanding that and they were told to drive the car away immediately. They were compelled to leave the steering lock intact and they hitched the car up to be towed, knowing that it was unsafe. At the same time the Superintendent who had organised the earlier police marches ordered the police to form up again with several dog-handlers to flank the vehicle. The car was towed away surrounded by dogs and police, and as the group moved off, the crowd started throwing missiles. The towing vehicle speeded up and slewed, hitting one of the doghandlers and knocking him over. The towing vehicle then sped out of St Paul's with the car swinging over the road.

7   Events in City Road and Ashley Road

The towing away of the car heralded the renewal of stone throwing by the crowd in Grosvenor Road. The police witnesses involved said that they were then ordered to fall back into City Road where a crowd of two to four hundred youths stood, though why they were there, when they went there, and their relationship to the crowd in Grosvenor Road was never explained. In City Road the police were formed into a cordon but they were dispersed by the crowd because they had no protection from the missiles being thrown. They were then issued with thirty riot shields and they formed behind these shields. They marched forward down City Road to the Ashley Road junction but as they were then exposed to the crowd on three sides they came under heavy attack. Again they had to retreat. Several police officers when cross-examined in court had no real idea of what could have been achieved by marching thirty police into a large, angry crowd and some denied that they tried to march forward, and said that they simply stood still across the road in a line trying to contain the crowd.

After the cordon broke up a second time the riot shields were withdrawn. In their evidence many of the police made it clear that they had little idea of who was in command or what was happening from now on. Sentences such as 'the riot shields seemed to disappear', and 'I have no idea why we marched', peppered their statements. Some picked up dustbin lids for protection, though earlier they had been ordered not to do this and by this time there was clearly a great deal of confusion and disarray. One Inspector said that he was in charge of the issuing of riot shields, while a Superintendent said that he was in charge. Different officers recorded being given orders by different senior policemen.

After this, events become very difficult to follow from the police statements. Some police were told to withdraw, others were formed up with riot shields again. Certainly none of the Task Force 'A' officers were used in the police cordon yet they were the only police highly trained in special riot shield manoeuvres; one policeman admitted in court that the shields discipline had been poor and the men untrained. In spite of the fact that Bristol had 55 Task Force officers trained specifically in public order, only one senior Task Force officer was recorded as being involved in any of these cordons. While some police formed up several times in City Road and Ashley Road, others were ordered to go and defend the police vehicles which were parked in Sussex Place outside Lloyd's Bank. As they arrived in a Landrover and a Sherpa van they came under attack though some police said that the stoning of these vehicles started only after the van had actually reversed aggressively into the crowd. Some police jumped out and attempted to defend the vehicles with riot shields, but those without shields were forced to retreat on foot down Dalrymple Road. Other police cars coming into the area were stoned by the crowd, the bank was set on fire, and sometime between 7.00 and 7.45 pm the order came from the police to withdraw. This final period was marked by crowd aggression, arson, stone throwing and shouting. Several police were hit and some were injured, including one police driver whose car came under very severe attack. But in spite of the numerous vivid police accounts of this period several key issues were left unresolved by their evidence, issues which the official versions failed to address.

It is far from clear how many police were on the streets at this time. Certainly many cars carrying police were coming into the area, two crashed into each other and several police commented on the congestion of police cars in St Paul's. Some said that they could not even get into St Paul's because there were so many police vehicles there already. Numerous 10:9 calls had gone out summoning police to come to the area, yet it seems impossible to ascertain how many police were there prior to the withdrawal. The official reports said that fifty-five to sixty police officers were involved, but as several hours earlier at least thirty police were on the street and many calls for help had subsequently been put out this seems a very low figure.

The size of the crowd is also difficult to ascertain. Many police put it at between two and six hundred, one or two talked of up to a thousand. Some said they were all black males; others said they were predominantly school children, black and white, age ten and less. Some said that a complete cross section of the community was involved; others that the women and children were solely spectators.

Another area of confusion involved the command structure of the police. Several police officers were giving orders by this stage and the chain of command was unclear. Different police constables said different senior police were in charge, and many in the cordons said that they did not know who was in charge of their operations. Senior officers named different people as being in charge of the same event.

Finally there were conflicting descriptions of the nature of the crowd after the panda car was towed away. While some police spoke of the uncontrolled fury of the mob viciously and consistently attacking the police and their vehicles, others gave a different picture. Some police said that it was the issuing of the riot shields that provoked the crowd and led to a mob fury and that every time the police cordons withdrew or broke up the crowd lost interest and the stone throwing stopped. While some accounts described a massive attack on the police, others suggested that violence only erupted when the police themselves took aggressive action such as advancing on the crowd with riot shields.

By 7.30 pm the police had withdrawn from the streets of St Paul's. Then followed a four hour period of looting and some arson carried out by people from many parts of Bristol, black and white, young and old. At 11 pm the police returned in great strength and met little resistance.

Not a Simple Account of 'The Facts'

Taking the sequence of the events on 2 April 1980 it is clear that the Chief Constable's report was not simply an account of the facts. While undoubtedly there was a raid, a crowd gathered, stones were thrown at the police and police vehicles, a police car was set on fire and there were confrontations between the public and the police using riot shields, the sequence of events is not clear from the police evidence. Nor is the nature of those events clear: how many people were involved and who was actually doing what? The Chief Constable's report did not confront the reality of the confusion of that day; instead he reported it as straightforward and simple. The Home Secretary found it so and had cause to remark to the House that the facts were clear; what was less than clear were the causes and solutions. The Judge was presented with this mass of confused and often directly contradictory police evidence and he did comment on the wide discrepancies and conflicts in their evidence in his summing up to the jury. He stressed however that the disturbance in St Paul's had been a uniquely frightening experience so that the jury should understand the consequent confusion and obvious contradictions in the police accounts. At no stage did the Government or the courts ask the police for any explanation about these diverse accounts. More importantly, questions were never asked in Parliament or by the public about what the police were actually doing at any given time. Nor did anyone ask officially what the police thought they were doing. No public issue was made of why the command structure of the police appeared to be so unclear during the afternoon. The police were effectively ruled out of the discussion and interest was focused only on the behaviour of the crowd. The police carried out a 'routine legal raid', and during the course of it they were fiercely attacked. No explanation was offered by the Chief Constable as to the reason for this attack, and the Home Secretary simply accepted the unexpectedness of the disorder, labelling it as sheer lawlessness. He made no attempt to provide any further understanding.

The only explanation provided by the police for the violence was presented in court. Apart from cultural explanations such as the anti-authority nature of West Indian youth, the only reason offered was that the youths wanted to recover the drugs removed from the cafe and so they attacked the drug squad officers. Once the attack had started it continued for several hours, and the ferocity of the attack forced the police to withdraw. The main issue thus raised was how the police can better prepare for spontaneous street violence in the future. No questions were raised about the nature of the policing and indeed in court the Judge specifically ruled that the police behaviour was irrelevant to the course of the afternoon and all attention was focused on the fact of an unprovoked attack, carried out by a mindless, lawless and criminal mob.

Once it is clear that the afternoon is not so easily reconstructed, that there are many areas of contradiction in the police evidence, and that their evidence throws a different light on some of the events, alternative accounts can be given, different questions can be raised, and other moments can be highlighted. A different account of what happend, and why, demands a quite different set of policy responses, as will be further discussed in Chapter 4.

Undoubtedly this was a legal raid on the Black and White cafe. But why was it thought a good use of police time and effort to use so many policemen to visit a small cafe used by a few customers who might be in possession of ganja or drinking beer illegally? Certainly these are illegal activities, but as Sir Robert Mark, John Alderson and many other police spokesmen have acknowledged a lot of petty crime is overlooked by the police all the time (Sir Robert Mark, 1978; Alderson, 1979.) There has to be a balance between keeping the law, protecting society and preserving the peace as all of these are part of the duty of the police. Within the terms of British justice both of these elements, arresting criminals and keeping the peace, must be there. The police knew that there was a risk of breaching the peace in St Paul's, they said so in court and they took over thirty policemen on the raid in case there was trouble. This clearly contradicts a crucial element of justice which is that good policing must be competent (Crown Office, 1976), a feature recently highlighted by a very senior police officer: 'The police have certain objectives, one of them being to enforce the law, but it is a higher, a superior objective to keep the peace' (Sir Kenneth Newman, *The Times*, 23.4.80). Newman goes on to say that the need to keep the peace could dictate alternative methods of law enforcement, and that the higher priority of observing the peace means 'you (as a police officer) have to consider very carefully the manner in which you enforce the law'. Alderson, the Chief Constable of Devon and Cornwall, was reported in the same *Times* article as saying that the issue of deciding between different objectives 'is fundamental to police work. At what stage do you enforce the law because you suspect you are exacerbating a situation?' Although Newman said that in his opinion the police could not have foreseen the trouble in Bristol, this is open to question and should at least have formed part of the official debate about the crisis of Bristol.

The raid was carried out without consulting the Community Liaison Officer and without using the Home Beat officer. It was done on the day when the streets were full of children on holiday. Thirty police went into a cafe containing about twenty customers; the scene was quiet and everyone was searched without resisting. Why then did the police not leave the area? The proprietor could have been summonsed, photos of illegal alcohol could have been used in court and the cafe could have been closed temporarily.

Instead, the police stayed in and around the cafe for up to an hour. They carried drinks out to the van through the crowd, they illegally searched the cafe for stolen property, they arrested one man and kept him in front of the crowd for about thirty minutes though they subsequently did not charge him. They handcuffed the proprietor, a man well known to all, and removed him, handcuffed, from the cafe. The Bristol Commission for Racial Equality report, written four weeks later, said that it was the removal of the proprietor under arrest that provoked the stoning of the cafe. That the police realised the arrest might be a provocative act was supported by the fact that no-one in court would admit to having authorised the arrest.

Many police said that their activities caused a crowd to gather in St Paul's, and arrests very often cause open hostility. In addition, police dogs are not officially supposed to be used for crowd control, yet they undoubtedly were. Whether it was dogs that started the crowd running or not, they were very much in evidence for most of the afternoon, on and off their leads. More than one police officer admitted to being frightened by the dogs himself! The Superintendent in charge of the raid saw that trouble was brewing and that the police were the focus of it, but he did not order the dogs off the street. In addition, at the same time as ordering police out of the area he sent out a 10:9 call asking for more police reinforcements to come in. Police cars came into the narrow streets of St Paul's at speed, some with lights flashing and sirens going. Whether this was 3.30 pm before any stones had been thrown or 4.30 pm is not clear.

Once trouble had started several factors provoked the crowd: the use of police dogs, the sight of police marching in military style up and down Grosvenor Road, the massive police presence flanking the towed car complete with dogs, and the advances of the police behind riot shields into the crowd. Much of the police evidence supports the interpretation that rather than a mindless, continuous outburst of sustained violence, the crowd threw stones every time the police took aggressive actions against them. It also suggests that the police command broke down and that many police were acting independently, or were receiving and reacting to contradictory orders; or they were obeying orders they simply did not understand. Who was in charge? What were the police trying to achieve? Why were untrained police officers using riot shields? Did the police withdraw because of the crowd violence or because their lines of communication had broken and they themselves were in disarray?

A different way of stringing the myriad pieces of evidence together can produce a very different picture of what happened on 2 April 1980 and consequently what should be done about it. An alternative scenario would raise questions about the police role: why they went into St Paul's in force on a quiet afternoon, why they used dogs and so many police, and why the command structure seemed to break down. These and other vital questions were made completely irrelevant by the way in which the story was told by the Chief Constable with the stress on the crowd rather than on the police; with the unprovoked rather than the possibly provoked nature of the attack; and with the criminality of the individuals in the crowd rather than the protest nature of the crowd behaviour against unjustified police practice.

3 Reporting the Bristol 'Riot' – 'the Media Version'

As demonstrated in the preceding chapter, the 'official version' of events in Bristol is perhaps best understood as a comprehensive description incorporating the perceptions, understandings, motives and concerns of a number of different institutions located within the state. Originating with the press releases of senior local police officers during and immediately after the violence, the official version found formal and coherent expression through the Chief Constable's Report. This was endorsed by the Home Secretary and as will be seen later shaped events in court. Notwithstanding its obvious importance with regard to the formulation of policy within the state, it was not the official version that came to constitute 'public' or common knowledge of the Bristol 'riot'. That knowledge was achieved primarily in and through media institutions. It is with the production of this media version that we are now concerned: in other words, 'How did the media report the violent crowd behaviour in Bristol?'

We could not, except in a book totally devoted to the subject, hope to explore the full public representation of events in Bristol as it was portrayed by television, radio and in the press. Thus, for convenience, and in order to penetrate in sufficient detail the various mechanisms by which a public event is reconstructed, we will concentrate on only one aspect of the media – the press. The way in which the crowd violence was represented in the press, however, was not dissimilar to its representation by both radio and television. It cannot be overlooked that although these different media institutions employ different technology and techniques, they share the same underlying professional ideologies or 'news values'. Our conclusions, therefore, though derived from a study of mass circulation dailies and Sundays, have broad implications for the media as a whole.

Before we address the specific issues involved, there remains the question of context. How the press reported Bristol cannot be abstracted from the way it habitually reports race. In this respect, as in this chapter as a whole, our primary concern is with the persistent distortion of race in the media. And though it cannot be dealt with here, the potential impact of biased and distorted reporting on the general public – black and white – should be kept firmly in mind. In a study of the role of the mass media on the formation of white racial attitudes, Hartmann and Husband found:

People in all-white communities are particularly liable to accept the interpretation of events offered by the media because they lack any basis of contact with coloured people on which to arrive at an alternative way of looking at things. (Hartmann and Husband in Cohen and Young, 1973, p. 273)

Clearly the overwhelming majority of white people live outside black areas, and have few readily available alternative sources of knowledge on race. On the other hand, what of the effect on black attitudes of continual malrepresentation in the media? Recognising the strategic location of the media in this context, Hugo Young, then assistant editor of the *Sunday Times*, argued that, when dealing with race, newspapers 'have a peculiarly delicate responsibility' (in Clement Jones, et al, 1971). The question here is how has that 'delicate responsibility' been discharged?

Race in the Press: A Distorted Mirror

No newspaper could hope to report even a fraction of the events that occur daily, nor do they attempt to. To produce a newspaper from day to day, journalists must operate a continual process of selection; a process that, in the first instance, decides for the reader what is and is not news. To some extent this process is prestructured, with a certain proportion of limited newspaper space being given over to specific categories of news, e.g. Home Affairs, Foreign Affairs, Crime, Parliament, Sport, etc. But within these categories, the selection process must further narrow down material by distinguishing between newsworthy and non-newsworthy events. The picture of the world as represented by newspapers then, is one that is continually and actively 'screened' by journalists and editors guided by some shared criterion as to what is of 'news value'. This criterion, as Stuart Hall observed, though 'nowhere written down, formally transmitted or codified', is nevertheless pervasive within dominant media institutions (Hall et al, 1978, p. 54). It embodies a continual search for the unusual, the unexpected, the dramatic, the conflictual and the problematic. It is particularly predisposed towards those issues and events surrounding, or of concern to, powerful individuals and institutions. It has a preference for events that may be simplified or more easily communicated through personalisation.

Newspapers then do not simply reflect the society of which they are a part. They are commercial undertakings, and no doubt the criterion by which news is selected or rejected – news values – is in part a product of the need to sell newspapers. But if news values account for the predominance in newspapers of conflict and disaster, they also help to account for the basic news approach to race. Of this approach, Hugo Young wrote:

By and large, unless a very conscious attempt is made to do otherwise, race only earns its place in the news to the extent that it is bad news.

Additionally, and by the same token:

Many events are felt to be newsworthy which if they did not ostensibly have a racial dimension would simply not be news.
(in Clement Jones et al, 1971, p. 131)

Thus a street robbery otherwise indistinguishable from numerous others that might occur in an average day, is rendered immediately newsworthy should one of the participants be of a different race; the same could be said of an industrial dispute, or a brawl between neighbours. Further, because the black population differs in culture, language and religion, this pre-selects them as a target for the media ever in search of the new-angle, the unusual, the unexpected. Young's conclusion in this respect is of importance. He pointed out that:

if newspapers judge by news value alone, they cannot avoid reinforcing the view that race is more of a problem than it really is (ibid., pp. 31–32).

One particular aspect of news values, already mentioned, deserves special consideration, and that is the predisposition towards those issues and events surrounding, or of concern to, powerful individuals and institutions. Newspapers are dominated by the need to produce 'reliable news' quickly. As a consequence, rather than a daily 'random search' for newsworthy events:

journalists position themselves so that they have access to institutions which generate a useful volume of reportable activity at useful intervals. Some of these institutions do, of course, make themselves visible by means of dramatization, or through press releases and press agents. Others are known regularly to produce consequential events.
(P. Rock in Cohen and Young, 1973, p. 77).

But this posture towards the powerful is more than simply a convenient and easy method of collecting news. As 'accredited sources', the statements of government officials, M.P.'s, leaders of industry, senior policemen, trade unionists, etc, are treated as implicitly more accurate, more factual, and more reliable than others. Not infrequently their practices are defended by journalists and editors in the name of those hallowed media principles, 'objectivity' and 'impartiality' and 'balance'. The result however, as Hall pointed out, is often a decided tendency towards an unbalanced and biased view of events:

the very rules which aim to preserve the impartiality of the media, and which grew out of desires for greater professional neutrality, also serve powerfully to orientate the media in the 'definitions of social reality' which their 'accredited sources' – the institutional spokesmen – provide.
(Hall et al, 1978, p. 58)

The impact of these standard and routine practices on the reporting of race has been, to say the least, significant. Hartmann and Husband in a study of race in the national press between 1963 and 1970 noted the gradual transformation of underlying conflictual themes, and how these came to be structured and dominated by issues of national political concern. The study found that over the period as a whole, the volume of race-related material appearing in the press increased, and that this was largely accounted for by an expanded coverage of domestic, as opposed to foreign racial issues and events. The study rejected the easy explanation that this increasing press interest was simply a consequence of the growing size of Britain's black population, since coverage did not increase evenly over the range of topics that the press might be expected to cover in relation to a given community. Rather, over the period, it was those topics that stressed the conflictual, the problematic, and the notion of blacks as a 'threat' that tended to predominate. In addition, the pattern of press coverage progressively moved away from those subject areas that would entail consideration of the underlying causes of racial conflict and came to concentrate on the actual manifestations of conflict itself. Notwithstanding the changes in the racial composition of Britain's population, the press continued to:

project an image of Britain as a white society in which the coloured population is seen as some kind of aberration, a problem, or just an oddity, rather than as 'belonging' to the society.
(Hartmann and Husband, 1974, p. 145)

As race became increasingly dominant in the political arena, so the politics of race tended to mould press coverage – reproducing political themes in broadly the same order of importance. Issues concerned with numbers, immigration control, illegal immigrants, citizenship and repatriation, subordinated race relations, prejudice, discrimination, and especially the representation of blacks as ordinary members of society. Of the extent to which the concerns of the powerful have defined the very assumptions on which the press coverage of race was based, Husband noted that:

faced with the frequently repeated statement that black immigration is a threat and a problem, the press, the race pundits and the audience, have not asked – 'Why is this so?' It has been an apparent truth that was beyond doubt; it conjured forth beliefs in the white audience which made it an impossible question to ask, for the answer would be literally incredible. (Husband, 1975, p. 26)

It is not the argument here that the media is in any simplistic sense the 'mouthpiece' of dominant groups and institutions. Rather, of the many influences on the selection and treatment of news with regards to race, the assumptions, definitions, interpretations and understandings of the powerful are accepted, often uncritically, as the basic frame of reference. It is largely within this basic framework that new themes are added, and existing themes elaborated, varied, reinterpreted, or extended. Where material cannot be readily fitted into this referential framework, it tends not to be covered. But this referential framework, it must be stressed, does not preclude the media from bringing pressure to bear on the powerful. Thus particularly of the area of race and Government policy, Young observes:

because of the emotional heat that the subject generates among the public, the Government's racial policies have been subject to constant change. Unlike the great majority of political issues, race and immigration are seen to be in flux . . . This gives the newspapers a relatively rare sense of power. It is open to them to raise the emotional temperature, with some confidence that this may have an important impact on policy.
(in Clement Jones et al, 1971, pp. 29–30)

It is perhaps within this context that the media phenomenon of Enoch Powell is best understood. Prior to his famous 'Birmingham speech', of 20 April 1968, Powell had said much the same things at Walsall in February of the same year, and at the Conservative Party Conference the year before. However, in the explosive racial atmosphere of April 1968, with the Labour Government about to move the second reading of the Race Relations Bill and the prospect of a new and unprecedented 'flood' of immigrants from Kenya, the press seized on Powell's speech. In both imagery and rhetoric, Powell re-emphasised the notion of black immigrants as a 'social evil', and dwelt on the social consequences should their numbers, as a result of misguided immigration policies, be allowed to increase. Though delivered to a mere handful of Tory faithful, blanket media coverage ensured that Powell's message reached over 90% of the adult population (Seymour-Ure, 1974). Transformed overnight into a major political figure, Powell continued to command the media's attention not only in relation to numbers and immigration, but as an accredited spokesman on all aspects of, and new developments in, the field of race relations.

In the case of Enoch Powell, the media used a then minor political personality to powerfully amplify the themes of immigration control, the threat of massive inter-racial violence and impending racial crisis. Since few newspapers questioned Powell's underlying assumptions, and most accepted that there was indeed some form of political conspiracy to understate the immigrant problem, subsequent editorial criticism of Powell's language counted for little. But the personalisation of particular issues around public figures is only one means by which periodic national 'panics' have been manufactured in the media. The 1968 crisis of British Asians in Kenya, for example, quickly came to be perceived and represented by the media as more a crisis for the British people than for Asian immigrants themselves. Improvising on the theme that there existed vast Asian hordes waiting at the drop of a hat to 'swamp' Britain, the *Daily Express* announced in bold headlines: 'A Million Chinese Can Arrive Here Next Week If They Want To' (1 March 1968). In the early 1970's the emphasis shifted to 'illegal immigrants'. Whether intentional or not, headlines like '40 Indians Invade' (*Daily Mail*, 2 July 1970), communicated an impression that the country was literally under siege. The journalist Derek Humphry well recalls the atmosphere that this issue generated within the media, and its consequences:

Real and imagined landings of Asians provided lots of spicey stories. In some instances, when small groups of men were seen landing in small boats, if they had healthy sun-tans and looked a bit swarthy, the police were called to suspected illegal immigrants. Often these stories got into the papers with the footnote that it was a false alarm with good intent . . . On the other hand, the success of the police in intercepting several groups of real illegal immigrants during the summer of 1973 provided a series of 'splash' stories on such a scale that it seemed Britain was undergoing a sizeable foreign invasion. In reality the numbers involved were a few score. (Quoted in Husband, 1975, p. 183)

These examples far from exhaust even the more notable cases of media distortion and amplification in reporting immigration and race. However, to illustrate another aspect of the referential framework surrounding race in the press, let us turn briefly to the treatment of two different types of crime. That overt conflict in all its forms constitutes the staple diet of newspapers and other media institutions is a point that has already been made. Where that conflict embodies a racial dimension, it is rendered all the more newsworthy. But where it involves whites attacking blacks this is often not reported because it does not always accord with the referential system defining racial understandings in the press. Of that system, Husband (1975) concluded that the media was unable to challenge the dominant assertion which represented blacks as a problem and a threat, since the alternative, 'white racism', was as 'incredible' as it was 'unacceptable' given the deeply held view of British society as inherently tolerant of outsiders. The reluctance to accept that whites could be an important part of the problem significantly structured the media approach to the coverage of the increasing incidence of individual racialised violence which began to emerge in the late 1960s.

What became labelled 'Paki-bashing' only began to appear in the press with any regularity after April 1970, prompted by an extreme case which resulted in the death, or rather the murder, of Tausir Ali. But, as pointed out by Derek Humphry and Gus John in 'Because they're black' (1971), London's Pakistani community had been complaining of the increasing frequency of racial attacks for at least two years. Those complaints were ignored by the press, as they were ignored by the Metropolitan Police, presumably for the same reasons – the police conviction that such incidents could be accounted for by the rising level of hooliganism, and were not motivated by racial hostility. Thus, it took a death for the issue of Paki-bashing to be recognised by the media. The act of recognition, however, was not to result in the media accepting racial motivation as an explanation of the phenomenon. Rather, as press coverage increased, the tendency was to concentrate on those actions taken by the Pakistani and Bangladeshi community in self-defence, and to ignore both the issue of motives of the whites and the inability of the police to counter the attacks (Leech, 1980).

By contrast, no such scepticism or restraint characterised the media's treatment of 'mugging', a phenomenon surfacing like Paki-bashing in the late 1960's and early 1970's. As Stuart Hall and his co-researchers demonstrated in 'Policing the Crisis' (1978), mugging came in for that peculiar one-sided or one-dimensional treatment reserved by the media for the coverage of violent crime. In the first place the media accepted, uncritically from the police, the label 'mugging' as a 'new' category of violent crime, when in fact that label merely regrouped under one heading a series of street crimes that had always been committed, many of which were not violent. Having accepted the label and its violent associations, it was but a small step to similarly accepting that the incidence of violent street crime was increasing on a scale that threatened to reduce certain areas of our major cities to the level of pervasive criminality found in the ghettos of New York or Chicago. The final element in the media's representation of mugging was the link between this violent new crime wave and black youth. This was equally suspect, based as it was on disputed police statistics. Not only did this progressively distorted media representation of mugging produce a climate of opinion and concern, where Judges felt obliged to respond with exemplary sentences and in which police were able to justify new methods of policing, but it also provided the basis for public figures like Powell to exploit the supposed racial implications of this new type of crime (Hall et al, 1978, p. 327). Insofar as the category mugging could be said to exist, the burden of Hall's argument is that it could not meaningfully be distinguished by either the race of the assailants or the racial composition of particular areas of the city. Nevertheless, it was as 'a racial crime', rife in black areas of settlement and committed by blacks against whites, that mugging came to be understood and represented in the press.

In summarising the treatment of race in the media, perhaps the most disturbing observation is that the systematic distortion and misrepresentation of black citizens, racial situations, events and issues are less a consequence of the racial bias of individual journalists and editors, and more of the routine ideologies and practices central to the production of news. Though media institutions cannot be abstracted from the hostile racial environment in which they operate, those supposedly sacred media notions of 'objectivity', 'impartiality' and 'balance' contrive to reinforce all that is negative, problematic and conflictual about race rather than lowering the racial temperature. This underlying perspective, sympathetic to and derived from definitions of race circulating in the political domain, at once 'over-selects' race as news and identifies and orders the various and changing themes through which race is reported. Transmitted with these definitions is the value and reference system within which race is understood, and from which explanations are generated. But if the definitions and understandings of the powerful may be said to provide the 'canvas', the media and its sense of what is implicitly newsworthy must take a large part of the responsibility for the resulting distorted 'picture'. How then did these mechanisms operate in respect to the violence in Bristol?

'War on the Streets' – The Newspaper Reconstruction

Having on the evening of 2 April 1980 been confronted with vivid television news pictures of the violence in Bristol as it actually occurred, the public supposedly picked up their newspapers the following morning in search of a more lengthy and coherent description of events. The question is would they have found it? It is here therefore, that our analysis of the newspaper reconstruction of the violent confrontation begins.

The first stage in that reconstruction is the reporting of the actual events that went to make up what the press labelled 'THE BRISTOL RIOT'. But the process of reconstruction implies more than just a factual sequential reporting of different actions. It includes a pre-history – the background to and circumstances of the event. It includes explanations and understandings of the event's broad social meaning and significance. And of particular importance in the case of newspapers, it includes editorial prescriptions of what ought and ought not to be done about the event and its related issues. These are the different elements that comprise the basic 'story'; and it is upon these that we focus in attempting to unravel the newspaper reconstruction of the violent crowd behaviour in Bristol. Our approach to these elements of the story will be essentially thematic, concerned with the nature of press representations of the various activities and participants involved. That the newspaper version differed substantially from events as critically reconstructed in the preceding chapter will soon become clear. Merely to establish these differences however is not enough; we shall want to know the means by which they came about and how the final and fearful press portrait of 'The Bristol Riot' was built up, step by step.

Notwithstanding the high concentration of ownership amongst British newspapers, or the argument presented earlier in this chapter that journalists share a common body of news values and practices, newspapers do nevertheless differ considerably. They have different party political leanings; they cater to particular audiences; and there are further differences of emphasis and approach between national and local mass circulation dailies, and between dailies and the Sunday press. In recognition of these differences our sample of national dailies included THE GUARDIAN, THE TIMES, THE MIRROR, THE DAILY MAIL, and THE TELEGRAPH. Of the Sundays, THE OBSERVER, THE SUNDAY TIMES and THE SUNDAY TELE-GRAPH were included. We also looked at the local Bristol newspapers in recognition of their greater proximity and access to events and information. The newspapers chosen here were the WESTERN DAILY PRESS and THE EVENING POST.

It should be stressed that in the rest of this chapter we shall be concerned only with the press treatment of those events that occurred in Bristol on 2 April, 1980.

Categorising the Event

In whatever form, be it a violent demonstration, clashes between rival football fans, or trade union pickets in confrontation with the police, civil disturbance is news of the first order. It is news in the first instance as a manifestation of conflict in its most intense and dramatic form. It is also news because such disturbances threaten the established social order; they breach and contradict that dominant consensual view of British society as inherently more united than divided, as devoid of major structural divisions, and as a society in which competing groups are supposedly all agreed that where a conflict of interest exists it ought to be resolved through negotiated, non-violent, discursive and democratic means.

Civil disturbances may be self-selecting as news, but clearly all are not of equal importance in a news sense. Questions of scale apart, the greater the perceived threat to the established social order, and by extension the greater the perceived threat to the state, the greater the news significance of a particular disturbance. Thus, a disturbance in which violence is collectively directed at the police is generally more news compelling than a seaside clash between mods and rockers which only indirectly involves the police. These considerations, as well as determining news' importance, also constitute the basic frame of reference within which different kinds of civil disorders are understood.

The importance of an event may be signalled by a newspaper in a variety of ways: where in the newspaper the report is located, the amount of space given over to it, whether or not the report is the subject of an editorial, and the use of photographs and different types of headlines. By these criteria, there could be no mistaking the importance ascribed to the violence in Bristol by the press. In all the newspapers surveyed the 'riot' commanded the number one, front page spot. It was the subject of dramatic headlines, extended reported accounts, and extensive pictorial coverage, particularly in the tabloids and local newspapers. Reflecting the greater local impact, the entire front pages of both Bristol papers were taken up with the events, with extended follow-up reports inside.

If the prominence attributed to the crowd violence revealed its perceived importance, the headlines gave the first indications why. Headlines are effectively the first stage in ascribing an event a social category through which its significance is communicated. Given that journalists and editors do not possess some inherent quality which enables them instantly to make 'sense' of any and every event – particularly where such are unfamiliar, complex and emotive – headlines are effectively the first stage at which news values may be superimposed upon an event. Here are a sample of the headlines appearing in newspapers on 3 April 1980:

Pull-out ordered as shops burn
19 POLICE HURT IN BLACK RIOT
Hundreds rampage after swoop on Bristol club
(*Daily Telegraph*)

Two hundred angry youths go on rampage after raid on black cafe in Bristol
19 POLICE HURT AS RIOTERS, BURN, LOOT CITY STREETS
(*The Guardian*)

Looting and fires as Riot erupts
MOB FURY
Gangs of looters go on Rampage
(*Daily Mirror*)

Twenty-five people injured and bank, shops and police cars set alight after raid on club
HUNDREDS OF BLACK YOUTHS BATTLE WITH POLICE IN BRISTOL RIOT
(*The Times*).

While subsidiary headlines indicated slants or aspects to be emphasised in the subsequent report, the dominant identity of the event is clear and simple. It is a RIOT. The RIOTERS are BLACK. They RAMPAGE, HURT POLICE, BURN and LOOT. Brief as they are, these headlines nevertheless manage to communicate the nature of the event, the main participants involved, what happened, and even how it was caused. As a bold statement of what are supposedly the essential 'facts', headlines have a disproportionate impact upon the readers' understanding of the event, whether or not it is qualified, fudged, or contradicted in the subsequent report. But are these the essential facts? In terms of accuracy, crucially, white participation in the crowd violence and especially in the looting did not prevent the singular label 'BLACK RIOT'. Indeed, taken as a whole, the headlines embody a series of emotive and value-laden labels, RIOT, RAMPAGE, MOB FURY. Whether or not these are justifiable descriptions will become clear. But already the basic framework within which the various activities are to be simplified and represented has been established: there is the criminal and therefore unjustifiable behaviour of the 'mob'; the 'MOB's' violence is directed primarily at the police in the execution of their legitimate duties.

The Initial Reporting

As regards an extended and coherent description of events, journalists – especially those working for national papers – were faced with one fundamental news-gathering problem: they simply weren't there. For 'hard' news, journalists were dependent on a few limited and readily accessible sources. Thus the first striking feature of initial newspaper reports on 3 April was their remarkable similarity, given that the events could have been reported from any number of different news angles. In newspaper after newspaper, whole paragraphs were virtually identical. It would not be inaccurate to describe the basic initial story as being entirely composed around the public statements of senior policemen and firemen, supplemented by the accounts of three or four eye witnesses.

From this limited supply of news sources, a number of consequences followed. First, in order to provide the reader with an extended account, the core material had to be enhanced, with the result that numerous inaccuracies of detail crept in. Secondly, events were portrayed as a series of images, rather than a sequential description of actions and activities. Thirdly, in the construction of these images, newspapers to varying extents (*The Times* least so, and the *Daily Mirror* most) reported as fact, versions of events derived from accredited official sources; sources which were both involved and interested. The end result was that only one basic version of what happened that afternoon and evening was available to readers on the morning of the 3rd, no matter which or how many newspapers were read.

The remarkable similarity of the initial reports makes it comparatively easy to break the story down into its component parts. These are, in the order of importance attached to them in the reports: the violent behaviour of the mob against the police and private property; the general difficulties of the police resulting ultimately in their withdrawal from the area; how the violence was initially caused; and the re-entry of the police to restore law and order. But in order to show how the referential framework already evident from headlines was substantiated by and structured into initial reports, we shall deal with events in sequential form.

From the beginning, the influence of the term RIOT, in its 'popular' rather than its stricter legal sense, is noticeable in the way initial reports retell the story of Bristol. Popularly, riots are sudden, an eruption, a total break with normality; they are characterised by wild, unrestrained, mindless violence and destruction; violence initiated, caused, and sustained by the 'mob', until it either wanes or is suppressed by the forces of law and order. It is this popular notion of riot that moulds the press reconstruction of the violence and looting. Where the facts did not 'fit', they are either omitted or relegated to a low status in reports.

Of the first critical element in the story, how the violence started, all accounts began with the police raid on the Black and White cafe in search of illegal drugs and alcohol. From there, the violence was represented as occurring with remarkable speed and suddenness. This representation of initial events as a sudden eruption was achieved by three different methods. First, with the exception of *The Times*, which early in its report suggests that the violence was related to 'friction which had been evident for several years', accounts did not include any relevant pre-history to the violence. Not only might such a pre-history have included the state of recent relations between the police and the community in St Paul's, it might also have inquired into why so large a number of police accompanied by police dogs were necessary on a raid concerned with only relatively minor offences, and whether a public order situation was envisaged by the police from the start. Secondly, in initial reports no times were given between the arrival of the police in the area and the occurrence of the first incident. Even in the official accounts, both the police and the crowd were held to be present in the area of the cafe for at least an hour before the first violent incident occurs. What happened in that hour is vital to any understanding of how the confrontation began, yet there were no accounts of it in initial press reports. Thirdly, in lieu of times, the violence was stated to occur soon after the raid began (*Mirror*), as the police 'left the cafe' – meaningless, since they left at different times – (*Guardian*, *Mail*, *Telegraph*), or 'within minutes' or 'within seconds' of the raid (*Times*).

Without a pre-history, and without an account of the immediate antecedents of the first violent incident, there remained the bare scenario: 'police raid cafe in search of illegal drugs and alcohol' – 'black mob attacks police'. In that scenario, the behaviour of the crowd is at best 'inexplicable', at worst it was 'explained' given the stereo-typical assertions that 'blacks are violent', 'blacks are criminals', 'blacks hate the police'. Either way, what essentially emerged from the story at this stage was a picture of a sudden, unprovoked attack on the police, for which the police, both in terms of their immediate and past actions, were not responsible.

✍ The next stage of the story involved the period from the first violent incident to the withdrawal of the police from the area at around 7.30 pm. Given the predisposition of news values for violent conflict, it is this stage that dominated initial reports. Within the referential framework operating at the level of headlines and in relation to accounts of how the violence began, this stage was recounted primarily by focusing on the behaviour of the crowd. The general difficulties of the police and their subsequent withdrawal were only subsidiary themes.

Two features typify the representation of the crowd's behaviour. First, all violence, whether it was directed at the police or at private property, was lumped together as if occurring simultaneously. Secondly, rather than describing a series or sequence of actions and events, the violence is stereotyped. The effect of both was to condense a multitude of different activities stretching over a period of some nine hours, into a few easily communicated, supposedly typical images. Thus the 'riot' and 'rampage' declared by the headlines was reproduced in reports. *The Guardian* reports 'six hours of vicious street fighting'. *The Telegraph* likens Bristol's 'coloured quarter' to a 'battleground' when 'gangs of West Indians went on a frenzy of rioting, looting and burning'. In the *Mail*, youths are reported as involved in 'hand to hand battle with the police'. While in the *Mirror*, with its account of 'rioters' sweeping through 'the streets of Bristol', it is initially difficult to establish that the 'riot', even at its height, was restricted to a few streets in St Paul's. Whereas the local Bristol papers incorporated greater detail based mostly on eye-witness accounts, their portrayal of the violence was, if anything, more alarmist. According to the *Western Daily Press*, 'Gangs of coloured youths ran wild; looting, stoning police and starting fires'. *The Evening Post* for its part insisted throughout on a war despatch style, reporting the 'WAR ON THE STREETS', direct from the 'RIOT ZONE', with '3000 rioters on the rampage', a 'horde' going 'wild'.

These then were the images used to communicate the 'RIOT'. Following on from the sudden and unprovoked attack on the police, the violence was said to have quickly escalated into general mayhem. This account from *The Guardian* is typical:

When they (the police) entered the club . . . a large crowd quickly gathered. As the police left they faced a barrage of bricks, stones, and bottles. Several officers fell to the ground with head wounds. As the rioting spread police vehicles were attacked, overturned and set on fire. Perspex shields were issued and dog teams appeared . . . (*Guardian*, 3 April 1980)

In so far as this description is accurate, and on several counts it is not, events separated in time by hours are concertinaed into a few minutes. The level of crowd violence is represented in most accounts as continuous and sustained until the withdrawal of the police from the area. These images may be consistent with the view of events as perceived and communicated by senior police officers, they may also be consistent with popular notions of RIOT, but they did little to inform the general public as to what occurred in Bristol on the afternoon of 2 April.

Unless the simplistic and closed position is adopted that whatever is done by the police in putting down riot is by definition legitimate and justifiable, then the changing character of the violence that afternoon and evening cannot be understood without reference to police decisions and actions. Such references were entirely absent from initial reports. Though the violence stemmed directly from the nature of the police intervention in the area, and though the violence had been directed at the police, press coverage of the role, methods and objectives of the police was almost totally uncritical. Indeed, many reports in opting for such headlines as '19 POLICE HURT.' (*Guardian*), in preference to for example, 'Twenty-five people injured . . .' (*Times*) indicated the value stance implicit in subsequent reports. By abstracting the police from the equation of responsibility in precipitating and sustaining the confrontation the essential facts that emerged concerning them were: that they were 'surprised' at the speed at which the disturbance developed; that they were outnumbered, beleaguered, poorly equipped, and very much on the receiving end of the mob's violence. Their subsequent withdrawal from the area was used to confirm this version of events and the degree of violence to which they were subjected. But if initial reports were more than a little uneasy with the implications of the police abandoning an entire area of the city of Bristol in the face of a hostile crowd, it was here that the deft hand of the official accredited source seems to have had its firmest grip on the story. Understandably, the police did not wish the withdrawal to be represented as a defeat. Rationalised by the Deputy Chief Constable, the withdrawal became an orderly, deliberate and even an humanitarian manoeuvre:

Every time we went in we increased what was a volatile situation and I feared for the lives of the policemen. It was a very, very dangerous situation, and in the interests of the safety of the policemen, and due to the inadequate number I had available, I felt it necessary to withdraw the police until such time as we had sufficient manpower to go in and establish law and order. (*Guardian*, 3 April 1980)

Thus prompted, *The Guardian* reported the withdrawal as 'an effort to cool down the situation', the *Mail* as 'an attempt to avoid further confrontation', and the *Mirror* as a 'brief "cooling off" period'. *The Telegraph* by contrast, unable to accept that the withdrawal could be easily 'explained' (instance the sub-headline 'Pull-out ordered as Shops Burn'), was obliged to stress instead the eventual police reoccupation of St Paul's. To this end it quoted the comments of a senior police officer as that re-entry was about to be effected:

We are going to show the public that we are very much with them and we will do our darndest to establish law and order again.

From the evidence submitted and tested under cross-examination during the trial, it is clear that the press grossly exaggerated the scale of violence and misrepresented that violence as being wholly and solely caused and sustained by black crowds. Not only could the different activities of the crowds, i.e. rioting, looting and burning, not be lumped together as if occurring at the same time, but the levels of violence described in the reports did not follow on directly from the initial incident, and were not sustained throughout the afternoon until the withdrawal of the police.

No-one can be certain how the violence began, but certainly the press version of a sudden and inexplicable attack on the police, while in or as they left the cafe, is wrong. According to the police, the disturbance began away from the cafe with an attack on four drug squad officers. Whether this limited attack was indeed the 'triggering incident', or whether trouble had already started as a consequence of the early use of police dogs, or by the arrival of a number of police cars, with sirens going and driving at speed towards the crowd and the cafe, cannot be said. Whichever was the case, the behaviour of the crowd cannot be understood except in relation to particular policemen or the actions and decisions of senior officers.

Nor, as initial reports would have it, did the first violent incident lead directly to generalised rioting. The period immediately following that incident was typified by isolated flare-ups. Police dogs were used and arrests were being made. But there were no battle lines. Crowds assembled, and, as quickly, dispersed. Individual or small groups of police officers were able to pursue individual stonethrowers through the crowds. Even after the first serious clash at about 5.30 pm caused by a military style police march towards the crowd and the cafe, the violence was not sustained.

There then followed an event that must be presumed to be totally without news value. For one hour, while the police were guarding a burnt-out police car near the cafe no acts of violence occurred in St Paul's. The police were greatly outnumbered by the crowd but were not attacked. The 'RIOT', even in media terms, was over. At the cafe, people were clearing up, and in City Road the area's main thoroughfare, rush hour traffic passed unhindered. By this stage according to the Chief Constable, no shops had been looted, and no buildings set on fire.

Inconsistent with the popular notion of riot these events and actions simply failed to appear in initial press reports. Nor were the police actions, which led to the breakdown of this period of calm reported. The police, having decided that a burnt-out vehicle had to be removed, assembled around the towing vehicle, and accompanied by dogs set off at a trot towards the crowd. The crowd responded with a hail of missiles, and the attack was kept up until the vehicle cleared the area. Subsequently, police tactics changed and the violence took on new intensity. Up to this point, in so far as police tactics and objectives could be discerned, no attempt had been made to confront and disperse passive crowds gathered on the streets and open spaces in the area. After the towing away of the burnt-out car, a decision was taken to confront and clear such a crowd in City Road. It is then that serious and widespread violence began in St Paul's. With the police now equipped with riot shields, the violence overspilled from City Road into adjoining streets, where police vehicles came under attack and a bank was set on fire. It is scenes from this stage of the evening's activities that initial reports used to characterise the whole disturbance. The withdrawal of the police from the area after several confrontations, an hour later, was perhaps as much to do with the confusion and unclear lines of police command as with the crowd's violence. Police reinforcements arriving in response to different emergency calls were unclear where to go and what to do. Riot shields were issued, withdrawn and re-issued. The shields were insufficient in number, and the men using them un-trained.

That press representations of the looting and arson bore little relation to events is hardly surprising, given the nature of the preceding elements of the story. Left open-ended in most accounts, it is difficult to determine when this aspect of the crowd's activities began and ended. Most accounts, however, were aware that the looting occurred largely during the police absence from the area, and this allowed yet another dimension of 'lawlessness' to be added to the story. To the basic theme conveyed by the *Mirror*, 'Gangs of Looters Go On the Rampage', *The Guardian* amongst others added this new dimension by linking 'reports of widespread fire-raising and looting' with 'rampaging crowds of youth' described as being in 'control of St Paul's'. By more accurate reporting, *The Times* initially managed to avoid this general view. But even *The Times* could not resist one of the more emotive quotes on which the description of St Paul's in the absence of the police was based. According to a local publican:

The youngsters, hundreds of them, are out of control. They are setting fire to houses and shops, smashing windows and destroying all they can. I have locked myself in, and I am worried we will be attacked next. (*The Times*, 3 April, 1980)

The essential picture needs little elaboration. With the withdrawal of the police, supposedly only the law of the jungle remained. Violent 'gangs', 'crowds', 'mobs' were in 'control'. Might this have been the purpose of the mobs in attacking the police so relentlessly from the beginning? This dimension of the violence remained only an undertone in initial reports; represented as a 'no-go' area it became explicit in subsequent features and editorials. For the moment, however, the point needs to be made that in the absence of the police from St Paul's for nearly four hours, these 'rampaging' gangs did far less damage than the media suggested. A total of thirteen shops had property stolen from them, and when looting, arson, and damage are added together, according to the police, twenty-four buildings were involved. Rather than widespread, looting was selective. Individual premises were singled out, and others left alone; older members of the community were able to prevent the local chemist from being looted. By the time the police re-entered the area at around 11.15 pm, the looting had already stopped, and the police were not resisted.

As 'news' in its truest sense, the initial report theoretically sets out to establish the facts, rigorously separating those facts from comment or opinion. Nevertheless, at the end of this first complete stage in the overall reconstruction of the violent confrontation in Bristol, there are already severe fractures between press accounts and actual events. Structured and simplified through popular or commonsense notions of riot, the violence is sudden, inexplicable, extreme and sustained. Reinforcing the perceived racial identity of the 'mob', initial accounts add brief background descriptions of St Paul's. In *The Guardian*, the 'riot' was described as occurring in, and against, the backdrop of the 'poverty-stricken black ghetto'. Blacks, in fact form only 30% of the population of St Paul's. The *Mirror* added another basic background feature that was later to become important in newspaper understandings of the 'riot':

Bristol's crime rate is one of the highest among provincial cities. St Paul's is Bristol's poorest area. It is known as a red-light district, with prostitutes openly soliciting on the streets. The area has the city's highest proportion of blacks. (*Mirror*, 3 April 1980).

Features and Editorials
For the purpose of media analysis, features and editorials are not normally dealt with together. Though in function they overlap and to an extent cover the same ground, they are derived through different news processes and the end products are different. Thus features and editorials occupy different 'places' in the production of news, and are ascribed a different status. The feature allows a deeper exploration of

the event, its essential social significance, its pre-history, its immediate and wider background and its causes. While this process is recognisably shaped by the political outlook of both the newspaper and the individual correspondent concerned, features yet conform to press notions of 'balance' and 'impartiality'. In 'weighing-up' the overall significance, implications and causes of an event, the correspondent brings to bear alternative and competing understandings and explanations. Editorials by contrast, make no such pretensions. They are the recognised political mouthpiece of the newspaper. Essentially discursive in style, only one argument is usually rehearsed, with the objective of prescribing remedies. It is through the editorial that the newspaper overtly attempts to marshall and mobilise public opinion to bring pressure to bear on powerful individuals and institutions.

Following on from initial reports, features and editorials are the next major stage in the newspaper reconstruction of events in Bristol. In looking at them together we wish to emphasise the extent to which, from the point of view of the social significances attached to events, the two were indistinguishable. But additionally, we also wish to draw attention to the essentially closed nature of the public debate. By ignoring the role of the police, it will be appreciated that this process of closure began at the level of the initial report. It was to attain full expression in features and editorials.

Race and racism: press rationalisations

Unanimously declared a 'black riot' in initial reports, features and editorials went on to explore wider implications and social significances in greater depth. One indication of emergent thinking on how the riot might be interpreted was the wide use made in initial reports of the comments of one Reverend Geoffrey Fowkes, a local key eyewitness:

It was not a race riot, because I am white, and I was standing there. Colour has nothing to do with this. I think it was a question of authority and reaction to authority rather than a question of colour. (*The Times*, 3 April 1980)

This 'on the spot assessment', however, did not strike a resonant note in initial reports. Could the violent activities be at one and the same time a 'black riot' and not in some sense racial? Additionally, though not formally mentioned, the black ghetto 'race riots' that shattered American cities in the 1960's were very much in play in shaping the initial reports. The possibility that Britain might be the scene of such riots having been voiced by politicians, pundits and the press for years, it was the most readily available and familiar social framework within which the events might be understood. Nevertheless, it was the Fowkes definition that came to dominate. Suddenly, journalists and editors became aware of the extent of white involvement. More to the point, from both Labour and Conservative benches, from the Cabinet, the Home Office, the police, and those local and national bodies concerned with ethnic and community relations came the chorus 'The Bristol disturbance was not a race riot'. While some newspapers had no difficulty in accepting and reproducing this peculiar non-definition, for others the tensions implicit in a non-racial black riot appeared to pose problems. Sceptical of what might now be termed the 'official' definition, an editorial in *The Times* left the issue unresolved:

Some have taken consolation in the opinion that what happened in Bristol was not a race riot. That needs qualification. The riot was not racial in as much as the only whites attacked by the black rioters were policemen, and it was the colour of their uniforms not their skins which counted; also there were some whites among the predominantly black rioters and looters. But the affair was racial in as much as it is traceable to a concentration of people of West Indian origin in that place . . . (*Times*, 7 April 1980)

The *Mail*, in its editorial, while accepting that the violence could not be described as a race riot felt obliged to add its own qualifications:

This was not a race riot. Yet it would be foolish to overlook that this was primarily a black expression of frustration against a primarily white authority. (*Mail*, 5 April 1980)

The Guardian was more expansive. In addition to Bristol it took the opportunity to declare that previous clashes in Notting Hill, Lewisham, Leeds and Bradford were also not in the classic sense of blacks against whites 'race riots'. These, it asserted, were in fact 'bitter anti-police riots led by black youth'. Yet again there were important and apparently contradictory racial qualifications:

It would . . . prove highly dangerous in the long run if by consoling ourselves with the thought that such are 'non-racial' we blind ourselves to the appalling tensions which now exist between black youths and the police. (*Guardian*, 5 April 1980)

Thus, though variously qualified, in principle newspapers accepted the official definition. The questions were, where did these RACIAL qualifications leave the understanding of an event that was 'NOT a RACE RIOT', and what was to become of the newspapers' own definition, 'BLACK RIOT'? The short answer is, both were imperceptibly blended. *The Times*, having noted the presence of the white rioter, and having firmly quashed any suggestion that there could be any significance in the colour of the policemen's skins, asked its readers to accept the simple proposition that where there are BLACK urban concentrations, there are RIOTS. The *Mail* and *The Guardian*, in identifying specifically BLACK frustration, tension, and conflict with white authority (particularly the police) leave the question begging as to whether the riot was racially caused. The implicit answer must be no:

whatever the qualification, if the violence was not perceived as essentially racial in origin, how could it be understood in terms of racial explanations? In essence what remained was a BLACK RIOT that was not racially caused. From this formulation, the white rioter is again missing. Indeed, throughout the newspaper reconstruction of events in Bristol, this figure is made to appear and disappear at the convenience of journalists and editors. Absent from initial reports, he appears briefly to witness the agreement between media and state that the disturbance was not a race riot, only to disappear as the media came to address the issues of wider implications and significances. In fact white participation in the violence and looting was a matter of some importance. It revealed both the nature of policing in areas like St Paul's, and that the shared experience of inner city could over-ride divisive racial ideologies. These were not however themes the media chose to explore.

The unwillingness to concede even the possibility that the violence might have been a 'RACE RIOT' could, *in part*, be attributed to – as in *The Guardian* – that 'traditional British reluctance to attribute trouble to tensions between the races' (5 April 1980). It could in part be attributed to simplistic and common sense distinctions between race riot and black riot (see Chapter 1). What, however, it most decidedly did indicate was the types of significances and explanations that were *not* to be pursued in the media. In other words, certainly the press were not about to abandon their fixations with blacks, but by ruling out race riot they were also ruling out any suggestion that the crowd violence in Bristol could be seen in terms of a reaction or revolt against WHITE RACISM, in both its incidental and institutionalised forms. Such a perspective would necessitate an examination of the black experience of, and protest against, racial practices within the state – a result of immigration legislation but also of the courts, prisons and at the hands of the police. It would necessitate an examination of racial discrimination in housing and employment, aspects compounded by the inner-city location of black communities, and concerning which government policies since the middle 1960's had been less than successful. It would necessitate an examination of methods used by the police in these inner city areas, methods that affect not only black but white communities similarly located. And last but not least it would necessitate an examination of the representation of race in the media.

Defined as a black riot not comprehensible in terms of a reaction to racism, how then was the violence to be explained? The first instincts of the feature writers were to return to the scene of the crime in search of a 'flashpoint' that might shed light on this unprecedented breakdown of law and order. The notion of a flashpoint, while totally ignoring any underlying circumstances, offered a ready explanation that the occurrence or non-occurrence of subsequent events turned on a single, possibly avoidable, incident. The search was most determined in the *Mirror* where it virtually replaced the need to examine background factors in any depth. But it also occupied to varying extents the serious press and the 'Sundays'. A 'TORN TROUSER' was the incident most commonly identified. Under the headline 'How a row over torn trousers led to . . . FLASHPOINT', the *Mirror* report ran:

> bad feeling boiled over when a beer crate being carried out by a policeman snagged on a youth's trousers. He demanded compensation for the rip. The officers ignored his protests. And soon all hell let loose. (*Mirror*, 5 April 1980)

Indicative of the confusion over this incident, in the *Mail* the youth in question was identified as Prince Brown, in fact Dr Prince Brown a local social worker and certainly no youth. In the *Sunday Telegraph*, Prince Brown, rather than starting a riot, is represented as strenuously trying to stop one.

The torn trouser incident occurred, but it certainly did not precipitate the violence. From the search for a flashpoint many feature writers went on to a wider exploration of the sequence of events. With the notable exception of the *Sunday Times* however, there was little to separate these secondary reconstructions from those available in initial reports. Though newspapers could no longer sustain the proposition that only black participants were involved, the representation of the crowd's behaviour as a sudden, inexplicable attack on the police flaring into generalised violence which continued until the withdrawal of the police, remained essentially intact. Proving that a more accurate account could be established where journalists chose to take the trouble, the INSIGHT team in the *Sunday Times* found that a protracted period had elapsed between the beginning of the police raid and the onset of serious violence; that early incidents were followed by a period of complete calm; and that this calm was broken by a 'fundamental tactical error' on the part of the police (*Sunday Times*, 6 April 1980).

The search for a flashpoint also provided features correspondents with an opportunity to pursue notions of impartiality and balance through incorporating the comments of local community spokesmen and personalities. It is here that the issue of police/community relations is first approached. Not only do black and other spokesmen outline a history of persistent police harassment, heavy-handedness and insensitivity, but they stress that these practices were often racially inspired and accompanied by racial abuse: 'they treat us like dirt' (*Mirror*, 5 April 1980). They 'regard black as "coons", intellectually subnormal and inbred criminals' (*Observer*, 6 April 1980). In reporting such remarks, newspapers could justly claim 'balance', i.e. reporting both sides. That, however, is not to say that such assertions were accepted. More often than not they were treated as 'claims', 'accusa-tions', 'hearsay', and even 'myth'. As such, they did not lead to any in-depth exploration of police/community relations. Nor did they divert newspapers from their primary area of explanatory focus – blacks, their environment, culture and behaviour. At best, as in *The Guardian* (5 April 1980), the police were portrayed as 'the symbols of white indifference'; mildly critical perhaps, but the very opposite of the picture community spokesmen were attempting to communicate. Else-where accusations of police harassment are taken to imply little more than an excuse on the part of rioters to justify their lawless behaviour after the event.

Confirming newspaper definitions and understandings, the basic explanation mobilised by feature writers and editors attempted to causally link the violence in Bristol with one or other forms of black pathology. These pathologies fell into two broad categories – socio-cultural, and environmental – with features and editorials often com-bining both types in explanations. However, in both main explanatory themes, the linking factor between the community, conflict and the police is *crime*, hence the closed or one dimensional nature of the press debate. The disturbance is criminal, it is a reaction to police executing a legitimate search for illegal drugs and alcohol, and the breakdown of relations between the police and the community is determined by crime.

The *Telegraph*, easily the most extreme proponent of the black socio-culture pathology thesis, lost no time in translating its opinions into print. In an editorial accompanying its initial report, it addressed the issue of 'tedious advice', by which it meant the kind of advice that attempted to explain the violent behaviour of the crowd in terms of the lack of amenities in areas like St Paul's. That this would be the cry of a 'host' of 'benefactors' already descending on St Paul's, the *Telegraph* was in no doubt. Hence the paper's anxiety to get in first. To the amenities argument the *Telegraph* posed a simple question to which, of course, there was only one answer: 'Is it really to be supposed that a craving for table tennis and coffee bars is at the bottom of this?' With the ground thus suitably cleared, in a brisk and authoritative style, the *Telegraph* homed in on its primary target:

The most serious problem confronting the police is undoubtedly a section of West Indian youths which is estranged from its families for a variety of reasons. These youths equally reject approach by the police or West Indians. The sub-culture has a substantial criminal fringe . . . we are dealing not with black immigrants, but with the irresponsible worst group of those immigrants. (*Telegraph*, 3 April 1980; see p. 54)

This substantial criminal fringe at once indicated that conflicts with the police were endemic and inevitable. On the one hand the police must enforce the law, on the other how could West Indian youth be but maladjusted products of their cultural environment. In restricting its first broadside to that estranged, irresponsible, criminalised section of West Indian youth, the *Telegraph* showed remarkable restraint. In its next broadside the black community, black history and culture were not to get off so lightly, and that was only for starters:

These unfortunate West Indian migrants emerged in the aftermath of slavery without any stable family framework to integrate into a wider society. Lacking parental care many ran wild. Incited by race relations witchfinders and left-wing teachers and social workers to blame British society for their own short-comings, lacking the work ethic and perseverance, lost in society itself demoralised by socialism, they all too easily sink into a criminal sub culture. (*Telegraph*, 7 April 1980)

It is difficult in this outburst to find a racist stereotype that is not rehearsed. Variously blacks are lazy, incapable, brainless, criminal, and without society or civilisation. Their behaviour is historically and culturally pre-determined. But for the *Telegraph*, even this does not in the last instance explain their resort to violence. That violence is part of a great left-wing conspiracy in which blacks are unwitting accomplices. Understandable then the *Telegraph*'s impatience with the advice givers: in this formulation what is there to discuss?

The themes of black criminality and pathological cultural imperatives also found expression in an *Observer* feature. In this instance, black criminal subculture and its violent consequences take on tribal proportions i.e. 'The Revolt of Britain's Lost Tribe' (6 April 1980). And the significance of the violence is not so much a non-racial 'anti-police' riot, but an action by blacks '. . . in defence of their freedom to drink beer in their own premises in the middle of a warm spring afternoon . . .'. Here, as in the *Telegraph*, the gap between the community and the police is irreconcilable. How could it be otherwise while blacks 'believe that in smoking ganja and drinking illegally they are indulging in harmless pleasures'? A young constable is left to draw the necessary conclusion:

When they talk of harassment, what they really mean is that we're carrying out our duty.

Explanations in the *Mail* seemingly fell between the two schools: black criminality, both culturally and environmentally caused, leading to antagonism with the police. In its feature entitled 'WHAT MADE BRISTOL BURN', the mainstay of black culture is identified as a shadowy world of 'clubs, pubs and cafes'. That most of these had been closed down by the police, for one or other reasons prior to the 2 April, meant that when the police raided the Black and White 'hostility was inevitable'. The material conditions referred to in the *Mail*, however, did not imply any close treatment of unemployment or housing etc. Rather, it was an image of the supposed behaviour of blacks in 'the ghetto' that the *Mail* sought to project: 'For the *majority*', the *Mail* held, 'a normal day in the ghetto . . . means hanging around the streets, listening to music and playing football' (6.4.80). Continuing with its editorial, the *Mail* outlined its own explanation of ghetto disaffection and here again we find a new list of black cultural pathologies:

The days when a few pingpong tables and a youth club could ease the problems of a deprived area are long since gone. Leaders of the black community must take some responsibility for this. If black children are playing truant from school and losing out from any benefits with which this society could provide them, then this is because their own *internal leadership* is weak and divided. (*Mail*, 5 April 1980)

Though variously employed, the central proposition informing this series of 'explanations' is that the origins of the violence in Bristol were to be found in blacks themselves and their culture. This argument does not quite voice the simplistic assertion that blacks are naturally violent, but it is only one step removed. Broadly, the guiding logic is that both historically and in its contemporary forms black culture is riddled with pathologies; certain items of that culture – such as practices with alcohol and drugs – are directly at odds with the laws of the land, but of greater significance, the culture reproduced a maladjusted, alienated and criminalised sub-culture amongst sections of its youth. Conflict between the police and the black community therefore is intrinsic, and is at its most intense where members of the criminalised sub-culture are concerned. This is the context within which the violence in Bristol is infused with meaning. It is an action – particularly by criminalised youth – in defence of their right to drink illegal beer and smoke ganja. As will be seen when we come to look at editorial prescription, the dominant issue raised by this formulation is black cultural practices and the law of the land. In so far as the violence is deemed to have significance outside this, then in deadly earnest the reader is asked to believe it was somehow bound up with ping pong tables, coffee bars, and youth clubs.

Supposedly those features and editorials that located the origins of the violence in environmental causes would be better able to grasp the larger sense of black grievance implicit in the crowd violence and founded in part on black confinement – along with other groups – to the inner city. This however was not the case. At its crudest, as in *The Times*, the environment, i.e. the inner city, was used not as a means through which the crowd violence could be understood, but as an object to which that violence was 'traceable' (7.4.80). Black concentrations in the inner city pointed not to the complex of discriminatory and other processes at work, but simply became another indication of the pathology and social status of the inner-city itself. Thus *The Times* could argue of St Paul's, that notwithstanding the remedial policies of local government:

the area is unmistakably at the bottom of the socio-economic table, *as is regrettably confirmed by the high concentration of blacks*
(7 April 1980, our emphasis)

Seemingly blacks both reflect and are part of the pathology of their environment. If, as *The Times* conceded, young blacks were four times as likely to be unemployed as young whites, this was 'not wholly' a consequence of 'prejudice and indifference' amongst employers, but also due to their own educational inadequacies. The end result is not dissimilar to the cultural approach above. Thus for *The Times* black youth in their 'estrangement' develop a 'racial self-consciousness' and descend into 'petty crime'.

If *The Times* illustrated the limitations of the environment argument as deployed within the press at one end of the scale then *The Guardian* illustrated its limitations at the other. Here the social location of blacks is described as that 'uneasy mix of racial disadvantages and inner city decay' (5.4.80). That mixture by itself however is not developed to account for the 'appalling tensions between black youth and the police'. And since the reasons for those tensions are not explained it may only be assumed to be a by-product of what *The Guardian* identifies as the inner city's 'most thriving industry', that being 'amateur prostitution, small scale drug peddling, and the running of illegal or after hours drinking establishments'. Nevertheless the crowd violence is seen as an outburst of black frustration, and it was directed at the police because they were the most immediate representatives of 'our uncaring society'.

Though the relationship traced between black inner-city concentration, crime, and violence is by no means as deterministic as in *The Times*, *The Guardian* follows essentially the same route. Without some explanation of why and how black communities came to be located in, and restricted to the inner-city, the concept by itself is not explanatory but merely an indication of material disadvantages. Nor is this explanation achieved through the notion of 'racial disadvantage', for unlike racial discrimination that notion is passive; it indicates socio-economic differences between groups of whites and blacks without addressing the question of why those differences exist. Clearly that question, along with the question of how black communities came to occupy the inner city cannot be adequately answered without some reference to the roles of racist ideologies and practices. This, however, is missing from *The Guardian*'s explanation of the violence in Bristol. Hence the ambivalence of the feature headline 'THE BRISTOL DISTURBANCES: RACIAL BUT NOT RACIST'. The imputation is that Bristol is not a race riot, but *The Guardian* has no explanatory alternatives to offer unless it is assumed that people who live in the inner-city are more likely to be violent. Ultimately the significance of the violence is minimal. If, as in the *Observer*, it is for the freedom to drink illegal beer, in *The Guardian* it is in the defence of the place where that beer is drunk, the Black and White cafe – the 'LAST REFUGE OF AN EMBATTLED COMMUNITY' (5 April 1980).

Editorial Prescription: Orchestrating the White Backlash

The process of reducing the crowd violence in Bristol to an easily understood occurrence to which 'obvious solutions' readily recommended themselves, began at the stage of initial reports. There the crowd violence was declared a black riot. The fixation with the race of participants was carried over into the features and editorials, only with racism ruled out of understanding and explanations. Thus at a stroke, one of the dominant factors shaping the experiences and consciousness of black communities in Britain was excluded. Without reference to the role and impact of racial attitudes and practices in British society, or to the prominence of race in the political sphere over the last two decades, or to the protracted struggle by black and other groups against racism, there could be no sense in which the crowd violence in Bristol could be seen as meaningful, justifiable, or legitimate. Instead the press offered up for public consumption the picture of a black community – either because of their culture or their location in the inner-city – literally prepared to go to war with the police over the right to drink beer and smoke ganja when and where they liked. Now here was something that editorials could really get their teeth into. To this dangerous, new, and unacceptable threat to our major cities, what was overwhelmingly prescribed was a healthy dose of 'law and order'. First, instances of crowd violence like Bristol had to be put down. But in the longer term, black communities were going to need even more rigorous policing.

That the police were unable to bring the violence under control and had withdrawn from the area at the height of the disturbance, provided editorials with their initial point of focus. Enhancing the significance of the withdrawal, and consistent with the portrayal of the violence as extreme, determined and sustained, the failure of the police was interpreted as allowing the creation of a 'no-go' area on the British mainland. Not only did that term superimpose the violent imagery of the political violence of Northern Ireland on events in Bristol, it in like fashion transferred political motivations. The imputation was that the creation of a 'no-go' area was in part the objective of the crowd. This the *Telegraph* saw as having important implications:

It is not easy to understand the conduct of the local Chief Constable in permitting the creation of a no-go area and creating a precedent for every other violent, thieving, and destructive group of untalented adolescents.
(*Telegraph*, 3 April, 1980)

So far as this editorial was concerned, the issues posed by the street violence were simple and singular. The only problem that remained was the present squeamish attitudes of society in general, and Chief Constables in particular:

A certain 18th century savoir faire and scepticism is called for, one which is free from paralytic anxiety about public images and which is rather less surprised when riots occur . . . Like fires, they are, correctly but firmly, to be stopped.

Sending 'shivers down the spine' of the *Mail*, the withdrawal of the police created not so much a no-go area, as a 'jungle' where civilisation itself was at stake. In an editorial entitled 'Defusing the Flashpoints', the *Mail* went on to propose a series of police measures almost identical to those that started the massive Brixton 'riot' one year later:

Inner-city ghettoes are going to need policing. That is going to have to be done with firmness and resolution . . . This may mean that we need more specifically trained squads – like the much maligned S.P.G. – able to disperse a mob before they can catch hold.
(*Mail*, 5 April 1980)

Delivering its editorial in the form of lessons, the *Sunday Telegraph* took as its primary theme the larger question of 'law and order'. The Bristol disturbance, it asserted, was in part the result of the disrepute into which law and order had fallen in recent years. Pursuing the theme, it went on to argue that no circumstance, whether police 'over-reaction' or 'mistakes', the use of force on arrest, or the social circumstances of youth in St Paul's could excuse or justify the riot:

Law and order are not some kind of welfare benefit to be applied on a selective basis. (*Sunday Telegraph*, 6 April 1980)

The theme was reproduced in *The Times*, *Telegraph* and *Mail* with much emphasis on the notion that one system of law and policing should apply to all equally:

Smoking pot or drinking alcohol in unlicensed premises cannot just be waved past as fairly harmless manifestation of cultural difference. If the fact of cultural difference is invoked as a reason for special treatment by, or under the general criminal law, the principle of equality before the law is lost, and with it the basis on which minorities' claims to fair dealing stands. (*Times*, 7 April 1980)

Along with other newspapers, *The Times* does not explain how the assertion that smoking pot and drinking alcohol are manifestations of West Indian culture, is arrived at. Further, had writers of such editorials demanding one system of law and policing, bothered to consult those customers sitting in the Black and White cafe on the afternoon of 2 April, they would have no doubt found them fully in agreement. For on the suspicion that laws were being transgressed, convictions for which no one was likely to be sent to prison some thirty nine policemen backed up by dogs descended on the cafe, thereby setting in train the crowd violence that later ensued.

Of the national dailies reviewed, only *The Guardian* found the hue and cry for law and order resistable. Calling attention to the disproportionate impact of Government policies on the inner city, it called for a 'programme to improve housing, job opportunity and . . . edcucation' for the black population (5 April 1980).

In marked contrast to the national press, the local papers adopted a more conciliatory note. The *Evening Post*, constructing its editorial around the Home Secretary's comment 'NEVER AGAIN', while recognising a 'protest' element in the crowd's behaviour, recommended 'no witchhunt', and stressed the necessity of all working together to 'remove the causes of unrest' (3.4.80). While in its news columns the *Western Daily Press* like the *Evening Post*, continued to give high prominence to continued law breaking in St Paul's, its editorial also struck a positive and constructive note:

The future of St Paul's is now Bristol's No. 1 problem. To say it is insoluble is to be defeatist; to say that it is a difficult problem with many complexities, is to be realistic.
(5 April 1980)

In conclusion, we point out that with the possible exception of the degree of hysteria, the press reporting of the crowd violence in Bristol did not depart fundamentally from the way in which the press habitually reports race. The nature of that reporting has to be seen as instrumental not only in the reproduction of racial stereo-types amongst large sections of the white population, but in the alienation of sections of the black population. That we have devoted a whole chapter to the press in a book primariiy concerned with the state is an indication of the importance we attach to the role of media institutions in defining the content and boundaries of the public discourse in relation to Bristol. The role of the 'official spokesman' in the construction of that public discourse is one link between the media and the state. But as we turn to a consideration of the perspectives and responses of state institutions it is important to keep firmly in mind the kind of political climate within which those institutions were operating, and the kinds of public pressure to which they were subjected. The newspapers – on 'behalf' of the public – demanded government action, but with few exceptions it was the kind of action that had led to the crowd violence in the first place – more police and more policing.

Part III Responses

4 Crowd Violence and the Political Process

Outside of rampant black/inner-city criminality, for the press the crowd violence in Bristol signified little. Criminality accounted for the initial police presence in St Paul's; it accounted for the intrinsically poor state of police/community relations; and it was the dominant inferential framework within which the behaviour of the crowd could be simplified, understood and communicated. In this and the following chapter, we turn to the various responses of different institutions and agencies within the state. Here, even without the promptings of the media, there could be little doubt that 'law and order' would constitute one of the core perspectives underpinning official understandings. Law and order is after all the first function of the state. And, as we sought to demonstrate in our introductory chapter, law and order concerns have increasingly intertwined with, and been punctuated by race. In the next chapter we shall deal specifically with those issues arising from the manner in which the law and the courts were used in response to Bristol. In this chapter we seek to evaluate the wider role of law and order as one of a number of official concerns raised by the street violence in Bristol. How were those concerns shaped and ordered within the state? And what were the roles of different state institutions in that process?

As would be expected the violence in Bristol compelled the attentions of a large number of institutions and agencies within the state. It called for questions, ministerial statements and debates in Parliament. The Home Office, Department of Employment, Manpower Services Commission and Department of the Environment were all involved. So also were the police, the twin levels of Local Government and local and national representatives of the Commission for Racial Equality. It is however, with the Home Office that we begin. In that public order, race relations and the inner city were the three most pressing issues thrown up by the violence in Bristol, responsibility fell most directly to the Home Secretary. Further, as we intend to show, though different political groupings and government departments were to bring to the discourse within the state their own priorities and concerns (in some instances differing sharply with the Home Office) it was Home Office understandings that prevailed. In other words it was the Home Office that was primarily responsible for organising and co-ordinating the wider institutional response and it was within its understandings that lesser and more peripheral bodies were obliged to operate.

National Dimensions: the Politics of Social Control

On the face of it, the first statement by the Home Secretary to the House of Commons on 3 April, signified little. Prompted by the massive media coverage of the confrontation, and by the need to be seen to act, the statement duly acknowledged the occurrence of a 'serious disorder' in the St Paul's area of Bristol, related a brief police account of events, and announced that the Chief Constable of Avon and Somerset had been asked to conduct an 'urgent' inquiry. In tone, the statement was intended to lower the temperature and to reassure. Accordingly, the Home Secretary was at pains to represent the withdrawal of the police from St Paul's at the height of the disturbance as tactical, rational, and most of all temporary; order had been re-imposed as 'soon as reinforcements were available', and the police were subsequently firmly in control of the area. The Home Secretary went on to emphasise that he would not be in a position to outline the Government's wider policy approach until he had received the Chief Constable's report. It was as yet, he intimated, too 'early to jump to too many conclusions'. But even at this stage in his responses to a series of questions from the floor, a number of understandings basic to formative Home Office thinking on, and approach to, the violence are clearly discernible.

Foremost was the Home Secretary's perception of the nature and significance of events in Bristol. Reinforcing the absence of any reference to race in his formal statement, the assertion that the violence 'was not *in any sense* a race riot' was later added. If, as the debate within the media demonstrated, journalists and commentators experienced some difficulty in equating this definition with explanations that identified blacks and black cultural characteristics against the background of the ghetto, these were not difficulties experienced by the Home Secretary. Consistent with and elaborating this stance, the Home Secretary resisted or ignored any question from the floor that attempted to causally link the crowd violence with race relations, the inner city and urban programmes, or the problems of West Indian youth. To one question which focused on black and white youth unemployment, and continued poignantly:

Will the Government take what has happened at Bristol as a warning that unless they reverse the cuts in the inner city programme they are taking a risk that in all our cities, including London, we shall have a British action replay of the American inner city tragedy?

The Home Secretary replied,

I note the Hon. Gentleman's remarks. What he is putting forward goes far wider than my particular responsibilities. I am aware of the importance of employment in all these areas.
(Hansard, 3 April 1980)

Variously stressing Bristol's 'good record in community relations', in which the local police were actively involved, and that substantial resources had already been injected into the St Paul's district, the Home Secretary effectively indicated that there were few areas in which an official explanation of the disturbances could be pursued and responded to outside of public order. Though at this stage the possibility of a 'public inquiry' into the wider causes of the violence was not ruled out, arguably such an inquiry was unlikely, for how could it fail to raise in some fashion the very social, economic and racial dimensions the Home Secretary seemed so anxious to resist.

In subsequent weeks these basic understandings were also communicated by other Home Office ministers. On 3 April, Timothy Raison – the Minister of State with special responsibility for race relations – was despatched to Bristol to make 'an assessment on the spot' and to get 'reactions in the area'. He 'strongly denied that Government policies, i.e. public spending cuts, had anything to do with the outbreak of street violence' (*Bristol Evening Post*, 5.4.80). The Minister also left executive officers of the Bristol Commission for Racial Equality (BCRE) with a clear impression of Home Office priorities and concerns. They reported that

Mr Timothy Raison . . . did not appear to support the idea of a public inquiry. He had listened with polite attention but his main concern was for the breakdown of law and order, rather than trying to deal with the reasons for the real tensions which exist up to the present time.
(BCRE Minutes, 16 April 1980)

At Cabinet level, the Minister for the Department of Employment appeared to be the only dissenting voice. His reaction to the disturbance was to announce a 'special inquiry' into black joblessness on the basis that his department had always recognised 'that unemployment amongst black youth is higher than amongst whites' (*Sun*, 3.4.80). Whatever the Minister's public stance, the 'inquiry' amounted to little more than a gesture. Having spent a day largely in consultation with local officials, Lord Gowrie, the Minister of State at the Department of Employment conducting the inquiry, 'was not convinced that there was a serious problem of unemployment in Bristol' (BCRE, Annual Report, 1980, p. 26).

The Government's policy responses were announced by the Home Secretary in a statement to the Commons on 28 April 1980. Supposedly these responses were based on the Chief Constable's report. We have already considered the substance of this report in Chapter 2, but it is important to recall here that the Chief Constable restricted himself largely to the events of April 2, and in particular to the withdrawal of the police from St Paul's. He did not address at length the immediate implications of the crowd violence for methods of policing, or for police/black community relations, nor did he attempt to deal with either the causes or wider significance of the violence. These concerns the Chief Constable – perhaps wisely – left to his political bosses, and at first glance certainly the Home Secretary's statement appeared to respond to these areas, For the record, three separate policy directions were envisaged. First a thorough and urgent examination of 'the arrangements for handling spontaneous public disorder' was to be conducted jointly by the Home Office, Her Majesty's Chief Inspector of Constabulary, the Commissioner of Police of the Metropolis, and the Association of Chief Police Officers. Secondly, a wider search 'for solutions to the underlying problem' was to be facilitated by the Select Committee on Home Affairs, which as part of a study on racial disadvantage intended to visit the St Paul's area of Bristol. Thirdly, an examination by Avon County Council (ACC) and Bristol City Council (BCC) of how best they could together 'further help in strengthening good community relations' in St Paul's was to be carried out (Hansard, 28 April 1980, Vol. 971–2). In concluding his statement the Home Secretary announced:

I am convinced that this threefold approach is the best way to respond positively and constructively to these events.

Perhaps the first thing that may be said of this 'threefold' approach is that on closer examination two of the folds disappear. Like an inverted version of the old three card trick, whichever card was plucked, it came up 'law and order'. In other words, while seeking to communicate the impression of a cohesive and concerted policy approach, the only initiative for which the Government was *directly* responsible was the review of arrangements for handling spontaneous public disorder. As the Select Committee on Home Affairs found it repeatedly necessary to stress, its decision to visit Bristol was autonomous, had been arrived at before 2 April, and was not 'intended as an inquiry into either *the immediate or underlying causes*' of the disturbance (Home Affairs Committee, 1981, p. xliii). In fact, the visit's brief, 'the extent to which local authorities recognised their crucial role in fighting racial disadvantage' could not accommodate a wider search for 'solutions' to the 'underlying problem', whatever the Home Secretary meant that to imply. Similarly, the decision of the two levels of local government to come together over the Bristol disturbance was made on the initiative of the Labour leader of the City Council (Minutes of Tripartite Meeting:

BCC/ACC/BCRE, 1 May 1980). And as will be seen, local interpretations of what was meant by 'strengthening good community relations' were to differ markedly from the Home Secretary's.

The Home Secretary's policy statement of 28 April effectively confirmed these Government understandings of events in Bristol which had been discernible since 3 April. The 'threefold approach' responded primarily to the public order implications of the violence while seeking to minimise – through localisation – the political, social and economic dimensions. The only sense in which the violence was officially perceived as having a larger and national significance, was in terms of the re-organisation of the police to cope with future spontaneous public disorders. Clearly then, official thinking allowed for the possibility that similar incidents could occur again, and elsewhere. Yet, while these larger implications were conceded in the area of law and order they were to be denied in all other spheres. More specifically, as perceived by the state, the violence indicated a new and specific crisis of policing spontaneous public disturbance. It did not indicate a crisis of policing, or of police/black relations. It did not indicate a crisis of current government policies, or a larger crisis of race reflecting directly on that complex of laws, policies and social agencies elected by the state to mediate racial conflicts and contradictions.

In the first place there was to be no form of official public inquiry, either independent, parliamentary, or judicial. Notwithstanding that a 'public disorder' on this scale was without precedent in post-war Britain, in the estimation of the Conservative Member of Parliament in whose constituency the disturbance had started, a public inquiry would have amounted to little more than a 'great circus which would have wasted time and would probably not have clarified anything very much' (Hansard, 28 April 1980, 974). In part, Home Office justifications echoed these sentiments. According to Timothy Raison, inasmuch as the 'facts' of the riot were 'already known', such an inquiry would be a 'forum for recrimination and rancour' (*Bristol Evening Post*, 20.6.80). These public pronouncements aside, there would be little doubt that the denial of a public inquiry was consistent with the Government's overall rationale. Having itself offered no explanation of events, and anxious that explanations linking the occurrence of violence to wider social and economic causes be avoided, it could hardly allow such explanations to be officially pursued. Not only would such an inquiry, if it were to remain credible, be forced in some form to examine the wider causes and implications of the disturbance, but any explanations, reforms, and recommendations arrived at would have more than just localised significance. In the face of street violence on a nationwide scale a year later, these aspects could no longer be denied. In the context of Bristol, however, the suggestion that the violence in St Paul's indicated a larger crisis of race and the inner city was severely frowned on by the Government. Addressing an audience in the West Midlands, Timothy Raison argued:

I do not think that we should talk ourselves into trouble. Prophecies of doom risk turning into self-fulfilling prophecies . . .

And to further convince his audience that all was indeed well, the Minister continued,

Moreover, only to dramatise trouble does not do justice to the whole picture. The day after my second visit to Bristol . . . I visited the Lord's test match. The crowd was full of West Indians. The atmosphere was good-tempered. The banter between the police and some of the crowd was lighthearted, and the only sense of the 'fire next time' that I could discern lay in the odd bumper from the fast bowlers.
(*The Guardian*, 28.6.80)

Nor did the Home Secretary's apparent offer of a visit by the Select Committee on Home Affairs, in lieu as it were of a public inquiry, amount to an official recognition of either the urgency or the scale of the issues thrown up by Bristol. Over and above the fact that it is to the House of Commons that the Committee reports and not to the Government, the Committee could not alter its brief to allow evidence relating directly to events on the 2 April to be accepted. Additionally, the Home Secretary's suggestion that the Committee's visit was in some way a ministerial response to the conflict severely damaged any chance that it might have had of fulfilling its brief insofar as Bristol was concerned. Spending only a day in the city, and only an afternoon receiving oral evidence, the Committee's visit was blighted by controversy and misunderstanding. The decision by local black associations, the Bristol Council for Racial Equality and other organisations with expert knowledge on the St Paul's area to boycott hearings brought the accusation of 'traitors' from the Committee's Chairman (*Western Daily Press*, 23.5.80). Nothing, however, could dispel the widespread local conviction that the Committee's visit was being used as a political ploy. Summed up by one local councillor:

The people in this city, the local community and the City Council, will not believe that the Home Secretary or the House of Commons have taken this matter seriously until we are given serious answers to serious questions.
(*Guardian*, 23.5.80)

With those dimensions concerned with the underlying causes of the street violence checked, obfuscated, or deemed to be only of local significance, it was the preparations for the 'suppression' of any like disorder that proceeded apace in subsequent months. There could be no mistaking the alarm that the violence had produced within police circles generally, and within the Avon and Somerset force in particular.

Articulating and pinpointing police anxieties, one anonymous contributor to the magazine 'Police' warned:

The issues have ominous significance for all major cities with inner areas like St. Paul's and large concentrations of alienated young blacks.
(*Police*, Vol. XII, No 8, April 1980)

Another article outlined what was perceived to be the basic issue at stake:

If anyone ever doubted that the police are required to stand between society and anarchy, St. Paul's has given the answer.
(ibid.)

In both cases, uppermost in the minds of the writers was the fact that the police had been forced to withdraw from St Paul's. And it was to the police withdrawal that the Home Secretary had most directly responded in outlining the terms within which the review of police methods was to be conducted. 'There can be no excuse for the lawlessness that then followed . . .' the withdrawal, he declared, and continued '. . . we must ensure that however quickly or fiercely public disorder may occur, the police are able swiftly to restore the peace and enforce the law' (Hansard, 28 April 1980).

Lest there be any doubt that this meant exactly what it said, the memorandum of the inquiry commissioned by the Home Secretary, in its conclusions, observed:

This review has been concerned with the handling of spontaneous disorder, and with the response to such disorder *rather than how it might be prevented*.
(Home Office Memo, 6 August 1980, our emphasis)

Put simply, the primary question posed by the review with regards policing in response to Bristol was, how hard could the police crack down on any future instances of street violence without *further* damaging the community's view of the police. The memorandum indeed makes strange reading. Given that the violence in St Paul's had been directed mainly at the police, thus signifying a spectacular collapse of that community's consent to the way it was policed, the review's point of departure was not what had caused this collapse to occur, but how the resulting public order situations could be more effectively and efficiently policed without further alienating consent. Within such a formulation, consent, at least the consent of communities like St Paul's, could not be an issue. Accordingly, the review did not go on to examine police/public relations, the effect of different methods of policing on those relations, or the policing of multi-racial areas. When in its conclusions the issues of community relations and consent were addressed, it was only to reiterate standard practices, i.e. 'the day to day work of careful and close community liaison by specialist officers' without having examined why and how such had failed in Bristol.

Recognising to some extent its own internal contradictions, the review refers on occasions to consent 'in the long term' and to the 'long term alienation of the public'. In the meantime, however, the question of what was to be done about policing spontaneous public disorders yet remained. The choice for the review was the same as it was for a prior consultative conference entitled 'OUR VIOLENT SOCIETY' attended by the Police Superintendents' Association, the Police Federation, and the Association of County Councils and Metropolitan Authorities. That choice was between the creation of a 'paramilitary' third force, supplying the police with aggressive riot equipment such as 'tear gas and water cannon', or a reorganisation of existing arrangements for the rapid assembly of large numbers of police officers. The dominant consensus in favour of the last option is probably better understood in terms of institutional inertia, the experience of paramilitary forces on the Continent, and the fact that most police forces had not yet directly experienced violent confrontations like that in St Paul's, than in terms of the explanations offered by the review. The intrinsic weakness of those explanations – the 'principle of minimum force', and that aspect of consent concerned with the further alienation of already alienated communities – were to be dramatically exposed a year later in what became known as the 'July Riots'. Then in the space of a few weeks riot equipment and tactics once considered unacceptable, i.e. crash helmets, new riot shields, new protective uniforms, and the use of police Land-rovers to break up crowds became the norm. CS gas was used and officially sanctioned, as were water cannons, plastic bullets, and armoured police vehicles as 'a last resort'.

Emphasising the choice to avoid rather than confront the wider social, economic and political issues implied by the crowd violence in Bristol, the review by focusing on the repression rather than the 'prevention' of public disorder laid the foundations for the continued changes in police ideologies, equipment and tactics a year later. The review recommended the setting up of 'logistics teams' to plan and ensure rapid mobilisation; a new look at 'mutual aid' arrangements between adjoining forces; a review of police protective equipment; and the training of all police officers in public order duties. These were applicable to police forces throughout the country.

Local Dimensions: the Politics of Stagnation

At the level of the local state, events of the 2 April were followed by a bevy of official activity. Acknowledging its basic responsibility, over succeeding weeks the Labour controlled Bristol City Council gave priority to widening the official base from which policy responses could

be generated. To this end, leading representatives of the Council met
with representatives of the BCRE, the Commission for Racial Equality,
and the Conservative controlled Avon County Council. From these
meetings two approaches emerged. Locally, the City Council in conjunction with the County Council and the BCRE undertook to meet in a
tripartite effort to examine how the problems of St Paul's could best be
tackled with a view to improving community relations (Minutes,
Tripartite Meeting, 1 May 1980). Secondly, formal requests were
issued by both the City Council and the BCRE for a public inquiry into
the underlying causes of the violence to be initiated by the Home
Secretary. Doubtful as to whether the City could cope alone with the
implications and consequences of a major social upheaval, initial
official local responses took place largely within the context of an
adjunct to expected Government action. Following the Home Secretary's statement of 28 April, however, the two local authorities found
themselves with the primary responsibility for dealing with both the
causes and aftermath of the violence.

In shifting primary responsibility to local government, the Home
Secretary rationalised that it was they who had been 'elected to take
responsibility within their areas' (Hansard, 28 April 1980, p. 975).
More to the point, the ploy completed the Government's broad policy
approach to the crowd violence. As has already been argued, according
to Home Office understandings, the events in Bristol signified a crisis
of law and order of sufficient importance to justify a revision of police
procedures for dealing with spontaneous public disorder. But it did not
at the same time, however, indicate a crisis of the nature of policing,
either in general, or in relation to black and/or inner city areas. By
leaving the crucial issues of causation and possible future prevention to
the initiative and perspectives of local government, the Home Office
denied the wider crisis of race and the inner city.

Restricted in scope principally to the specificities of local conditions
and local policies, the 'findings' of any local official inquiry could
represent no serious threat to the broad direction of Government
policies. This was so particularly with regards employment, youth
unemployment provision, housing, education, spending cut-backs in
the inner city programmes, and the continued persistence with immigration concerns through the mechanism of nationality legislation.
Even so, it may not be assumed that the Home Secretary was prepared
to accept without qualification either the formulations or recommendations of local government. Indeed, it is worth looking at the exact terms
within which the Home Secretary intended what he described as 'action
at the local level'. In the light of what had just occurred, the Home
Secretary continued to identify the objective of the proposed joint local
authority inquiry as an 'examination' of how best they could 'further

help in strengthening good community relations in the area' (ibid., p. 972). In this, it was promised that 'experts' from all those Government departments concerned would play a full part, but in fact, with the exception of the local department of the Manpower Services Commission, a 'full part' amounted to very little indeed. The findings of the local inquiry would in no sense be binding on Government, and consistent with the strategy of localising the non-law-and-order implications of the violence, no undertaking was given that the findings would be published or otherwise communicated to other local authorities. Nor did the Home Secretary give any indication of how the basic objective was to be achieved. To the already limited areas of local government responsibility and autonomy of action, the Home Secretary's repeated reference to public resources already expended on St Paul's added the important constraint that throwing money at the problem was decidedly not a recommended option.

It must be stressed that the local authorities did not intend to undertake a formal inquiry into either the immediate or underlying causes of conflict between the community in St Paul's and the police. Rather, primarily through the involvement of the BCRE, an attempt was made to identify the problems of St Paul's, and to examine how existing statutory provision might be extended or improved. But notwithstanding the sense of official urgency in the immediate aftermath of the violence, even this limited project was to prove far from straightforward. Given the difference in party political control between City and County Councils, inevitably representatives of each arrived with their own perspectives and concerns. Like central Government, both were anxious that the whole issue should not reflect badly on their past and current policies. Additionally, the BCRE brought to the inquiry its own, often quite different, understandings. Not least amongst these was the very question of local official attitudes and policies with regard to race and the inner city. Indicative of the causal importance the BCRE ascribed to local official attitudes in relation to the events of 2 April, the Senior Community Relations Officer wrote:

Blame must be laid fairly and squarely at the feet of the policy makers and those who hold the purse strings. . . . The Senior CRO was called alarmist on many occasions before 2nd April, when she tried to warn many people, including representatives of the Police, Education, Housing and Social Services Department . . .
(BCRE, *Annual Report*, 1980, p. 9)

In many ways the inquiry came to represent, in condensed form, the politics of race at the level of local government. The acceptance of the BCRE as being able to 'communicate the black community's views', reflected on the one hand the lack of black representation within local party machines and on local elected bodies, and on the other the unwillingness of the local authorities to adopt more direct methods of canvassing black opinion and grievance. To the local authorities the BCRE provided an easy and convenient method of 'consulting' the black community. As a demonstration of the grossly unequal power relations between the two parties, it was the perspectives and concerns of the local authorities that determined the scope, direction, and eventual outcome of the inquiry.

Significantly, the BCRE was not able to force the inclusion of issues of policing on the inquiry's agenda. Having attributed the immediate cause of the violence to 'heavy handed and ill-timed police activity', the BCRE put forward for 'urgent action' fresh initiatives on police training, and an examination of ways to improve the relationship between black youth and the police (ibid., p. 24). In the absence of a public inquiry, clearly the tripartite meetings on which the Avon and Somerset Constabulary were represented, remained one of the few platforms on which the police issues could be officially pursued. Nor was it a case of the urgency of the issues receding with time: there existed very real dangers that the post-'riot' policing of St Paul's would lead to renewed violent confrontation. With few arrests having been made on the 2 April, over the next two weeks some one thousand five hundred people in the area were interviewed by the police mostly in connection with looting (*Guardian*, 12.4.80). One local activist described this period as 'ten days of terror', and according to the BCRE the level of police interrogation was interpreted 'as a vendetta against the black community in an attempt to regain police authority, lost when they withdrew from the area' (BCRE, Annual Report, p. 25). In an effort to restrain police activities, the BCRE was obliged to act unilaterally. As early as 4 April, representations were made to senior police officers eliciting the promise that the 'interviewing of looting suspects would be over in seventy-two hours' (ibid., p. 25). However, as late as 16 April, resolutions were still being passed demanding an end to further police inquiries and arrests (BCRE, Mins, 16 April). Where the police made concessions, it was decidedly on their own terms. On 11 April, while the Chief Constable accepted the need to allow representatives of the BCRE to visit police cells proving that no one was then being held, he said that further inquiries would cease only if black social workers were prepared to contact those persons still wanted and 'accompany' them to the police station. A 'wanted list' of some twenty-five names was promised by the police but only six names were eventually delivered. This was perhaps fortunate, given the potential divisive implications of black social workers 'policing' the community.

On the grounds that matters relating to policing could more properly be dealt with by the visiting Select Committee, the leader of Bristol City Council, chairing the first tripartite meeting on 1 May, dismissed the subject. Nor did the City Council on its own account raise any of the issues. On receiving the Chief Constable's report, the Council's Police Committee extended its 'strong and unanimous' support for the 'courageous and responsible way' in which a 'very difficult and totally unforeseen situation' had been handled. On the question of blame and responsibility, the Chairman of the Committee commented:

If there is any blame to be laid, no doubt the police will analyse it carefully. There are a number of inhabitants who are determined to live a way of life which is not what most of the residents of this country wish to live, and there is an element, not all black, who are not prepared to accept our way of life. (*Guardian*, 24.4.80)

The issue of policing was to disappear even from discussions between the police and the BCRE. Thus six months later when the police suddenly announced a plan to establish 'cop shops' in St Paul's, it was a decision taken without consultation with the community or the BCRE.

The local authorities also determined the wider context within which the problems of St Paul's were to be situated and explained. While that context – the inner city – appeared in large measure to overlap with BCRE understandings, it soon became clear that both sides meant entirely different things by the term. To representatives of the BCRE, the inner city constituted past and continuing structural disadvantage and deprivation. Not only had immigration, racial attitudes and practices resulted in the black population being over-represented and later confined to the inner city, but the same factors differentially affected their social and economic location within it. Whilst the local authorities could accept that racial 'discrimination' sometimes did affect blacks in employment, racism as such had no part to play in wider explanations. This difference of perspective was to form a major point of contention from the very onset of the inquiry. At the first tripartite meeting, a senior councillor on behalf of the City Council expressed concern at the number of times the word 'racism' had been used. He felt 'that it was being misused far too frequently and that if discussion polarised on racism alone, nothing would be achieved' (Mins, p. 5). Reiterating sentiments expressed by the Chairman of the Police Committee, to representatives of both Councils, race was a two-edged affair. If 'racial discrimination' affected blacks in some spheres, then according to one County Councillor the practice 'could be overcome (only) if the black community would fully integrate, but many seemed to be reluctant to do so' (Mins, p. 4). Similarly in the view of a City Councillor 'many black youths whilst endeavouring to adopt an African culture, were not really sure what their real aims in life were'. He professed that he could not 'understand the conflict between the black and white cultures, especially as many black youths were second and third generation and had been educated in the English system'.

Insofar as racial discrimination was relevant, then, it was as much a consequence of separatist cultural and other tendencies within the black community, as of white attitudes. As such, the concept implied no fundamental contradiction with the authorities' largely 'colour blind' approach to a wide range of policies affecting the black community. But in part the local authorities' posture on race also reflected official fears that accusations of racial practices might also be levelled at them. Not only was their poor response to Urban Aid Schemes originating in the St Paul's area a source of bitter local complaint, but neither authority had responded meaningfully to a BCRE call a year earlier for discussions on local government implementation of the relevant sections of the 1976 Race Relations Act, particularly with regards equal opportunity. Such considerations continued to prove a major constraint to constructive discussions with the BCRE. Well into the inquiry, the BCRE commented:

So far it cannot be said that meetings with the local authorities have been particularly productive. There appears to be a basic lack of acceptance of the discrimination and disadvantage experienced by black people in our City, as distinct from other disadvantaged sectors of the community. While this basic misconception persists, the elimination of racial discrimination and the establishment of a truly multi-racial society will be impeded and such expressions of frustration and alienation as occurred on 2nd April are bound to continue. (Annual Report, p. 29)

In practice the real work of the inquiry was conducted by three smaller working groups addressing the areas of employment, education and community facilities. Though the promised Government 'experts' attended the larger tripartite meetings, none participated in the work of the smaller committees, with the exception of the MSC who assisted the Employment Working Group. In explanation, the Home Office representative declared that his department 'did not profess to know any answers to the problem or be able to provide solutions . . . Government financial assistance has already been made but this had not solved the difficulties' (Mins, 1 May 1980). The representative of the Department of the Environment found that his department was not 'specifically involved', but asked to be kept informed. However, as will be seen, when the reports were compiled and submitted to the Home Office, many of the recommendations did concern the Department of the Environment, and it was this department that was given the final responsibility for delivering the Government's detailed response.

For the Community Facilities Working Group and its concerns with inner city housing, environmental and recreational provisions, the St Paul's Local Redevelopment Plan provided the basic point of reference. However, consistent with the City's anxiety that the disturbance was in no way a consequence of inner city neglect, the plan was approached more as evidence in mitigation, than as the basis from which a critical examination could proceed.

Certainly with regards those underlying conditions that the Plan was intended to alleviate, there was little to distinguish the experience of blacks settled in Bristol from those in other cities. Though relatively small in terms of overall numbers, estimated at some 17,000, the 'non-white' population comprised 4% of the population of Bristol (HAC, 1981, p. 41). This compared with 6.4% Greater London, 6.3% Birmingham, or 4.9% Bradford – cities more commonly considered areas of intense 'immigrant' settlement (Booth and Drew, 1980). Like these larger metropolitan conurbations, the black population of Bristol became highly concentrated in a few wards geographically located in the city's problem ridden inner area. Between them, the wards of St Paul's, District, Easton, Eastville, and Windmill Hill (Totterdown) contain approximately 60% of Bristol's black population. Though the proportion of blacks in the population of these wards varies greatly, the 30% in St Paul's is similar to that found in the London boroughs of Brent or Hackney. It is in the St Paul's and Totterdown wards that the majority of the city's substandard accommodation is to be found. Additionally, both the Local Plan and the Community Facilities Working Group identified a deficiency of suitable premises given over to communal use, poor quality and limited open spaces, dereliction, poor street lighting, road and footpaths in very poor and sometimes dangerous conditions, and an excess of extraneous through traffic (Report, Joint Working Groups, 25 March, 1981).

On the question of the past and continuing black concentration, the local authority maintained that its housing policies, which were based on 'the simple principle that all individuals are treated fairly and equitably, irrespective of race, colour or creed', were in no way responsible. The local authority, however, had kept no ethnic records on any aspect of housing (HAC, p. 100). While in relation to underlying conditions the local authorities claimed a 'vigorous inner city programme', involving the expenditure of £13 million, which resulted in 'massive' improvements particularly in housing in the St Paul's area, to the residents in the area the programme has brought what may only be described as mixed blessings.

In its attack on inner city housing, Bristol was a late starter. As early as 1950, the City's own first redevelopment plan recognised St Paul's as an area in urgent need of urban renewal, yet a start was not made until 1975. In its implementation and effect, the St Paul's Local Plan could best be described as modest and piecemeal. Rather than taking the option of declaring Greater St Paul's a 'General Improvement Area', a twin strategy of part renewal and part replacement was adopted, concentrating activity in small 'housing action areas' scattered in and around St. Paul's. The strategy of renewal, in particular, attracted criticism. Not only was the cost per unit comparatively high, but complaints have persisted as regards both the quality and durability of the work completed (HAC, pp. 149–50). Further accentuating the uneven and piecemeal impact of the plan, little attention thus far has been given to aspects like the environment, community amenities and facilities, the area's economic base, shopping, and traffic problems. Of the last aspect in particular planning interventions in the past have compounded general environmental problems. A major intrusion into the area, the construction of the M32 motorway, at once destroyed a third of the area's available residential housing stock, in addition to dividing St Paul's from Easton.

The basic posture struck by the Community Facilities Working Group was that if Bristol's inner city problems persisted, this was not for the want of effort and expenditure incurred by local government, but due in large measure to the failure of the city to qualify for additional Government aid under the Urban Programme, either as a 'partnership' or 'programme' authority. As the City Council itself continually stressed, redevelopment in St Paul's had been financed largely on a self-help basis with only limited grant assistance from central Government. With these local sources of finance exhausted, and Government assistance for the year 80/81 substantially reduced, all 'starts' on new schemes had had to be frozen, and loans and grants to individuals and to housing associations reduced. In fact, the whole inner city programme was 'in danger of floundering' (HAC, p. 117). Within local official circles, then, the violence was perceived as powerfully reinforcing the local authorities' case for special access to Government funds. And it was with this clearly in mind that the Community Facilities Working Group compiled its final report. The report envisaged and recommended some thirteen different schemes involving the creation of new community facilities, recreational amenities, and general environmental improvements. Most had originated from the St Paul's Local Plan, and those involving large expenditures, particularly the St Barnabas Community Centre facility – could not be undertaken by the local authorities in the absence of considerable Government assistance in the form of Urban and other grant aid (Report, JWG, 25 March 1981).

Quite clearly an area involving Government rather than local authority responsibility, the report and recommendations of the Employment Working Group also depended crucially on the need for special Government assistance. With regards the scale and nature of ethnic minority unemployment in Bristol, little of substance was discernible from official figures. Though the overall number of black unemployed could be estimated (subject to non-registration at unemployment offices especially amongst West Indian youths), in the absence of accurate figures about the size of the black working population, the differential and comparative impact of unemployment on the black community remained largely unknown. The statistical device of expressing black unemployment as a percentage of all unemployed represents one attempt to overcome this problem, but it is particularly ineffective where, as in Bristol, the size of the black working population is small. Accordingly, for November 1980, the MSC found that for the Bristol area ethnic minority groups represented 2.9% of all unemployed. Compared with the average of 4.0% for the country as a whole, 7.8% for the South-East, and 8.9% for the West Midlands, the MSC concluded that 'there is no evidence to show that coloured workers fare any worse than others in times of a changing labour market' (Report, JWG). However, when the area for which these figures are expressed corresponds more closely to the area of black settlement, then more meaningful information is obtained. For the Bristol inner city areas generally, ethnic minorities were found to represent 6.6% of all unemployed; and for the last year that small area statistics are available, unemployment was found to be 20.3% and 26.4% in the two zones that corresponded most closely to St Paul's (Gazetteer Zones, 1976).

The only firm and up-to-date information that could be obtained related to the ethnic minority unemployment statistics for Britain. Here it was found that 76% of all ethnic minority unemployed were West Indians. Furthermore one-third had been out of work for over a year, with the burden of unemployment being borne slightly more by youth than by the adult population. The Joint Working Group held that racial discrimination i.e. 'the attitude of some employers and employees to young blacks' (Mins, 29 September 1980) was of only limited significance in explaining this youth unemployment. So it was to factors involving educational qualifications, job preferences, religious and cultural constraints, and social background, that they turned. Continuing their inner city deprivation and disadvantage perspective, solutions were envisaged on three levels. First was the creation of new long term industrial employment opportunities in and around the St Paul's area by promoting and undertaking the development of suitable land. This had to some extent already been started within the terms of the St Paul's Local Plan, but because of the costs involved was not to be submitted as part of the package to central Government. Secondly, the local authorities, in collaboration with the MSC, were to actively promote small businesses within the St Paul's area, and to seek to ensure that a greater proportion of local labour was employed. Thirdly, the existing provision for the support, training and retraining of the local unemployed, particularly black youth, was to be expanded. At all levels the Government's direct involvement and financial assistance was of central importance. Arguing that the 'area's special needs on a comprehensive basis' had to be recognised by Government, the report called for Government assistance with regards the early release of suitable industrial sites, the purchase and development of those sites, special consideration in respect of the Government's new Community Enterprise Programme, and additional resources for specialist careers officers to service the inner city area.

It was in the area of education that the basic posture of the local authorities came most into question. Rather than questioning the extent of Government funding under Section 11 of the Local Government Act, 1966, the Education Working Group focused directly on local authority attitudes to, and policies on, multi-cultural education. Indicative of these education policies and the official rationale that informed them, the Bristol City Council had 'deliberately' closed the only secondary school in St Paul's in the 1960s, on the grounds that the school would reflect the ghetto characteristics increasingly evident in the area with the 'large influx' of West Indians (HAC, p. 3). According to the leader of the City Council, the children had been 'spread around' amongst other comprehensive schools. Dispersal, however, did not include the secondary school (Fairfield Grammar) which is closest in proximity to St Paul's and from whose catchment area St Paul's is excluded. Further, both the logic of the policy and its continuation by the Avon County Council appear all the more curious given the current ethnic composition of primary schools in the St Paul's – Easton area. One study of Easton Ward found that:

> In no primary school in the area is the proportion of New Commonwealth/first generation British lower than 50%, except in the Whitehall schools. The average white component is 30% and the split between Asian and West Indian is levelling off at a similar ratio.
> (Clarke, p. 8)

An interesting additional feature the author thought worthy of note was the '. . . virtual absence of coloured teachers in the schools'.

Discovering in the late 1970's that the City's schools were a long way from meeting the specific needs of West Indian and Asian children, the County Council unified its efforts through the establishment of a Multi-Cultural Education Centre. Voicing local criticisms of the Centre's impact, however, a member of the visiting House of Commons Home Affairs Committee reported that 'most black people have never heard about it and know little about (its) policy and objectives' (HAC, p. 8). Certainly those objectives did not become clear as a result of official evidence submitted to the Committee. Over and above concerns with teaching English, the Centre's other principal aim could only be articulated in terms of the vague notion of promoting amongst teachers a recognition of the 'multicultural society in which we all now live' (ibid., p. 7). The leader of Avon County Council did not see the need to pursue an active policy of recruiting black teachers. And on the crucial question of black under-achievement, its assessment was perceived as neither a function of the Multi-Cultural Education Centre, nor an area it could competently research.

Undoubtedly, the County's broad approach to multi-cultural education has to be seen in the context of the philosophies emanating from top officials. In evidence to the Home Affairs Committee, the leader of Avon County Council argued, that if young coloured people were unemployed, this was because they happened 'to be less academically inclined' (p. 5). Similarly, the Director of Education, when asked to identify the specific difficulties presented by black children, responded:

What we have in the inner city areas are the problems of children, regardless of the colour of their skin, living in socially deprived areas. If additionally there are intellectual limitations that is another problem. If children have those disabilities and their skins are black they are trebly disadvantaged. (p. 9)

Aside from the recurring themes of the children's intelligence and background, rather than the standard of provision in inner city schools, not only are the problems of black and white equated, but race is inverted so as to signify a disability seemingly embodied in skin colour and not in a specific set of official attitudes and practices. Against this background, the meetings of the Educational Working Group constituted less an inquiry and more a protracted confrontation between official perspectives and those of the BCRE. Reflecting these tensions, the Group's report took the form of an official reply to three BCRE proposals: that the Authority issue and adopt an acceptable policy statement on education in a multi-ethnic society; that steps be taken to research black under-achievement; and that the possibility of 'mother tongue' teaching be considered (JWG Report, 25 March, 1981). Of the last, the authority declared itself sympathetic so long as mother tongue teaching did not take place within 'normal school hours'. But on the first of the two proposals some ground was conceded. With regards to underachievement the County agreed to pursue the possibility of co-operating with the Rampton Committee's investigation, while on multi-ethnic education the County was at least prepared to adopt in statement form the dimensions of racial equality, anti-discrimination, and equal opportunity.

The local authorities' inquiry was to take over ten months to complete, and it was another four months before the Home Office was in a position to receive a deputation to hear its first response. By then, the whole situation had changed. What the Government had been pleased a year before to treat as an unfortunate episode of crowd violence for which responsibility could be delegated to local government, had developed into a full blown storm raging throughout the country. The local authorities could not but see 'July Riots' 1981 as adding weight to their case.

The deputation, consisting of leading Councillors and executives of both authorities and two members of the BCRE, met the Home Secretary on 22 July 1981. From a minute of the meeting submitted to the Resources and Co-ordination Committees of both councils:

An extended discussion took place on the reports and specific issues involved and the Home Secretary acknowledged the efforts which had been made. Sympathetic and positive response by the Government was recognised and indicated.

Accordingly, the Home Secretary promised that the funding of those proposals for the creation of long term industrial employment in the city would be conveyed to the Cabinet; an application by ACC for a social worker to work with Asian women was agreed; the ACC's entire application for funding under Section 11 for the year 1981/82 – £1,141,000 – was approved in full; proposals in the area of Higher Education would be discussed with the DES; specific cases relating to housing provision would also be discussed; and support was indicated for the major project put forward by the Community Facilities Working Group – the St Barnabas Community Facility – in addition to discussions on other minor schemes.

Crucially the Home Secretary took the trouble to make it clear that with the exception of the social worker and ACC's Section 11 funds, 'no specific financial commitment could be made at this stage'. Taking that as the basis on which the Home Secretary's response is assessed, and given that the Home Office had already had four months to consider the report, the only positive Home Office response to the deputation was in fact the funding of a solitary social worker. The £1 million Section 11 funding thrown in by the Home Secretary in passing did not in fact form part of the response, but represented the results of negotiations already agreed with ACC in principle since December 1979 (HAC, p. 43).

The full implications of the Home Secretary's response were to become clear to the local authorities on the occasion of a subsequent visit to Bristol by a representative of the DOE. According to the minutes of that meeting, the representative:

. . . indicated that the Government's ability to respond to the City Council's request for financial assistance towards meeting the needs of the St Paul's area were limited by the availability of Urban Aid funds: there were no other funds available for allocation to St Paul's, and any projects which the City Council wished to promote with Government assistance would have to be submitted as part of the Circular 20 procedure.

In effect, the local authorities were back exactly where they started, with exactly the same criterion of access to Urban Aid funding. With the exception of a scheme under the Community Enterprise Programme for workshops in St Paul's which when completed would provide one hundred jobs, all other employment and community facilities schemes, including the St Barnabas project, would have to be submitted in order of priority under the 'old' Urban Aid programme. The majority of the lower order schemes would therefore fail. Nor could the DOE offer any better news on housing, which would again have to be re-submitted to Government in order of priority.

Summary and Conclusions

As an instance of collective violence Bristol confronted the Government with two broad choices between law and order responses on the one hand, and remedial responses cognitive of the underlying causes of the violence on the other. Given that the violence had been directed largely at the police the implicit contradiction between these two strands of policy will be immediately obvious. This, however, was not a contradiction experienced within the state in relation to its overall reponse to the violence in Bristol, for it was law and order that dominated to the almost total emasculation of social, political and economic responses. More accurately the remedial dimension was simply 'squeezed out' of the decision making process within the state. That squeezing out process began with the means by which the state chose to inform itself about events in Bristol – a means which could not accommodate the wider political significances and implications of the violence. It continued with the localisation of those implications to the city of Bristol. And ended with the less than enthusiastic response of National Government to those specific proposals that were to emerge from the local political process. It must be stressed here that at no stage in these local negotiations were either the community in St Paul's or participants in the violent confrontation involved. Thus the perspectives that were 'squeezed out' were not, as it were, the 'demands of the rioters' but the very perspectives evolved within the state – dealing variously with race and community relations, police/black relations, employment, education and the inner city, and based on extensive research. At the very least, supposedly the crowd violence in Bristol signalled the need for these perspectives in their respective policy areas to be re-evaluated and the result ascribed new political priority. This, however, was not an outcome in respect of Bristol. Further, the virtual abandonment of the political sphere has to be seen as going hand in hand with what was at the same time going on in the courts. Both, we intend to argue, were to have important implications in relation to the renewed crowd violence in 1981.

5   Charged with Riot

In spite of the many expressions of concern about a wide range of issues affecting black youth in the inner city, issues which included poor housing, poor education, serious and growing unemployment and police/black relations, the central focus quickly became 'law and order'. The crisis that Bristol marked was almost immediately identified as one of policing street hooliganism rather than a crisis about the position and experience of black people, especially youth, in the society. The primary concern quickly became how to prevent such a thing ever happening again and solutions were sought in improving police efficiency rather than looking deeper into the problems. The Chief Constable's report demonstrated that it was the severity of the inexplicable street violence that had caused the police to withdraw, so the Government had to act decisively, first looking into police procedures and improving the police ability to suppress spontaneous public disorder. Secondly, it was necessary to bring those responsible for causing the crisis to account, and to be seen to be doing so. The 'criminals' involved must be punished and because the crime was so grave, the need was for severe punishment. As so many times before the response to violence on the streets was simple, to stamp it out and come down harshly on those involved. The political content of the disturbances has, historically, been abstracted and Bristol was no exception. By defining out of the situation the causes of the violence, the way is left clear for dealing with the situation in terms of criminality. In this chapter we look at the way the full force of the legal system was brought to bear on the St Paul's community, both in order to bring about immediate punishment and to serve as an example to the other black communities in Britain.

One hundred and thirty people were arrested in Bristol in the days following the 'riot' and over a hundred were later charged with offences such as looting, threatening behaviour, and possession of offensive weapons. The majority of cases were heard in the Magistrates Courts and most people were found guilty, and received heavy fines for looting. Sentencing was severe because of the grave view of the trouble on the streets taken by the Magistrates. As the NCCL found after the Southall trials, the Magistrates appeared to conceive of themselves 'as engaged in teaching a lesson to some group' (NCCL, 1980, p. 10). But the matter did not end there, and three months after the disturbance sixteen people had their charges changed. They were charged with 'riotous assembly' and were ordered to appear together in September 1980 to stand before the Magistrates who would decide whether they had a case to answer. If they did, they would have to stand trial in the Crown Court.

Riotous Assembly

The charge of riot is extremely serious, it is second only to the charge of treason in the canon of English common law and it carries a maximum sentence of life imprisonment. Sixteen people who were initially charged with offences such as possessing an offensive weapon and threatening behaviour which carry, at most, a few months in prison, suddenly found themselves facing the prospect of a massive trial and the possibility of years in prison. The nature of the charge and the fact that they were to stand trial together invested their behaviour, in the eyes of the public and the prosecution, with a gravity and criminality that the actions of others in the crowd who had been charged individually and with less serious offences, lacked. The very use of the charge emphasised that what had occurred in St Paul's had been a serious criminal outbreak.

The charge of riot is one which, even within the context of a law and order response to Bristol, was exceptional. This charge has rarely been brought in this century and, as will be described later, when it has it has been used in clearly defined circumstances. The situation in Bristol did not conform to previous usage at all, yet clearly the charge was brought with the expectation of a conviction. The Director of Public Prosecutions who authorised this charge presses charges only when he is over fifty per cent sure that a conviction will follow. He chose this charge precisely because of its severity, necessary in the face of such a perceived threat of violent social upheaval:

in Bristol (referring to the St Paul's disturbances) we originally decided to prosecute 12 defendants for riot, because we thought that the evidence was good enough to get a conviction for riot and we thought that it was in the public interest to prosecute as hard as we could those who in our view had been responsible for what happened in Bristol.
(Interview with DPP, *Times*, 11 May 1981)

Yet, as with so many similar cases before (see Chapter 2) the charge failed and no-one was found guilty. This failure, however, did not lead to any questions being asked about the quality of the police evidence upon which the charges were based, or about the suitability of the charge, or about the real nature of the disturbance. Rather it led, as had happened before, to several public criticisms of the jury system and a move to change the law. Another obvious result was to avoid using the same charge again in the same circumstances and in 1981, when the scale of violence and damage in Moss Side, Toxteth, and Brixton was far greater, there was no similar riot trial.

It was in the law courts, rather than anywhere else that the details of what happened in Bristol were examined. Because of the nature of a legal trial only the accused were on trial; the actions of other people involved were effectively irrelevant. There was never a public inquiry into the role of the police on that afternoon and questions relating to their role were dismissed in the court; as the Judge said, they were not on trial. This practice of examining the issues only within the limited confines of the law courts has been well established in Britain and was not really broken even a year later when Scarman was asked to inquire into the Brixton riot. The behaviour of the police, the issues lying behind the outbreak of violence and the nature of the police case are not, and indeed cannot be, part of the legal debate in front of the Judge. The position of black people in the society and on the streets do not form part of the legal considerations. Indeed the reverse is the case: the law is used to repress any violent protests. Thus trials such as Mangrove, Chapeltown, and Bristol are seen by many black people to be part of the process of legitimising the way the police behave, and further marginalising and 'criminalising' the black community. Such trials stand, along with the use of the 'sus' law (now repealed), the stop and search laws (now in the process of being widened), the 1971 Immigration Act and the 1983 Nationality Act, as part of the legal process of isolating and undermining the black community, and of ignoring their complaints about their situation and the conditions they face in this society.

The crisis of Bristol was relegated to the law courts, the disturbance was labelled illegitimate and criminal. But even within the narrow parameters of the concern to stamp out such violence and punish those involved, this case raised very serious issues. This chapter will concern itself only with these. How valid was the bringing of such a charge? How were the defendants selected? Who were they? How adequate and in order was the police evidence? Was it really the law of riot and the jury procedures that needed changing when the charge failed? The examination of this trial in detail throws light on factors that have been consistently apparent in similar trials including the exceptional nature of the charges, the breach of the Judges' Rules by police, questionable evidence presented in court and a reluctance to accept the validity of the jury verdict when they reject the prosecution case. These together inform our understanding of how the legal process is used to suppress and punish violent protest.

The legal requirements of the charge of 'riotous assembly'
As already noted the charge of riot is little used in this country; David Williams wrote in *Keeping the Peace* (1967),

indeed even where there has been an undoubted disorder involving numbers of people, and even where the ring-leaders can be identified, actual prosecutions for riot are undertaken only with reluctance. There were, for instance several outbreaks of disorder during the General Strike in 1926 . . . yet . . . there were no prosecutions for riot, rout or unlawful assembly. (p. 240)

The Law Commission (1982) noted that 'the offence of riot is not frequently prosecuted' (p. 91), rather it is the common practice to use charges under the Public Order Act or the Prevention of Crimes Act, or even charges of affray in cases where there is street disorder. The charge of riot was not used in Southall 1979 where the police/public confrontation was sustained and violent. It has not been used when there have been major clashes between 'mods' and 'rockers', skinheads or other organised groups. While there have been many occasions where violence has occurred on the streets in the past few years the charge of riot has rarely been brought. For example, between 1976 and 1980 there were only twenty individual offences of riot recorded by the police, in contrast to over two thousand of affray and offences against public order. Affray itself was not much used as a charge until the mid-1950's.

Williams noted that while the charges of riot and unlawful assembly were very widely defined, and that the definition of riot in law was 'broad enough to cover a wide variety of conduct', the charge of riot was in his opinion only an 'appropriate crime to be used as a deterrent when speedier, summary prosecutions have apparently ceased to have an effect' (p. 241). Clearly in Bristol the concern with an exemplary deterrent, in circumstances where the police had withdrawn from the streets, was paramount.

A riot in law is not the same as the dictionary definition of riot, 'thus the offence may not be committed even though a layman might readily say of an event: "it was a riot" ' (Law Commission, 1982, p. 26). In order to establish that there was a riot in law five essential elements must all be proved. These elements are most clearly stated in Hawkins, *Pleas of the Crown* (Vol 1, C65, ssl–5), and in the case of *Field vs. Receiver of Metropolitan Police*, 1907 (Law Reports, 2KB, p. 853). Although these five points have never been individually contested in front of the Court of Appeal or the House of Lords, they were upheld in the case of *R. vs. Caird and Others* (the Garden House Hotel Riot) in 1970 (Law Reports, 54 Cr. App. R. p. 499) in the Court of Appeal. All the lawyers and the Judge in Bristol accepted this definition as correct in law.

These five essential elements are clearly set out in the case of Field:

In order to constitute a riot five elements are necessary – (1) a number of persons not less than three: (2) a common purpose: (3) execution or inception of that common purpose: (4) an intent on the part of the number of persons to help one another, by force if necessary, against any person who may oppose them in the execution of the common purpose: (5) force or violence, not merely used in and about the common purpose, but displayed in such a manner as to alarm at least one person of reasonable firmness and courage.

It is broadly accepted in law that the common purpose in riot must be private rather than public in order to prove riot. A public purpose such as the levying of war, would be treason.

If the purpose is a private one, the offence is a riot; but if the purpose is public and general, it is a levying war. The same assembly with the same aims might, by a mere difference in the intent . . . be either a riot or a levying war. (*R v. Downing*, 1848, Law Reports, 3 Cox c.c. p. 514)

It was argued at some length at the trial that if there was the common purpose as suggested by the prosecution, the common purpose of attacking the police, that this would in fact be treason. Some lawyers argued that a concerted attack on the police would be treason because the police are representatives of the state, to attack them would involve a public purpose. The Judge listened to the argument but ruled that the attack was only on Bristol police and because it was thus geographically limited it was not an attack on the state; the crowd was attacking individual policemen who were not defined by them as representatives of the wider state. This reasoning might appear convoluted but it was, of course, necessary. If a common purpose was proved and it could be shown to be an attack on the police and the authorities in a wide sense then the appropriate charge would be treason. Such a charge of treason would clearly be an absurdity and could never be brought.

The DPP could have brought the charge of affray rather than riot, a charge which does not demand the proof of a common purpose and is much less complex to prove. Indeed towards the end of the Crown Court trial, the leading prosecution barrister asked if the charge could be changed to affray. The fact that the DPP did not use the most obvious charge, but a more serious one, further underlines our proposition that the state wanted to get a maximum charge and so heavy punishments to serve as an example and a deterrent.

The defence lawyers at the trial vehemently contested the use of this charge of riot. The primary legal argument hinged around the issue of a private common purpose. This area of dispute marked the Bristol case as unique, because in previous trials for riot the purpose was clearly known and usually stated: 'in the great majority of cases, however, no question will exist or arise as to the purpose of those charged with rioting' (Wise, 1907, p. 35). In the case of *Field*, for example, it was the declared intention of the crowd to knock down a wall; in *Ford v. Metropolitan Police District Receiver* (1921, 2 K.B. 334) it was to destroy a house in order to build a victory bonfire to celebrate the end of the war; in the *Garden House* riot the stated intention was to disrupt a Greek Junta dinner party. In direct contrast to these, in Bristol there was no stated or overt common purpose and the defence argued that there was no hidden, deducible purpose either. That there must be such a purpose was not in dispute, as without a common purpose there could be no riot in law and people could only be held responsible for their own individual actions in court and not for the overall behaviour of the crowd.

At the committal proceedings, the prosecution argued that there was a common purpose, namely to drive the police out of St Paul's *in order* to loot and to do damage. They argued that although they would not put a time on the start of that common purpose (they said that was a task for the jury in the Crown Court), once it was in existence it continued to give the crowd coherence until 11 pm when the police re-entered St Paul's. In the Crown Court, they altered the argument. Firstly, they put a time on the start of the riot; they said that the common purpose had emerged by the time the drug squad officers were attacked. Or if not by then, certainly a few minutes later there was a common purpose when there was stone-throwing in Denbigh Street. The Judge concurred with this assessment and said that by the time the events were underway in Denbigh Street there was 'open riot' according to the law. Secondly, the common purpose offered by the prosecution in the Crown Court was somewhat different; they said it was *a show of force against the police*. There was no further mention of the primary aim given at the committal, to loot and do damage. The Judge accepted this wide common purpose but ruled that because this was the common purpose then the riot must have ceased once the police left St Paul's at 7.30 pm. His argument was, unlike the one put forward by the prosecution, that if the common purpose was the show of force against the police, it could only have existence while the police were present. Once they left St Paul's it was not possible for the crowd to make a show of force against them, so according to the Judge, the riot ended at the time that the police withdrew. That was exactly the time when most of the damage, arson and looting began, and it was the films on this period that people watched on their TV's. This was not, however, a riot in law. The prosecution argued, and the Judge accepted, that once the common purpose was in existence it continued throughout the afternoon. Once there was a riot in law it continued without a break until 7.30 pm and anyone who joined in, for example by shouting or stone-throwing or offering encouragement, was guilty of riotous assembly. Importantly, the period of calm was glossed over and was not accepted as representing a break in the flow of events.

One leading defence barrister, Mr Edward Rees, challenged this construction of common purpose on several grounds, and other defence lawyers supported his argument. First, they argued that there was no common purpose in law. The crowd had at no time discussed a purpose:

it had no coherent, united intent within the terms of the law of riot. They challenged the prosecution to say when the crowd could have formed a unifying purpose on that afternoon, where separate groups were involved in distinct, separate encounters with the police. They argued that the violence had occurred in response to different stimuli; stones were thrown at the drug squad, and later at the police who were using dogs in Denbigh Street. Some people threw stones when the police marched military style to the cafe, and when they marched again to the burnt-out car, and the most severe violence broke out in response to the march of the police and their dogs beside the towing vehicle, and the later march of police into the crowd behind riot shields. Different people in different crowds had responded to different police actions.

Secondly, they argued, that if there was a common purpose, and that was a show of force against the police, then this was a public purpose; an attack on the police represents an attack on the state whom they represent. This would thus constitute treason and if the prosecution insisted that this was the common purpose then they should charge the youths in the dock with treason.

Thirdly, they argued that even if the prosecution could establish beyond any doubt that there was a common purpose in existence during the attack on the drug squad and the cafe, this must have ceased to have any existence during the 'uneasy peace' when no stones at all were thrown. The Chief Constable had himself said that this period had marked a complete break with the trouble and that he had thought that the violence was over. According to the case of Jones, 1974 (an affray case), the Lords ruled that once a show of force or fighting is terminated, the offence ceases (*R. vs. John McKinsie Jones and Others*, House of Lords, February 1974). While the majority of the police spoke about this period of calm in their evidence, the Judge over-ruled their evidence and said that in his opinion this had not been a real break, merely a period of re-arming. Fourthly, the defence produced evidence to show that the force was not only directed against the police: several civilians gave evidence showing that they too had been subjected to hostility from people in the crowd.

Further the defence said that the evidence produced to show that people committed violent acts could not also be used as evidence to show their intent to do these things, so the fact that they threw stones did not show a common purpose of a show of force. There have to be five elements in riot and it is legally incorrect to combine (1) the execution of a common purpose with (2) the common purpose. The fact that people threw stones did not justify the inferring of a common purpose as required in law. The Judge ruled that the common purpose could come into existence just seconds before the outbreak of violence and that as long as it existed prior to stone-throwing, even by fractions of a minute, this was sufficient in law.

This is a very tenuous argument and there is, of course, no way of proving the emergence of a common purpose in a case like this except by inference. This is not normal procedure in cases of riot, and indeed the police evidence in this case in fact showed individuals often acting alone, reacting to a series of quite separate police actions. The police evidence was suitable for bringing charges of threatening behaviour or even assault or affray, but it could not sustain the interpretation put on it by the prosecution of a continuous, united show of action. By bringing this charge the defence argued that the prosecution completely ignored what was really happening on the streets and why. They challenged the prosecution to explain why the police frequently raided black cafes, why they used dogs, why so many police were briefed, and why they had used military tactics against civilians on the narrow streets of St Paul's. They argued that the defendants in the dock had reacted to each of these separate provocative activities, and that they had had no single overall shared intention.

The Judge said early on in the trial, that in his opinion there was a common purpose and sufficient evidence on which the jury could find there was a riot, but the defence continued to argue the point throughout the trial. In his summing up, the Judge repeated to the jury that he accepted that there was a common purpose, and they had to decide whether each of the defendants had or had not shared that common purpose. The inception of that purpose (a show of force against the police) and the execution of it by throwing missiles were and could be almost simultaneous. He ruled that the crowd acted together, that they acted only against the police and that their unifying purpose had lasted all afternoon; it had 'ebbed and flowed' through the streets of St Paul's, informing every individual action.

Throughout the trial the Judge rejected all the arguments put forward by the defence relating to police behaviour on the streets of St Paul's, saying that the police actions were irrelevant to the legal case. Even if they had been aggressive it would be no defence, and he warned the defence several times that it was not the police who were on trial but the twelve people in the dock. Two defence lawyers (Narayan and Khadri) argued throughout that it was the police, not the people, who had acted together and that it was they who had had a common purpose, not the crowd. Being in a court of law this argument, though coherently developed, was not admissible because the legal forum is one which 'permits the police to carry out their work with the firm knowledge that they will only rarely have to account for their behaviour and then in an environment – the courtroom – in which the dice are heavily loaded in their favour' (McConville and Baldwin, 1981, p. 193).

The DPP accepted the brief of the prosecuting barristers that the five points of riot were present in St Paul's and charged sixteen people with 'riotous assembly'. But if the whole crowd acted together, why were only sixteen charged? How were they selected, who were they and how were they singled out from all the others who had been arrested?

Arrest, search and interrogation

Only two of the defendants who appeared in the Crown Court charged with riot had actually been arrested and charged with any crime at all on 2 April 1980. The events of the afternoon had been marked by confusion and by 7.30 pm the police had withdrawn. After they had left, the most serious arson and looting took place. How did the police know whom to arrest when they were not present for four hours and when previously there had been lots of people and a lot of activity on the streets?

The Chief Constable in his report to the Home Secretary said that after the uniformed police withdrew, 'plain clothes officers entered the St Paul's area and some were successful in obtaining information and reporting it' (Chief Constable's Report, 1980, p. 6). How much information they obtained during the evening was never revealed in any of the court cases. What did emerge clearly was that on the days following the disturbance the police subjected the people of St Paul's to some very intensive policing. They needed information and they carried out many house to house searches; items they discovered in these houses were used to bring charges of looting. As a result of these searches people were charged with looting jars of coffee, packets of cigarettes, even toilet rolls as well as larger items such as cloth, radios and bicycles. In addition to house to house searches, many young people were picked up by the police, taken to the police station and questioned about their activities and the actions of their friends on 2 April. The police denied at the time, and later in court, that they had grilled young people for information, but it is significant that in the Crown Court more than one police officer had cause to ask permission to change the words in the transcript of an interview held with a defendant while he was detained in the police station; they asked to alter the wording of one question from 'how many did you *know*?' to 'how many did you *throw*?' They insisted in the court that they had been asking how many stones the defendant threw, not how many people he knew on the streets that afternoon. But during the trial it became clear that somehow people must have been closely examined for information while in police custody. Indeed, one officer confirmed this by telling the Court that they had had to pick up people, take them to the police station and question them intensively because the police had little information about that afternoon. This kind of police searching and questioning was used after the Chapeltown troubles and was certainly seen again in

Brixton in 1981. Yet in court most officers deny such police practices.

The Commission for Racial Equality in Bristol complained to the police about the way in which they were policing St Paul's after the disturbance. Some of the defence lawyers also talked to senior police officers in the week following the trouble asking them to change their tactics and stop arresting and detaining so many youths. In a letter to the Director of Public Prosecutions in July they referred to the way the police had behaved in St Paul's from 3 to 10 April. They accused the police of having made numerous arrests, creating more ill-will and increasing the level of fear and mistrust beyond that which was already clearly in existence between the police and the black community. By the time the police stopped this house-to-house searching and the arresting of people for questioning, they had collected a great deal of information. They had opened action files on individual suspects in which police intelligence was recorded, and which could be referred to by any police officer who was involved in the examination of witnesses and suspects. These files were also used in the writing up of officers' notes concerning the events seen by them on 2 April.

In addition to their own enquiries the police were able to make use of TV coverage of the disturbance: 'Policemen saw video films of television news coverage taken during the St Paul's riots while they were questioning suspects' (*Evening Post*, 28 September 1980). These, in conjunction with press photographs (both published and unpublished – the latter were made available to the police by the press) were used to pick out and identify individuals who were on the streets. Some individuals, so identified, were later arrested and charged by the police.

Of those arrested in the weeks following the troubles, many were interviewed at the police station at length several times. From the evidence presented in the committal and Crown Court proceedings in relation to the sixteen youths charged with riotous assembly, it is possible to point to several things that happened to those youths who were detained at the police station. Some juveniles (people under the age of sixteen) were undoubtedly interviewed without their parent or guardian being present. This is a clear breach of the Judges' Rules, which though they are not legally binding are guidelines that the police should follow during their interrogation of suspects. They are designed specifically to protect the rights of the individual in police custody when 'the suspect is most vulnerable and where . . . that disparity in resources between the state and the accused is greatest' (McConville and Baldwin, 1981, p. 5). Under these rules the individual held by the police has the right not to reply to questions (the right of silence), the right to see a solicitor, and the right to have a parent or guardian present if he or she is under sixteen. All interviews should be logged, as should the provision of meals and other activities, including phone calls requesting a solicitor. A person is not to be held at the police station for any length of time without being formally charged with a particular crime though this is legally a rather grey area, (an area which the new Police Powers Bill addresses – to the detriment of the detainee). In Bristol many young people were interviewed with no parent present, at least one person was kept in police custody for over twenty four hours without being charged and without his actions or the police interviews being properly recorded. More than one of the sixteen defendants said that they had asked for a solicitor and had had their request refused. Solicitor's calls in relation to one case were certainly not recorded.

This disregard of the Judges' Rules in the treatment of suspects fits in with what other people have previously described: 'in England, there is a considerable body of legal and social scientific research which demonstrates that the safeguards provided for suspects in the Judge's rules are very often flouted' (McConville and Baldwin, 1981, p. 56). Indeed it conforms well with what many police officers themselves say:

The Rules afford, I think, the classic example of the enormous gulf between those who enforce the law and those who administer it . . . it is hardly surprising that the Rules, the conduct of police interrogations and the so-called right of silence should today be the subject of such controversy.
(Sir Robert Mark, 1978, p. 54)

According to Mark, the way to resolve this controversy would be for the police to obey the Judges' Rules, and so show their ineffectiveness in fighting crime; 'the effect would quickly be disastrous. Only the weak, the spontaneous and the intellectually underprivileged would continue to be amenable to the law' (ibid., p. 55). The Fisher Report (on the Confait case) makes it plain 'that the provisions of the Rules regarding access to a solicitor are a complete dead letter. Not only are they disobeyed, many police officers do not even know of their existence' (Blake, 1980, p. 29). Sir David McNee has even asked the Royal Commission on Criminal Procedure to abolish the suspect's right to silence and he has called for an increase in the length of time a suspect can be held by the police for questioning. He asked for a general power to detain people for seventy two hours without charging them; the proposed bill will in fact grant the police ninety six hours.

In many police stations, the Judges' Rules are applied in a limited way, if at all, and 'it is plain that the Judges lean over backwards to give the police great latitude in the conduct of their investigations – often to the extent of ignoring the breaches of their own rules or conniving in the "pious perjury" that Commissioner McNee talks about' (Blake, 1980, p. 25). Yet it is in the police station that the individual is most vulnerable. The person does not know if he is a suspect or a witness, he is isolated from other people and 'the very relation of interrogator and suspect is a relationship which implies the exercise of power by one over the other'

(Blake, 1980, pp. 26–27). Under unfamiliar and hostile circumstances many people are overwhelmed and frightened and it is at this stage that many people 'confess' to the police, even if they have not committed a crime. Research has shown, and certainly the cases to be presented from the Bristol trial uphold this, that confessions in police custody can most readily be obtained from the young and the ill-educated. Confessions, once obtained, play a crucial and often central part in the prosecution case. Our evidence certainly supports the contention that once a confession has been given, under whatever circumstances, it 'may be a devastating piece of evidence against him (the accused)' (McConville and Baldwin, 1981, p. 126).

Charging
Of those arrested in Bristol, questioned and detained at the police station, over a hundred were charged with criminal offences. All those who were charged were charged with crimes such as theft, receiving stolen property, threatening behaviour or possession of an offensive weapon. A few were charged with assault and criminal damage. Many people were not charged in April but bailed to return to the police station in May or June when they were charged with some of the offences mentioned above. During May and June many defendants appeared in the Magistrates Courts and were found guilty and fined for theft of such goods as a briefcase, an eiderdown, TV's, radio cassettes, and net curtains. Others were convicted of threatening behaviour, possession of an offensive weapon, or stone-throwing. Of the ninety cases that went through the Magistrates Court almost all resulted in a guilty verdict.

Sixteen people were eventually selected out of those originally charged for the much more serious charge, that of riotous assembly. Their actions, by and large, were difficult to distinguish from many of those of people whose cases were heard in the summary courts. For example, one man who threw a brick (and there was photographic evidence to support that fact) was charged with threatening behaviour, a charge that carries a maximum of three months in prison. He was found guilty in the Magistrates Court, but acquitted on appeal. Yet suddenly a small group found that their charges were drastically escalated and they were separated out from everyone else to be charged with a crime that encompassed much more than their individual actions; indeed, some of them had not done as much as throw a brick. At the committal the prosecution dismissed as irrelevant the charge that these were sixteen arbitrarily selected people. The point was only that they had been present. The rather random nature of the selection was indicated both by the selection of only sixteen and by the fact that they all had the charges against them changed many times, and charges were even dropped during the committal. Some defence solicitors wrote to the Director of Public Prosecutions complaining about this arbitrary selection of sixteen people, an act which they said would inevitably be seen in St Paul's, by the black community at large and by many other people as a public punishment of people randomly selected to represent the St Paul's community. Rather than allowing the situation to settle down in order to allow the examination of the grievances of the community, the nature of police/black relations and racial disadvantage, a handful of people, many juveniles, were put on trial.

The defendants involved were not told until mid-June that their papers had been sent to the Director of Public Prosecutions for consideration for the bringing of serious criminal charges. The Magistrates, who delivered this information to the defendants between 16 and 18 June in the Magistrates Court, themselves 'expressed their extreme concern' that the cases of the defendants involved would be prejudiced in respect of their possible defence if they were actually charged at this late stage with serious crimes. They even asked the defending lawyers to make their feelings known to the Director of Public Prosecutions. The defendants were not in fact charged, i.e. told of their precise crime, until 11 July 1980, over three months after the events in St Paul's.

The Director of Public Prosecutions, constitutionally a curious character, is hired and fired by the Home Secretary but is in fact not answerable to him. He is responsible to Parliament through the office of the Attorney General. His decisions about when to bring charges and when not to bring them are based on a variety of *legal* and *political* considerations, one of which is that the prosecution must be in the public interest; in his own words 'does the interest of the community require us to go on?' (*Times*, 4 May 1981). Many factors go into making these decisions, many of which are politically controversial such as those to prosecute Jeremy Thorpe, and not to prosecute Sir Peter Hayman or any of the SPG involved in the death of Blair Peach, 1979. In the Bristol case, the Director of Public Prosecutions decided both that the police evidence was good enough for a prosecution and that it would be in the public interest to bring the charge of riot, in spite of the concern expressed to him by the defence lawyers and the Magistrates. The Director of Public Prosecutions decided that the demand for severe treatment for the people involved in the disturbance outweighed any local community relations considerations. This interest clearly related more to the political considerations of teaching 'rioters' a lesson than to any legal necessity or concern with the people of St Paul's.

The DPP took eleven weeks to decide to bring this charge. During this three month period the police had had time to prepare their accounts of what had happened, who they saw and what they were doing. In contrast, the defendants were unable even to start preparing their cases, their identification evidence and their alibis. They did not start collecting the defence evidence until months later when even recalling exactly where they were, who they were with and at what time things happened was extremely difficult. The defence argued that this, in fact, seriously undermined the position of the defendants and that such a delay could not be acceptable by the criteria of either fairness or justice. At the committal there was reference to the fact that such long delays contravened the European Convention on Human Rights. It was patently unjust to wait so long before bringing such serious charges carrying life imprisonment. Yet the charges brought by the DPP, were allowed by the Magistrates to stand against twelve of the sixteen young people initially charged.

The decision to go ahead clearly indicated a preparedness to spend a great deal of time, and therefore money on a trial; in the event it cost over half a million pounds. There was a vast amount of police evidence, much of it repetitive. Even when the prosecution was advised by the Judge to slim down the volume of evidence at a pre-trial hearing in December (the Summons for Directions that occurred between the committal and the Crown Court hearing), this advice was ignored and indeed fresh evidence was added. Some defence lawyers made it clear to the DPP right from the start that if he pursued this charge the hearings would be long and the cost prohibitive. However, the DPP decided to proceed with the case stating that in his opinion the committal would only take about three days; in fact it took six weeks and the Crown Court trial took a further seven weeks.

'I Swear That the Evidence I Shall Give'

The police evidence was the foundation upon which the charge was brought. Initially the evidence presented by the Chief Constable described the events in St Paul's in such a way as to largely exclude police behaviour from the situation and to blame the crowds for what happened. Later the evidence presented by individual police officers – evidence which had in some cases been altered or amended – played a key role in the DPP's decision to prosecute, and the police evidence played a crucial role in court: 'the police remain firmly the central figures in the prosecution process' (McConville and Baldwin, 1981, p 95). In Bristol tens of policemen were called to the witness box to give evidence, first to establish that there was a riot in St Paul's and secondly to prove the involvement in that riot of those in the dock. A great deal of the police evidence in fact related only to establishing what happened on 2 April, how frightening it was and that it was a riot. Well over half the police officers called made no identifications of specific people at all. Consequently, relatively few police officers were called to give particular eye witness evidence against the individuals accused, and in four of the cases, not a single police officer had seen the accused at all that afternoon. In several other cases only one or at most two police officers had seen the defendant on 2 April. Only in a few cases had more than two police officers seen the accused, even though several of the youths in the dock were familiar to the police in Bristol prior to the disturbance.

Police evidence in court is essentially of two kinds: eye witness reports of an event, and reports of conversations and confessions made by a suspect while being questioned by the police. In relation to the first it is customary police procedure to record any unusual, suspicious or obviously criminal event in a notebook that is carried at all times while on duty. The kind of information that is normally recorded covers the time of the incident, the details of what happened and descriptions of the people involved if they were clearly seen. At a later time, if a decision is taken to proceed with a particular case, the police officer writes out his notes into a coherent and comprehensive statement. This is signed and dated and handed to a senior officer. The accuracy and verity of the notes and subsequent statements are crucial as they form the core of the prosecution case in court. Once the case comes to court the police officer will be questioned and cross-examined about the evidence given in his written statement. The police usually bring their notebooks into court to help them to remember the exact details of the case because they are not allowed to look at their statements during cross examination. Sometimes the defence will ask to look at the notebook during the course of the trial in order to verify the recorded details of timing, place and identification.

It is admissible in England for police officers to write up their notebooks together. This raises problems, because obviously the statements of two police officers giving identical condemnatory evidence carry more weight than one lone statement, or two statements containing discrepancies. Concern has been expressed before about the fact that collaboration is officially accepted practice (see Humphry, 1972, Chapter 2) because this can too easily lead to unfair collusion.

There were several disturbing aspects to the police evidence in this case. While the bulk of the evidence consisted of statements recounting eyewitness accounts of the events of 2 April 1980 almost every policeman who came to court to give evidence came *without* his notebook. The committal proceedings and the trial were marked by this notable absence of notebooks. Police officer after police officer said, on oath, that they did not need to bring their notebook into court because they could remember in vivid detail exactly what they had seen on that dramatic afternoon. But the trial in the Crown Court did not start until ten months after the disturbance and under cross-examination it became clear that officer after officer was really confused or very unclear about crucial issues, issues such as the timing of events, where people were actually standing and what they were wearing. Even more general details such as which police officers acted together were forgotten or contradictory and it became difficult to establish the course of events. The details of this confusion will become clear as the individual cases are documented. This lack of notebooks caused the defence great concern, and because few officers produced notebooks the defence was unable to ask to see them and check them. They could not verify whether or not what an officer was saying in the dock actually accurately reflected their original eye-witness accounts and, as there was a lot of contradiction in evidence and some officers altered their accounts about timings etc., this was a serious handicap to the defence. This absence of notebooks gave the police a leeway which may not have existed if the defence could have checked on their original notes. While it is not legally compulsory to use a notebook in court, it is such usual procedure that their absence was glaring in the Bristol case. Some defence lawyers challenged police to admit that they had been ordered not to bring their notebooks into court because their notes would contradict the evidence they were giving in the witness box in court. The police consistently denied this accusation but the fact remained that for the majority of police witnesses there was no written evidence available in court with which the defence could check the police oral statements against notes made at the time of the disturbance.

A second almost universal theme was that contrary to normal practice, the majority of the police said that their statements had been written before their notebooks. Very few notebooks were apparently written up on 2 April, many were not written for two or three days and others were not written until weeks later. The police produced a variety of explanations for this unusual procedure. There had been no time for some to write notes up on 2 April because they had been posted to other duties; for others their notebooks had been lost in the disorder; for yet others their notebooks were full. In a few cases an injury had prevented the officer from being able to write for some days. While the police agreed that this was an unusual way to proceed they repeatedly stressed that it was because the circumstances too were very unusual and they denied the interpretations suggested by the defence. These interpretations included one that statements had been written, often together, following briefings by Senior Officers and after seeing films of the events, rather than from memory. This breach with normal procedure suggested to some of the defence a degree of control over written reports of the events by senior Police Officers.

Statements were certainly written, by and large, after the police had been briefed by senior officers and after many of them had seen television news video tapes of the afternoon. Many statements were written by police officers in collaboration and, throughout the period of statement writing the police were discussing the events together, naming names, writing up action files on individuals, looking at published and unpublished newspaper photographs and watching videos. Although none of these are unlawful, this police procedure must have affected some of the statements.

Some of the police statements about the events were further marked by specific irregularities. Several statements carried a date which was said to be correct at the time it was signed but later, in court, was said to be incorrect. Several other errors were also referred to in court; a few statements were not signed, and one had a nine line addition after the signature – the latter evidence was dismissed by the Judge. Several police asked for particular words to be corrected in their statements; as where the word 'know' had apparently been repeatedly mistakenly typed as 'throw'. The details of these peculiarities in the evidence are carefully described in relation to the specific cases.

Arguably, police evidence should be precise in order to secure a conviction, this being especially so for identification evidence. The Devlin Committee inquired into this issue after a series of alleged wrongful convictions on identification evidence in the 1970s. Instead of bringing in legislation to deal with the problems of identification evidence, a ruling was made in the Court of Appeal. In 1976 in the case of *Turnbull*, the Judges ruled that a trial Judge must be cautious about accepting identification evidence. If the Judge believes the evidence is good enough to stand, he must give a special direction to the jury, and he must tell them that they can only accept such evidence under certain circumstances. These circumstances must take into account factors such as the length of time a person was seen, under what conditions they were seen, how good or bad the light was at the time and whether or not clothing was clearly identified; they must also consider whether there was any corroborating evidence. This directive was crucial in the Bristol case where the identification of anyone was almost impossible, a fact to which many police officers testified under oath. Judges themselves are obliged to drop cases if they think that the identification evidence is too weak.

A second kind of police evidence used in court arises from conversations and confessions made while a suspect is being questioned by the police. When the police are interviewing someone, usually in custody at a police station, that interview is not tape-recorded (such procedure is apparently permanently at an experimental stage). Instead, the police officer or officers concerned write up the interview themselves, usually after, rather than during the interrogation. This kind of evidence has two aspects. The first is the police account of what questions were asked and what answers were given based on notes of the interview. These accounts are often the focus of intense conflict in court, and as the repeated attempts to introduce tape recordings have so far failed in England this evidence about the content of an interview rests solely on the integrity of the police officers recording the encounter and also on the sharpness and clarity of their memories. Police evidence about what suspects say while they are in custody is often powerful evidence against the accused and is difficult to refute. Even more powerful is the second aspect of evidence which may be obtained at this stage: a written confession which may be written either by the police officer or by the person accused. It should be written in the person's own words and voluntarily given, it should not have been obtained by a question and answer session. In an English court 'verbals' or written confessions can be used to convict a person even if there is no other evidence against that person; this is not possible under Scottish law where there has to be corroborating evidence. In practice, in England, it is often difficult for the accused to refute the police evidence because their word is less forceful than the written statement of one, or often two, police officers. It is clear that, even where the Judges' Rules which protect the suspect have not been implemented by the police, the courts still give great weight to interview, verbal and confession evidence. This was certainly so in the Bristol trial, especially in the cases of some of the younger defendants where the only evidence against them was their confession given to the police while in custody.

In order to bring a case such as riotous assembly before the Crown Court the prosecution evidence has to be presented in a lower court (a Magistrates Court) and has to convince the Magistrates that each of the accused does have a case to answer. During these proceedings in the Magistrates Court four of the Bristol defendants were found not to have a case to answer. Twelve were sent on for trial in the Crown Court before a jury.

No Case to Answer

The committal proceedings are not a trial. The prosecution only has to present sufficient evidence against each individual at these hearings to show that there is a case to answer. The defence may challenge that evidence and attempt to discredit it but they do not present a full defence. The Bristol proceedings took place in front of three Magistrates, and was observed daily by a public gallery filled by people from St Paul's. One demonstration was held during the hearings outside the court demanding an amnesty for the sixteen accused. The interest, significant attendance and the many protests made in the court during the proceedings by people from the St Paul's community attested to the crucial importance of this case to them (Kettle and Hodges, 1982). There was much distress – when twelve were sent to the Crown Court – ameliorated only by the dismissal of four cases. What was the police evidence against these four that led the DPP to charge them but the Magistrates to dismiss them?

Originally *Colin Coke* was charged with possession of an offensive weapon and he appeared twice in the Magistrates Court in relation to that charge on 1 May and 16 June 1980. In July he was charged with riotous assembly on the basis of evidence that he had thrown a brick through the window of a police Landrover which contained six Task Force officers from Bath. The precise timing of this event was never clear. While the driver of the Landrover said in his first statement, written on 3 April from notes taken at 10 pm on 2 April (and he brought his notebook into court), that it happened at 6.40 pm, in his second statement made 3 days later he altered this and said that at 5.40 pm he was en route to St Paul's and it was soon after that the incident happened. At the committal he reverted and put the time at between 6.20 and 6.40 pm and said on oath that they had left Bath at 5.40 pm, contrary to the time put in his second statement. All the other officers put the incident earlier by saying that at 5.40 pm they were already en route to Bristol.

At whatever time, these Task Force officers answered a 10:9 call to go to St Paul's and drove straight from Bath to Trinity Road police station where they picked up an Inspector (who was never named and who did not give evidence) to guide them around the unfamiliar streets. The driver, in his second statement, said that on arrival in the area he saw two police cars parked irregularly in Ashley Road surrounded by a hostile crowd of screaming and stone-throwing black and white youths. There were more black youths standing at the mini-roundabout at the end of Ashley Road and as he drove past this crowd, they started to stone the Landrover. When he heard the missiles hitting the vehicle he accelerated out of the way while the other officers crouched down to avoid being hit. As he accelerated down the road he saw Colin Coke standing on the corner of Ashley Road and Norrisville Road, on the driver's side of the vehicle, and as he drove past Coke threw a piece of concrete which hit the Landrover roof. Coke ran off up Norrisville Road. They stopped the Landrover and chased Coke, who climbed onto the roofs of some nearby houses and shouted 'I don't give a damn, you're all bastards', and later, 'You're all fair game, we'll have you all, you bastard.' Coke was arrested, put in the Landrover and driven out of St Paul's hidden under a coat so that the crowd could not spot him.

Aspects of the statements given by the four other officers who submitted written evidence were similar to that given by the driver, though there were discrepancies about who was sitting where in the

Landrover, who got out to chase Coke, precisely what the object was that was thrown, and whether the vehicle was moving or stationary. The driver and one other officer came to give evidence at the committal and three discrepancies came out clearly. The driver said that, contrary to his previous written statements where he had said that he was accelerating out of St Paul's, the car was in fact not moving, it was stationary when Coke threw the brick – a red brick; he was sure of this because he remembered being in a traffic jam. The other officer said that in fact they were moving at a speed of perhaps 15–20 mph, and the traffic was not heavy. Secondly, there were problems about where Coke was; one of them placed Coke about twelve feet from the vehicle, but the other put him at a distance of seventy-five yards. Thirdly, in their written statements the object thrown was said to be concrete, but in court they said that it was a red brick.

While there were many discrepancies in the evidence against Coke, what was not in dispute was that he was acting alone. The prosecution argued that the fact that Coke was standing alone was of no consequence, he was clearly part of the riot 'in spirit' and he shared a common purpose with them against the police as was demonstrated when he had shouted something to the effect that '*We'll* get you, pigs.' The Magistrates rejected this argument and said that because Coke was acting alone he could not be said to be sharing a common purpose with anyone. They referred his case back to a lower court to be tried for possession of an offensive weapon, but the prosecution offered no evidence against him on this charge in the Magistrates Court so his case was dropped.

Trevor Edwards was arrested on 16 April, not until a fortnight after the trouble. He was in fact picked up by the police on a charge quite unrelated to the events of 2 April, but during his interview at the police station he was cross-examined about what had happened in St Paul's. He was interviewed twice, once by a single police officer and later by two officers together. Edwards claimed that he had asked for a solicitor to be present but the officers denied that he had made any such request. There was no record on the police log of a phone call which had been made by a concerned person to ask if Edwards wanted to see a solicitor, and he was not given access to one.

The police denied that they had used the occasion of Edwards' arrest to pump him about the events of 2 April and they asked that a typographical error on their statements relating to his interview be changed; the typist had mistakenly typed the words, 'how many did you know?' and they had signed it as correct without noticing the error. They insisted the question was 'how many did you throw?', even though it followed the question 'how many people were throwing stones at the police?'

Edwards refused to make a statement, though verbally he was said to have admitted to running about and shouting on 2 April. One police officer who had seen Edwards on that afternoon (an officer whose evidence about the timing of events was seriously at odds with the majority of police evidence throughout the trial) said that he had seen Edwards when the crowd started to run past the cafe after the drug squad officers had left and that Edwards was at the front of the crowd, leading the chase. But his fellow officer on the grass with him did not see Edwards in the crowd, and indeed said under cross-examination that there were no leaders to the crowd. Only one other policeman saw Edwards that afternoon, around 5.30 and 6 pm when there was no trouble in St Paul's.

During the committal proceedings Edwards appeared very disturbed and he was ordered to be removed from the court several times. He was the only defendant who had his bail withdrawn, and was kept in police custody during most of the proceedings, at the end of which his case was dropped – presumably because there was not sufficient evidence against him.

Errol Haddad was initially arrested on 8 April for threatening behaviour. The case against him rested solely on the evidence of one police woman who said that she had seen Haddad outside the Black and White cafe at the start of the trouble, and that he had been acting as a ringleader. In her first statement, made on 4 April, she said that following the altercation over the trousers between a West Indian man and a police officer she saw Haddad shouting at the police and pushing them. He was a leader, acting with two others, and together they were pushing and shouting, increasing the agitation of the crowd. She said the crowd was already noisy and pushing, though many other police said that people were quiet and in good spirits at this stage. Her second statement, made on 7 April, gave a fuller account of Haddad's behaviour, where she described him as shouting abuse at the police, using terms such as 'Rassclat' and 'Bloodclat'.

In the Magistrates Court this woman officer said that she had written up her notebook on 3 April in conjunction with a male police Inspector. On the 4th she had written her statement alone and had opened an action file on Haddad. The defence challenged this and they showed her the signed copy of her action note made on 2 April, at 11 pm. She said that she must have misdated the note because she had certainly not written it on the 2nd; later she said that she must have meant to write 11 am, 3 April 1980 on the note.

When Haddad was arrested on 8 April he was interviewed by two police officers. He told them that he had been sitting on the wall outside the cafe watching the events, but as soon as the police van had arrived and the crates of alcohol were being loaded he left and went to see his girlfriend at her house. He arrived there just after 4 pm and stayed until 2 am in the morning when he went to a blues. He was sure that he had been sitting on the wall because he was suffering from a bad corn on his foot, and he denied absolutely any involvement in the trouble, and he refused to make a statement. The evidence against him consisted only of this uncorroborated statement which he rejected and the Magistrates dismissed the charge.

Jimmy Walsh was one of the only two white youths involved in this case and, like several of the defendants, he was only sixteen when he was arrested. Although he was legally a juvenile at the time, he was not dealt with in the juvenile court because the charge of riotous assembly is not triable in a juvenile court.

Walsh was arrested on 4 April on suspicion of burglary. Apparently he fitted a description that had been given by a witness of a young lad who had been seen looting the betting shop. He was first interviewed in the police station by two police officers, without a parent or guardian present, at 7.50 pm in the evening. In their accounts of this interview, written two days later, these officers said that Walsh had denied going into the betting shop. He told them that he had been at work until 4.30 pm and then he had gone home and stayed with his Mum until 6.45 pm, when he went to look at the burning cars in Sussex Place which a friend had told him about.

He was re-interviewed after a night in the cells, at 11 am the following morning by the same officers. During that second interview he agreed that he had watched the crowd running down Ashley Road and that he had followed it, he had also followed when the crowd charged the police, but then he had left to go and meet his uncle in Campbell Street. He refused to make a statement to the police about what he had done, but he did agree to make a witness statement about what he had seen; this was written and signed. At 2.30 pm he was interviewed for a third time by the same two officers. This time there was no discussion about the alleged burglary; instead they told Walsh that they had heard that he and two other youths had seriously assaulted a police officer in Ashley Road. Walsh strenuously denied this, but the officers, according to their own statements, had insisted that someone had identified Walsh and that they had evidence that he had joined in. Walsh then asked who was 'grassing' on him; they refused to tell him and he refused to say any more.

He was interviewed again at 3.45 pm by a different police officer who saw him alone. He asked Walsh what he had been doing on 2 April and then accused him of rioting in City Road. Walsh said that he had done nothing and that he had not hit a police officer. He was cautioned and then made a statement admitting some involvement but saying that he did not throw anything and he had only shouted because he got caught up in the events. After making his statement he was returned to the police cells and later that evening was allowed to go home.

At the committal proceedings concern was expressed by the defence about the number of times Walsh had been interviewed in a short period of time and the fact that the exact number of interviews had not been properly recorded at the police station. There was no accurate logged account of who had interviewed Walsh, and when, while he had been in police custody. Initially Walsh was picked up because he fitted a description that had been given in relation to some looting. The police admitted that by Saturday morning they were satisfied that he was not the person referred to, but they did not release him. They never checked his alibi about the time that he was at home with his mother because, as one officer put it, they had already formed the opinion that Walsh was lying.

During the first two interviews on Saturday, one of the police officers agreed at the committal that they were trying to get general information about the disturbances because they had very little evidence about the events and they were trying to compile eye-witness accounts. Walsh refused to co-operate and provided very little in the way of information: he named no names and he only admitted to being on the streets in the late afternoon/evening. In the third recorded interview (it was not clear whether he had been interviewed more times than were recorded) the police suddenly accused him of seriously wounding a police officer. In court the officer agreed that Walsh had been obviously surprised at this accusation, but he vehemently rejected the defence suggestion that Walsh, who was only sixteen, and had been isolated in custody overnight and repeatedly interviewed, was really frightened. He also denied that Walsh ever requested to see a solicitor. The third officer who interviewed Walsh alone at 3.45 pm on Saturday said that he was asked to do so because he knew Walsh of old. He had been told that Walsh was accused of throwing stones and hitting a police officer.

During the court proceedings it was made clear that Walsh had been held for an extended period of time in the police station without being charged. No notes of the interviews had been made by the officers until 7 April, two to three days after the interviews. Many of the things they reported Walsh as saying in their interviews conflicted unaccountably with the signed statement that was finally obtained from Walsh. In addition this statement was written in language which Walsh did not use. The police officer concerned denied obtaining the statement by suggestion, or by question and answer, but the defence challenged this. They said that the many strange confusions of time and place contained in the written statement arose because the officer who obtained it did not know at what time or where Walsh was said to have been involved. He (wrongly) had thought that Walsh was accused of being involved in the events in City Road at 5 pm and so the statement followed that assumption. In addition this officer was very vague about the geography of the streets and this accounted for the confusion of places in the statement. The officer denied all this in court, and he also denied seeing an action file on Walsh before he went to interview him. But the defence put it to him that he himself had opened an action file on Walsh two days before, on 3 April at 8.45 pm. Before he left the witness box the officer remembered that he had opened such a file after all because he thought Walsh might have been the looter, described as a punk, in the betting shop. He also remembered noting on that sheet that Walsh 'ran' with the Mighty brothers. This was important because the only police eye-witness evidence against Walsh was contained in a statement made a day later, on 4 April, where an officer described seeing Walsh with the Mighty brothers at the Black and White cafe. This officer had made no notes prior to 4 April because, he said, he had lost his notebook in the chaos and he had not been issued with a new one until the 4th. He agreed that he had written up his statement and his notes on 4 April after talking to other officers and certainly after the action file on Walsh was available for him to consult. His evidence was unique, because while many police officers reported seeing the two Mighty brothers throughout the afternoon none of them, either in their statements or under cross examination, had seen a white punk in their company.

On all these points the defence challenged the admissibility of the evidence against Walsh. He had been repeatedly interviewed without an adult present, he had been intimidated and frightened when the police told him that they had concrete evidence (which they never produced) that he had wounded a police officer. The only evidence against Walsh, apart from an admission that he was present, was one police statement written after the action file was opened and unconfirmed by any other officers. While Walsh had been picked up for burglary he had not been charged with such an offence, and the statement he eventually signed was not in his own words because the officer had obtained it by question and answer. It was a confused statement because this officer was under the mistaken impression that Walsh had been involved at 5 pm rather than later, and because he did not know the relationship of the streets in St Paul's. This officer threw further doubt on the accuracy of the statement by asking in court for the word in the sentence 'how many did you *know*?' to be changed to 'throw'. The case against Walsh was dismissed.

In Front of the Judge

Of the twelve cases that were tried in the Crown Court one was dismissed by the Judge after the prosecution had presented its evidence, ruling that the accused had no case to answer. The case was that of *Raymond Jones* who was arrested on the day after the troubles and kept in police custody overnight. He was interviewed by a police officer acting alone at 10.05 am on 4 April. This officer accused him of causing damage in St Paul's on the 2nd and said another police officer (unnamed) had identified him as throwing missiles at the Black and White cafe. Jones denied it. He agreed that he had been in the cafe at the time of the raid, and had been searched which made him uptight as he was 'clean'. Afterwards he had left and gone home. He admitted later that he had thrown a bottle at the wall of the cafe, where it had smashed, damaging no-one. Jones then made a statement and signed it. There was no other evidence against him, although the interviewing officer had told him that a policeman had witnessed his behaviour. No such evidence was ever produced. The drug officer who had searched Jones did not even make a statement naming him until 7 May 1980.

Jones was originally charged with threatening behaviour and subsequently with riot. But the Judge dismissed the case of riotous assembly against Jones in the Crown Court because throughout the whole of the prosecution case his name was never mentioned. Not one piece of evidence was offered against him during the trial.

Two more cases were dismissed on the direction of the Judge after the defence evidence and they did not go to the jury for a decision. These were the cases of *Sidney Clarke* and *Nicholas Walker*.

The initial evidence against *Clarke* came from a young man who lived in St Paul's and was himself taken into police custody for questioning in relation to looting offences after the disturbance. This man gave the police a witness statement about some of the events of 2 April, though he was not charged with any offences himself. His evidence was that at 9 pm on the 2nd he saw Clarke standing by a burning car holding a fire extinguisher; the police could not provide any corroborating evidence since they had withdrawn from St Paul's by that time. However, Clarke himself did refer to the incident when he was arrested nine days later on 11 April. He told the police that he had gone to St Paul's at around 6.15 pm with a friend, because he had heard about the troubles. He had watched the police tow away the burnt-out panda car and then he had stayed to watch and he saw the police leave the area. He insisted that he had only been an observer of the 'real trouble'. Eventually Clarke admitted that after the police had left St Paul's, he had seen the stationers being looted and set on fire and in the excitement he had picked up a fire extinguisher and thrown it through the window of a red car. As he walked away from the car he saw some children trying to overturn it and he had returned to help them; some young girls had then set fire to the car. This version differed from the witness account, in which he was seen standing by a burning car holding a fire extinguisher. Clarke said that he had left St Paul's later in the evening and when he was stopped at a police road block his car had been searched. No stolen goods were found as he had not been involved in any looting.

The Judge dismissed the charge of riot against Clarke saying that if the common purpose was a show of force against the police then Clarke could not have been party to that. First, neither he nor the eyewitness were aware that the red car that was attacked was an unmarked police car. The prosecution argued that they would have known it was a police car by its aerial but this was rejected by the Judge. Secondly, Clarke's only involvement in any trouble came after the police withdrawal, when the Judge said it was not possible to make a show of force against them. Thirdly, although Clarke was admittedly excited by the events he was not part of the main crowd and he had taken part only in an isolated incident for reasons unknown, even to himself. He had admitted that he had 'no idea' why he did what he did.

Nicholas Walker. The case against Walker rested solely on the evidence of one officer, a Detective Constable in the drug squad, so the reliability of that one statement was central. Walker was arrested on 10 April on suspicion of having been involved in the riot on the 2nd. He was interviewed twice before he saw his solicitor. He gave no written statement to the police, though verbally he said that he was in the cafe and searched during the raid. He had left the area soon after and spent the rest of the afternoon with his girlfriend.

The drug squad officer who named Walker, and who had searched him in the cafe, made his first statement on the evening of 2 April but Walker's name did not appear in it. Nor did his name appear in the officer's second statement, made almost three weeks later on 18 April. It was not until 23 April that Walker was named, in his third statement, where the drug squad officer said that he had searched Walker in the cafe. He found nothing but Walker had been generally abusive. Later he saw Walker in the crowd pushing and jostling them (drug squad officers), as they left the Black and White cafe. The crowd chased them and when he was kicked he turned to defend himself, and saw Walker taunting and pushing. When they reached Denbigh Street the officers were hemmed in by two crowds, and he again saw Walker who was throwing stones and running with the crowd.

At the committal this officer said that he had forgotten to write about Walker in his first two statements, though he was aware of the critical nature of his evidence in any court proceedings. He said that during the evening of 2 April he had remembered Walker and had noted his name down in his notebook, but he did not bring his notebook into court. He said he did not see the need to make a statement naming him at this stage. On the 3rd he named Walker in an action file in the incident room, but although he was asked to write a statement as well he did not do so for three weeks because he was too busy with other matters. Nevertheless, he was sure that it was Walker he saw standing at the bottom of Denbigh Street on the grass verge throwing stones, (or at least a stone) at the police and their car. He was adamant about the identification even though the situation was certainly confusing and one of his fellow officers said that it had been impossible to make any identifications in the moving crowd.

In the Crown Court the defence challenged this officer. Why had he not brought his notebook to court? Why had he failed to make a statement about Walker for three weeks? They argued that the reasons he gave, i.e. the labelling of drugs and a week's holiday which had prevented him writing up crucial evidence, were unsatisfactory. They cast doubt on the accuracy of his statement both because it was not written until 23 April and because it was written from memory. They queried the clarity of his memory because in the Crown Court the officer changed his positioning of Walker, moving him from the bottom to the middle of Denbigh Street. The Judge leant forward across the bench and asked him which of the two versions was correct; he chose the version he was giving then, not the one that he had given at the committal weeks earlier. Doubt was cast on the accuracy of the officer's memory and the feasibility of making an adequate identification under the circumstances that surrounded the chasing of the drug squad and the stoning of their car. There was no other evidence against Walker.

The Judge initially said that Walker did have a case to answer, but a day later he withdrew the case. Thus seven of the sixteen defendants had their cases dismissed by the Magistrates and the Judge. Only the following nine cases were actually put to the jury. It is necessary at this point to look at the composition of the jury, because after the trial it became the focus of much critical comment.

The Jury
Given the legal principle and practice over the past centuries that a person on trial should be tried by their 'peers', it has been generally accepted that the jury must genuinely be peers of the accused. Thus 'the justification for defence challenges to jurors based on their political opinions, their race or their occupation is grounded in the traditional constitutional doctrine that the accused are entitled to be tried by their "peers" '. (*State Research*, Vol. 3 No. 15, p. 44).

In this case, the defence argued that given that the experience of blacks in this country is very different from that of the white population, in order to ensure a fair trial there must be black people on the jury. This was problematic because blacks are consistently under-represented in jury service, and a one week survey in the Bristol Crown Court during January 1981 had shown that not a single black juror was sitting, although many of the defendants were blacks. This under-representation is clearly documented in research from Birmingham where there should have been twelve to fifteen times as many blacks on juries as in fact there were, where 'for the years 1975 and 1976 there appears to be a serious under-representation on Birmingham juries of those from the New Commonwealth (particularly the West Indies, India and Pakistan)' (Baldwin and McConville, 1979, p. 98). The defence asked the Judge to take special measures in this case because of the under-representation of black people on juries. As has been observed:

There are good reasons for ensuring that at least some of the jurors come from the racial or cultural minority to which the accused belongs. The role of the jury in the process of adjudication presupposes a certain instinctual rapport with the accused which cannot be taken for granted in an increasingly heterogeneous society. For example, if a charge of riot is brought against coloured demonstrators, it may be difficult for white jurors, who are not familiar with the mental and emotional atmosphere in which the defendants live, to decide whether they really intended to use force if necessary, in order to assist each other against anyone opposing their common purpose.
(Dashwood, 1972, p. 87)

The Judge listened to the lengthy arguments on both sides. He rejected the request that at least half the jury must be black and said that he would not deviate in any way from the normal processes of jury selection. He advised the defence that they must choose the jury from the usual panel of a hundred, using their right to reject three potential jurors on sight. They each had that right and in this way up to thirty six people could be rejected. The Judge gave the defence the option of dismissing the panel of a hundred and drawing the jury from a different panel, but he could not guarantee there would be any more black people in another panel, and he hinted that there were certainly blacks in the waiting jury panel. The defence accepted this panel and selected the jury according to the normal legal processes. A total of thirty-four people were rejected on sight before the jury was finally selected, consisting of two West Indian middle aged women, one young West Indian man, a middle-aged Asian man, two white men in their twenties and six white women, mostly under thirty. The defence had chosen to reject on sight predominantly older, white men. The details and significance of the controversy surrounding jury selection and jury decisions will be discussed in the final chapter.

Trial by Jury
Nine cases were tried by this jury. The first three cases to be discussed were cases where the Judge warned the jury to be very careful about the evidence against the defendants.

The evidence against *Clinton Brown*, like that against Walker, rested predominantly on the evidence of only one police officer, though in this case another officer had seen Brown in the crowd, milling around in Campbell Street when the dog handler was lying unconscious in the road. But the only officer who saw Brown doing something wrong was one of the Task Force 'A' officers, an officer whose evidence was also used against several other defendants, and which proved problematic in each case.

This Task Force Officer wrote his first statement quickly and it was dated 2 April 1980; in this he recorded what happened from 5 pm onwards. In a second statement made on the 6th he described events, starting at 2.30 pm. In his first statement he said that he saw Brown, who was well known to him, throw a bottle containing liquid from forty feet at police who were retreating after the march five abreast to rescue the police officers trapped in the cafe. The bottle, similar to those being taken from the cafe, burst on the ground. Twenty minutes later he saw Brown get into a car, drinking from another similar bottle. He confiscated the bottle but did not arrest Brown as he had been instructed not to by a senior officer. In his second statement he said that he first saw Brown outside the cafe when he went to collect handcuffs for the cafe proprietor early in the afternoon. Four pages later in this detailed statement he said that Brown threw a bottle at him from a distance of thirty to forty feet as he marched to the cafe. The officer then picked up a dustbin lid to protect himself. He subsequently saw Brown swigging from a looted bottle which he confiscated and Brown got into a car.

Brown was arrested the day after the disturbance by a police officer who thought he was somebody else, and said 'I have reason to believe you are Franklin Rapier and I am arresting you for criminal damage.' Brown resented this arrest and asked why he had not been arrested when he went to report to the police station on another matter on the evening of 2 April. Brown was interviewed by two officers and while he agreed that he had been present during the raid he insisted that he had done nothing wrong. During his interview Brown accused the police of starting all the trouble, he said that they are always pushing blacks around and harassing them, and that the Black and White is the only place blacks have to go and the police do not even want to let them have that. He consistently denied doing anything wrong and complained that the Task Force officer had been harassing him by wanting to arrest him for drinking and driving when in fact he was walking along the road! He said the officer was lying about the bottle throwing because he never threw a bottle. The police interviewing him accused him of injuring the police and putting them in hospital, he denied this repeating that they had caused all the trouble, they had picked on the blacks for too long. He vehemently refused to make a statement.

At the committal proceedings, and subsequently in the Crown Court, the defence examined this Task Force officer closely and several significant facts emerged from these two cross examinations. This officer's evidence about the general events differed substantially from that of many other officers in several ways. For example, he said that Superintendent Arkell had told him to handcuff the proprietor Wilkes but the Superintendent adamantly denied this. Where most officers said that the drug squad car which was attacked was red, he insisted that it was green. When many officers (including the other constable to name Brown) saw a crowd of twenty people throwing stones at the cafe, this officer saw 'several hundred negroes'. When the bulk of officers involved in the rescue march to the cafe agreed that the identification of any individual was impossible because they were sheltering from stones, this officer insisted that he could identify Brown even though his description of the attack was far more terrifying than anyone else's, and by his own admission he was hiding behind a dustbin lid at the time.

Then it emerged that he had not written his first statement until 3 April. He had written his notebook first which took him two days to complete, so his first statement should have been dated 3 April, not 2 April. Similarly his second statement was also misdated, it should have read 7 April not 6 April. He said that he had not noticed either of these dating errors when he had signed the statements as correct, nor had his senior officer. In relation to the bottle throwing episode itself, his written evidence was contradictory about whether Brown threw the bottle as the police approached the cafe or as they retreated from it, and this was never resolved. There was conflicting evidence about why this officer had wanted to arrest Brown, whether it was for disorderly conduct and theft of a bottle of beer as he said, or drinking and driving as Brown and another policeman said.

In his summing up the Judge commented on both the general and particular contradictions in the evidence against Brown and said that he believed that this officer was 'no doubt honest but mistaken'. The identification evidence was poor because of the confusing circumstances, the reasons why Brown was arrested were unclear and there were many problems with the evidence. He told the jury that they must be sure of the accuracy of the evidence before they could accept it. They were also instructed to take into account the fact that Brown himself had consistently and vehemently denied any involvement, both in his written statement and in his statement from the dock.

Brown was the first defendant to be acquitted by the jury.

Clifton Mighty was sixteen at the time of the trouble. He was one of the 'Mighty brothers' referred to in Walsh's case. His brother, who also featured in the police evidence disappeared from St Paul's after 2 April and was never brought to trial. Clifton was arrested on 8 April on suspicion of being involved in the riot and although he was a juvenile he was interviewed alone in police custody. He denied being involved in any stone throwing though he did agree that he was an observer of many of the events on 2 April. He had been at the cafe for a while before going home to Campbell Street, from where he watched the police arrest Clive Edwards. Then he went out and watched the police rescue march to the cafe, from there he went to his girlfriend's house. Later he saw fighting, he saw the police car set on fire and dogs going into the crowd and he finally went home between 7.30–8 pm. He wrote and signed a statement. He also gave evidence in court under oath repeating that he was merely a spectator on that afternoon, and that he had popped to and fro between his house, his girlfriend's house and the streets. He witnessed a lot of things but he did not join in or throw stones.

Four police officers mentioned Clifton Mighty in their statements; two of them only saw Mighty but they did not see him do anything wrong. Their evidence was not in dispute as Mighty himself said he was there. The other two officers gave evidence that Mighty did dispute. These were the two officers who said that they had come to St Paul's to answer an emergency call at 3.30 pm, one hour before Superintendent Arkell said that he sent it. Their evidence about timing conflicted with others in relation to events all afternoon. They said that they saw Clifton Mighty throw a stone at the cafe when it was under siege; one of them said he saw Mighty in a group of six throw stones at the cafe, he was the only one to throw a stone. He was able to see this clearly even though he was sitting in a police car at the time, Mighty was about a hundred yards away in a moving crowd, and people were running about between this group and the officer. The other officer, sitting in the same car, said that Mighty was standing in a group of fifty people, half of whom were throwing stones. Neither of these officers could say what Mighty was wearing and they agreed that there was a lot of confusion in the area.

These two officers said that they identified Mighty while they were sitting in a car, but from the position they described themselves to have been in it would be difficult to see a group a hundred yards away, especially if the car was parked at an angle. They each placed the car in a different position in their evidence, so the exact angle of viewing was unclear. Also, at the time that most officers said the cafe was under siege (4.30–5 pm) many police said there were no cars parked in Grosvenor Road. Mighty's defence lawyer documented the whereabouts of each police vehicle during the afternoon and she argued that these two officers could not have been in a car watching the cafe at the time it was being stoned, because all cars had been removed from the immediate area by then.

The Judge cautioned the jury about the poor identification evidence; the crowd was moving, the angle of the viewing was unclear, no clothes were identified and the evidence conflicted over several important details, such as the size of the group Mighty was in and how many were throwing stones. Mighty had denied any involvement throughout and had given evidence on oath that he was only a spectator.

The jury returned a 'not guilty' verdict.

The case against *Clive Edwards* rested primarily on the evidence of the same Task Force 'A' officer who gave the evidence against Brown described earlier. The same general problems with his evidence applied in this case as they did in Brown's. Other officers gave evidence against Edwards but their evidence all related to events that occurred *after* Edwards had committed the alleged offence.

Edwards, who was sixteen, was arrested during the course of the trouble in Campbell Street. He was taken to the police station and charged with disorderly conduct; later he was charged with riotous assembly. The case against him was as follows. In his second statement dated 6 April (but written on 7 April as he said in court) the Task Force officer described the arrest of Edwards, which he had not mentioned at all in his first statement. He described graphically the stoning of the drug squad car in Denbigh Street, his chase of a man into Campbell Street and up some scaffolding, and the stoning of the police by a crowd of twenty youths in Campbell Street. He was in the company of a doghandler in Campbell Street when he saw Edwards pick up a rock and throw it. He chased Edwards who got away, but another officer ran and tackled him and together they arrested Edwards. The Task Force officer then saw the doghandler lying unconscious on the road and went to shield him from the crowd with another officer. All the other Task Force 'A' officers and police constables who gave evidence against Edwards were clearly under the impression that he was chased because he had thrown the stone that had knocked down the doghandler. The officer who chased Edwards never explained to them that he had seen the rock, allegedly thrown by Edwards, harmlessly hit the ground, nor did he go to give evidence to that effect when Edwards was tried in a lower court for wounding the doghandler.

There was confusion among the officers both about why Edwards was being chased, and who he was. The Task Force officer who started to chase him called him Raymond Mighty, the officer who tackled and grounded him (Edwards got some bruises on him) called him Michael Edwards, and others said that the youth looked very like Mighty. There was confusion in the police evidence about which police officer was working with whom; for example, the doghandler in his evidence did not say that he was with the Task Force officer, and there were contradictions about who arrested Edwards. The details of most of this confusion will be dealt with under the case of Maye, because she was arrested minutes before Edwards by many of the same officers. The Task Force officer who knew what Edwards had done was the arresting officer and he should have taken Edwards to the police station, but he left that to someone else who thought that Edwards was actually being arrested for wounding the doghandler. Again this case was further complicated by the fact that the officer who did take Edwards to the station denied that he had searched the youth and was surprised to be shown the charge sheet showing that he had done the search. In addition the date on his statement had been changed, it looked like the 2nd; he said that it was the 3rd but he had changed it to the 4th because it took him two days to finish. Both leaving a statement overnight before completing it and altering the dates on it are abnormal police procedure. The Judge, looking through his magnifying glass, said the date did look like 2 April to him.

Edwards gave evidence in court under oath. He said that he had gone to the cafe and watched what was going on from the grass. People were swearing but not pushing. He watched the drug squad leave and then he went off to join his girlfriend. A little later he went into Campbell Street where he saw the Task Force 'A' officer armed with a dustbin lid and drawn truncheon chasing a man down the street which he (Edwards) was walking up alone. The officer suddenly turned and grabbed him when the man he had been chasing got away. Edwards said that he had thrown no stones and there had been no chase but that he had been arrested wrongly when the man the police officer was chasing escaped. The defence lawyer argued that the place where Edwards was arrested was inconsistent with a story of a police chase down Campbell Street. In addition many of the police involved thought that he was Mighty, and were confused about his identity.

The Judge said that the fact that they called Edwards Mighty could imply a wrong arrest. Edwards had consistently denied throwing stones or showing violence to the police, and no one had seen him actually throw a stone that hit anyone. The only real evidence against him, which was that he threw a stone which hit the ground, rested on the Task Force officer whose statements contained many discrepancies. The other officers only saw Edwards after he was being chased and simply assumed, wrongly, that he had thrown the rock that knocked out the doghandler. The jury found Edwards 'not guilty'.

Two more of the defendants were found 'not guilty' by the jury after long deliberations. These were *David Royal* and *Franklin Rapier*.

David Royal was also sixteen at the time of his arrest. He was arrested in the Shady Grove cafe on 26 April almost a month after the disturbance and then interviewd in custody by two police officers, prior to the arrival of his father. Royal told the interviewing officers that he had been in the Shady Grove cafe on 2 April and that from there he had seen a dog handler try to arrest Franklin Rapier, who managed to escape. Subsequently, Royal said, he went down to the Black and White cafe where he met someone, and together with the proprietor of the Shady Grove they had driven off to Castle Cary to shop. The interviewing officers then told him that they had pictures of him on the TV videotapes showing him throwing his arms about in Ashley Road at the time the police were in cordons with riot shields. Royal then said that he had been there at that time doing his boxing exercises! When he was subsequently interviewed in the presence of his father the police accused him, and his friends, of injuring many policemen. Royal denied this strongly. He said he was there alone and not with his friends and he was just standing, waving his arms. He refused to make a statement.

In court, Royal brought witnesses to support his alibi for the earlier part of the afternoon. The cafe proprietor said that Royal was at the Shady Grove till 5.30 pm, when he went with him to a garage in Totterdown. The garage man gave evidence supporting this. From the garage they went to the 'cash and carry' and went late through the checkout at 8 pm. Though there had been a third man in the car he did not give evidence. There were discrepancies in the alibi concerning for example who drove the car, how many people were in the car, and why they went out driving. In court, the alibi was undermined by the verbal police evidence that Royal admitted to being present in Ashley Road doing exercises shortly before the police withdrew at 7.30 pm. He did not make a written statement about this to the police, however.

The main evidence against Royal involved several police officers. The two officers who had arrived at the cafe at 3.30 pm had some evidence against him. One of them said he had identified Royal running past him while he was standing on the grass opposite the cafe, chasing the drug officers. The other officer said that he could not identify anyone at that stage. They both said that they saw Royal later on throwing stones at the cafe, but this evidence was the same as the evidence against Clifton Mighty and suffered from the same weaknesses of identification. Two other officers, acting separately, said that they saw Royal later in the day throw stones at the police behind riot shields. One who knew Royal well said that while the police were behind the riot shields they were being bombarded by youths throwing stones; he saw Royal throw a bottle. This officer had been involved right through the afternoon as he was in the initial raid, but he had not seen Royal until that incident. The other officer said, in his statement on the 4th, that he saw Royal run up to within five feet of the riot shield cordon at 6.40 pm, throw an object, transfer another from his left to his right hand and throw that. He spotted Royal a few minutes later running with the crowd. In court, this officer said he remembered seeing Royal earlier in the day in Campbell Street and he thought he had told him to go home then.

In court it was apparent that both of these officers had identified Royal from behind riot shields at a distance of thirty to forty yards, in a moving hostile crowd while police were being pelted with missiles. Both these officers had access to the video-tapes where Royal was apparently to be seen waving his arms, and one of the officers said that he had discussed the events of 2 April with other officers before writing up both his notebook and his statement.

One of the interviewing officers was closely questioned in court. He had interviewed Royal without a parent present because he said Royal had wanted to talk. This officer said that he had a photograph which clearly showed Royal standing next to a Mini throwing a stone. Under oath he said that this could not be a picture of anyone else, but the defence questioning revealed that the height of the person in relation to the height of the car made the person in the photograph taller than Royal. In addition, the man in the photograph was wearing a ring which the officer agreed Royal never did. The officer concluded that, after all, he was no longer one hundred per cent sure that the photograph was of Royal.

The evidence was, according to the defence, insufficient to secure a conviction. Royal had an alibi for much of the day, the photographic evidence was far from certain and identifications made from many yards away behind riot shields must be open to serious question. David Royal denied being in St Paul's until late and he consistently denied playing any part in the attack on the police. But the Judge in his summing up laid stress on the discrepancies and inconsistencies in Royal's alibi (more stress than was laid on police inconsistencies) and noted that several police officers had seen Royal that day, and that there was a photograph of him throwing a stone. The jury, however, returned a verdict of 'not guilty'.

The case against *Franklin Rapier* was very different. Rapier was a man in his thirties, a person well known to the police as, among other things, a critic of their methods of policing in St Paul's. Rapier had been wrongfully imprisoned for seven months in 1979 and was outspoken about that experience. He is a tall man with a moustache; on 2 April he was wearing a blue track suit. Rapier was arrested on the day after the disturbance and was told that he was being arrested for throwing a brick through a police car window in City Road. He denied this vehemently and said that only kids had been involved. He denied the police accusation that he was a ring leader and said that he himself had been hit by a brick while attempting to stop some trouble. He agreed that he had been chased by a police dog, but explained his fear of dogs and lifted his shirt to show the interviewing officer scars of a previous encounter with a police dog. Rapier insisted throughout his interview that the police were trying to pin responsibility on him, 'You have got to have somebody and you are trying to make me a martyr.' When he was reinterviewed on the 4th he had seen his solicitor and refused to answer questions. The interviewing officer told him several police had named Rapier in their statements and on action sheets to which Rapier replied, 'I don't want to talk to you, you are trying to frame me'. He accused the police of lying and refused to make a statement. He maintained this position throughout the committal and the Crown Court trial, saying that the police had set him up in order to try to pin the blame on him for the trouble in St Paul's. His defence lawyers concurred, adding that it was the police who had created trouble; but in order to exonerate themselves with the Government and the public, they had painted a picture of an outburst of unprovoked violence and labelled Rapier as the instigator of this inexplicable crowd aggression. So many police gave evidence that they had seen Rapier in so many places, doing so many things that, the defence argued, they had created a mythical 'superman' figure who had whipped up different crowds, at different times and in different places, thus causing a riot. These allegations were denied by the police.

Unlike the majority of other defendants who were seen by at most one or two officers, some twenty police officers named Rapier in their statement. This evidence was not, however, corroborated by any of the civilian prosecution witnesses.

Two drug squad officers gave evidence against Rapier. One said that he saw Rapier that afternoon though he recognised nobody else. His fellow drug squad officer, who had identified Walker in the crowd, also named Rapier as being present running with the mob. These two officers made statements to this effect on the day of the trouble, but at the Crown Court trial new evidence undercut the second officer's evidence. This officer (who had named Walker on 23 April) had described Rapier in detail – in nine lines – in his first statement made on 2 April. At the committal he had implied that Rapier was the man who kicked him in the back. In the Crown Court he agreed that he had not seen who had kicked him from behind and in accusing Rapier he was only repeating what he had been told. After questioning it became clear that the nine lines which documented Rapier's involvement so coherently had been added *after* the statement had been signed by the officer; there was no way of knowing when this addition to the statement had been made. It is not admissible to add lines to the end of a signed statement; rather a supplementary statement must be written, signed and dated. The Judge therefore ruled that this evidence must be withdrawn from the prosecution case because of the dubious nature of this undated addition. As the officer did not bring his notebook into court, the truth of his claim that Rapier's name was indeed written there on 2 April could not be verified.

Several of the Task Force 'A' officers gave evidence against Rapier. Taking their evidence together they said broadly that they saw Rapier when they arrived at the cafe at about 3.20 pm. They saw him shouting in the crowd while the prisoner was sitting outside the cafe in the police car; he was seen hitting the police vehicle containing the alcohol and he was one of the main agitators. He was variously seen standing or sitting on the wall by the cafe, jostling and shouting abuse and when the drug squad officers left the cafe Rapier chased after them, leading the crowd and shouting 'let's get them'. Some of them saw Rapier kick the drug squad officer, who then fell to the ground.

There were discrepancies in the details of their evidence, even though several of them wrote their evidence together, for example the crowd Rapier was said to be leading ranged in size from about thirty to forty to fifty people, to a mere twelve youths. Overall these officers did draw a vivid picture of Rapier prancing about stirring up the crowd outside the cafe, though other Task Force officers who also described the chase did not see Rapier in his blue tracksuit at all. At the committal and in the Crown Court some details about this evidence emerged. None of them had written up their statements or notebooks until at least 3 April, by which time they all agreed that they had discussed the events with each other and with other police officers and Rapier's name had already been mentioned several times. One did not include Rapier's name until his second statement; another had not written his notebook until the 9th because of injuries; and yet another never wrote his notebook up at all though he had never omitted to do this before. A fourth made his statement on the 5th and wrote his notebook after-wards on 6 April.

The defence cross-examined the Task Force officers about their evidence that they saw Rapier kick a drug squad officer to the ground, they asked how they could possibly have seen that when, by all accounts, the drug squad officers were surrounded and were masked by a jostling crowd. The defence also challenged their evidence because the drug squad officer, by his own admission, was not pushed over. The defence pressed one officer on two further points; one on the loss of his vital notebook and the other about altering the date on his statement. The defence argued that these officers did not see Rapier kick anyone and that they had deliberately not brought their notebooks to court because there was no mention of any such incident in them. Most of them had written their statements together, after Rapier's arrest and after discussions with senior officers. In addition it perhaps could have been pointed out in court (but wasn't) that while four drug squad officers left the cafe together all these eyewitnesses only saw three, raising serious questions about how well they had been able to see what was going on.

A third group of police officers who said that they saw Rapier outside the cafe at this stage were three detective constables sitting in an unmarked police car by the Inkerman pub. These were the men who went off to town for coffee and found that on their return at 4 pm the cafe was under attack. One of these officers said that while they were sitting in their car watching the cafe someone in the car pointed Rapier out to him: he was doing nothing wrong, but he was pointed out purely for 'local intelligence purposes'. When they returned from town they saw a police car drive past the cafe at 4 pm and get stoned (other police evidence put this event much later), and Rapier was one who threw stones at this car. He then ran off into Campbell Street with the crowd which was being chased by dogs. This sequence contradicted the story that Rapier had run into the side street chasing the drug squad and only later was the police car stoned, and whether dogs cleared the crowds from the Black and White or whether people ran following the drug squad did not become clear in court. One of these officers agreed in court that he had not named Rapier until his second statement and as he himself had not actually seen Rapier do anything wrong, he was unable to say why he had named him at all. Perhaps, he said, it was because an officer had told him to do so.

One of the doghandlers also gave detailed evidence against Rapier. In a statement dated 5 April this officer said he was standing on the corner of Grosvenor Road and Brighton Street during the cafe raid. He saw two hundred youths outside the cafe at that time, then he saw the drug squad officers chased and a police car stoned. This officer followed the crowd into Campbell Street with his dog, then he went up to City Road where he was bombarded with missiles. At the junction of Dalrymple Road with City Road he saw Rapier shout, run off down the road to a skip where he collected a brick, run back through the crowd and hurl it at the window of a police car. This officer and his dog chased Rapier and cornered him in Ashley Road outside the Shady Grove, but a crowd gathered and enabled Rapier to escape. In the Crown Court, he was unable to say which police car Rapier had stoned. It was pointed out to the Judge that a charge of damage had been dismissed in a lower court because of this lack of certainty about which police car it was; also this officer had at least one of the street names wrongly recorded in his statement and many of his times were also wrong. However, the Judge ruled that his evidence was admissible for the purposes of a riot charge.

The doghandler said in court that he had not used his notebook on 2 April because he had had no time and in fact he had written his statement before his notebook. He did not bring his notebook into court because he could remember his evidence so well, though under cross-examination he became extremely hazy about times and places and kept prefacing his answers with 'as far as I can remember'. He repeatedly pointed out that he had had no sleep and that he had been under intense pressure on 2 April. It gradually emerged that although this officer had only submitted one statement to the court, he had in fact made two. He was recalled to the witness box the following day when this missing statement had been found and made available. Both the statements were dated 5 April but the doghandler then insisted that *both* these dates were incorrect; one statement had been written on 3 April and the other on 6 April. The dates on both statements were wrong due to administrative error; although he had never made such an error before, he had now made it twice. It was a mystery to him how no-one had spotted the mistakes until they reached the Crown Court.

While Rapier agreed that he had been chased by this officer and his dog, he said that he had run, not because he had done anything wrong, but because he was afraid of the dog. He said the officer was chasing the wrong person and one civilian witness for the prosecution gave evidence to the effect that this officer was indeed misguided in running after Rapier.

The defence hammered home the contradictions in the police evidence; the conflicts over timing and the sequence of events; the irregularities with the writing of notebooks and statements; and the fact that all the evidence was written after lengthy discussion and after Rapier had been arrested on 3 April. It was, according to Rapier and his defence, a frame-up, an attempt to blame someone in the community for the trouble to shift the spotlight from the police. The Judge rejected this argument and told the jury not to worry about the inconsistencies, contradictions and confusions in their police evidence, nor about their lack of notebooks in the court. But he did remind the jury that Rapier had consistently denied any involvement and had insisted that he was being framed from his first interview with the police to his final, emotional statement from the dock. By showing the court scars inflicted by a police dog he had convinced them of his fear of dogs. The jury found Rapier 'not guilty' on the third day of their deliberations.

It was here that the role of the jury came to an end. The Judge dismissed them on the third day, leaving four cases undecided. Though the jury indicated they could reach a decision on Maye, they were deadlocked on three cases. They had deliberated on and given verdicts in five cases only, they found five youths 'not guilty'. In three of these cases the Judge himself had cautioned them to be very careful about the quality of the identification evidence which rested on one, or at most two police officers, operating under very difficult conditions.

'In the Interests of Good Race Relations'

Four cases were undecided and referred back to the DPP. He decided, on the advice of the Chief Constable, to drop all the charges in the 'interests of good race relations'. One of these cases involved several police witnesses, but the last three were based solely on confessions given while the defendants were in police custody.

Doretta Maye was the only woman defendant and the only person in the dock to have retained other charges against her in addition to riot, those of wounding a named police officer with intent to do him grievous bodily harm, and unlawfully and maliciously wounding another policeman under the 1861 Offences Against the Person Act. She was also the first of the defendants to be arrested, between 4.30 and 5 pm in City Road/Campbell Street on 2 April by the two of the same Task Force officers who were later involved in the arrest of Edwards in Campbell Street. Five officers gave evidence against her, the general gist of which was that while three of them (a Task Force officer and two others) were busy arresting a young man for throwing a stone, and pushing him into a police car they were surrounded by a hostile crowd. Maye was in this crowd when she threw a stone which hit one of them. She was arrested almost immediately, after a short chase.

One member of the Task Force said that he saw the stone hit the officer but he was unaware that this officer was actually arresting a man at the time. He saw Maye throw a brick from a distance of twenty-five to thirty feet while the officer was standing on the corner of City Road and Denbigh Street. At the trial his evidence was different and he said that the policeman had in fact been standing by a car when the stone was thrown. The stone passed over the head of a police driver and hit the officer, wounding him. This officer said that the police driver then chased Maye and caught her within about fifteen feet; she was put in a police car and driven away. The police witnesses gave conflicting and contradictory evidence about who actually arrested Maye and who drove her to the police station.

The police driver, referred to above, gave a somewhat different story. This officer said that he and another officer drove their car into Denbigh Street, saw a crowd at the bottom and so reversed up this street with their lights flashing and sirens going in order to distract the crowd and allow the drug squad car to leave. However, none of the Task Force officers who were in Denbigh Street and who saw the drug squad leave saw any other police car there, with or without lights or sirens, and indeed one of them maintained that the drug squad car was still in Denbigh Street when Maye was arrested. The driver said that after leaving Denbigh Street he had stopped the car to arrest a man whom he and his colleague had seen throw a stone. A Task Force officer came to help them to get this man into the car, but as he did so Maye threw a stone at him from behind. She threw it from a distance of only four feet; the stone did not pass over his head, and he did not have to turn to chase Maye as the first witness suggested because he was facing in her direction at the time. Indeed, that is how he saw her throw the stone in the first place. Under cross-examination he said that the Task Force officer was crouching when the stone hit him on the back of the head. At the time they were surrounded by a crowd of about six women but no-one else was throwing stones at them; only Maye threw a stone, one stone, from a distance of four feet and she was arrested immediately. The Task Force officer who was hit said in his evidence that they were surrounded by a group of about twelve people, that lots of stones were thrown and that four or five missiles passed him before he was hit. He said he was standing up when he got hit.

The second officer in the police car also gave evidence. He saw the drug squad car leave Denbigh Street, then they reversed their car out of Denbigh Street and were quickly involved in trying to arrest a man. In his statement made on 3 April, he said he saw a stone hit the officer and that his driver took the wounded man to the Bristol Road Infirmary. But the driver said that after this incident he walked on into Campbell Street and participated in the next event.

Another Task Force officer who was with the others said that he did not witness any of these events at all, but arrived on the scene only in time to see Maye's arrest. At the trial when he was giving his evidence he sought to explain this. He said that when he was walking up Denbigh Street he had panicked and stopped dead in his tracks, and this delayed him reaching City Road. The defence asked why he felt the need to explain his absence from the scene: they said that he must have talked to the other officers during the committal or trial proceedings in order to discover that another Task Force officer who had been in Denbigh Street with him, and was hurt and limping, had reached the top of the street before he did. He had produced this story about being 'paralysed with fear' before the defence had even indicated that they wanted an explanation for his absence. He had not mentioned this moment of fear in either his original statement or during the committal proceedings in September 1980. The defence asked to see his notebook so they could see exactly what he had recorded about these events. However, although the officer had had his notebook in the Magistrates Court, he had subsequently lost it. He could not think where it was, nor how it had got lost; it had simply disappeared.

The prosecution were never able to pinpoint the exact position of Maye, her distance from the group of police officers, their position, where she threw the brick from, whether the driver had his back to her or was facing her, or who actually arrested her and where, because the Task Force officers' evidence and the evidence of the two officers in the police car were so contradictory. Maye, herself, gave evidence on oath and had one witness, a woman friend. Maye said that she saw the arrest of a man and she saw the police kicking him and pulling his neck. She said that at that time there were twenty people around; there was shouting and bricks were flying. She started to run because a friend told her to run; not because she had thrown a brick, but for safety. She was caught and arrested. By her own account she was chased right into Denbigh Street before she was actually arrested, she was not arrested within a few feet of the incident. She was very abusive to the police because she had not done anything wrong and she was initially charged with insulting behaviour. She was later charged with wounding, and then riot. She never made a statement at any point.

In his summing up the Judge suggested to the jury that maybe they would not find Maye guilty of riot if they thought that she had acted alone and that she had had a very specific and limited purpose in throwing a brick: namely to free her friend whom the police were arresting. But the jury failed to reach a decision on either of the charges before they were dismissed by the trial Judge.

The cases of the last three to be dealt with here were similar in two ways. All three people were young; two were sixteen at the time of the trouble and one was nineteen. None of them had been named by any of the police in the ninety or more statements, and the only evidence against them was what they themselves had said to the police. Two of them admitted to having been quite seriously involved, the third only marginally. The defence of the two who were more seriously implicated, Binns and Sharpe, was that while they were guilty of criminal damage they had no common purpose running through their actions and they had no links to the crowd around them. The third youth, Minter, said that he had hardly participated at all during that afternoon.

It was *Paul Binns's* defence lawyer who so consistently throughout the trial argued that there was not a riot in law in St Paul's on 2 April 1980. He said that there was no common purpose in the crowd, and Binns certainly could not have been said to have a defined purpose that day, let alone a shared one. Binns went voluntarily to the police station on 14 April where an officer formally arrested him for being involved in the rioting and looting on the 2nd. He was cautioned, booked in and placed in custody. Later he was interviewed by one officer alone. After initially denying any involvement he said that he had been involved and agreed to make a statement, because he was anxious to leave the police station. He said that he had been outside the cafe when the trouble started, that he was then in City Road and Campbell Street throwing stones at the police and dogs, that he threw stones in Grosvenor Road and that he later led a charge against the police behind their riot shields.

He said that he broke windows and helped to turn over police vehicles, and he even marked their position on a map drawn for him by the police officer. He was originally charged with causing damage to a police vehicle to the tune of £2,600. This charge was dropped at the committal proceedings.

At the trial Binns did not deny these activities: he admitted that he was guilty of breach of the peace, criminal damage, assault, and even perhaps affray. But he denied being a part of riot, and insisted that his statement was not in his own words but that it had been obtained by question and answer. His lawyer argued that Binns, by his own admission, had no idea what was happening that afternoon. He was overwhelmed by what he saw and he had no idea why he acted as he did. He could not be said to share a common purpose both because there was no common purpose and the prosecution's choice of a common purpose was totally arbitrary. Also Binns was bewildered and had no purpose beyond throwing stones. He acted alone; he did not talk to anyone. He would not have understood if he had been asked at the time whether he was involved in a 'show of force' against the police. This common purpose was a fiction of the prosecution superimposed on a series of disconnected responses to particular actions by the police.

The Judge in his summing up repeated that in his opinion there had been a riot in law and he accepted the prosecution's definition of common purpose. He noted that, by his own admission, Binns had been involved in every incident, and that as there was a riot in law he had been part of that.

Carlton Sharpe, sixteen, was originally picked up on 6 April on suspicion of stealing from the APT stores. While he was being questioned he made a statement to the police which included an admission of causing serious damage to the Post Office. Originally he was charged with causing damage under section 1(1) Criminal Damage Act 1971, but this charge was dropped at the committal.

In his statement Sharpe admitted being in St Paul's and smashing up the Post Office. He was charged with criminal damage on 1 May and 16 June; he was then charged with riot on 28 July. At the committal proceedings his defence lawyer suggested that he had been included in the sixteen because he had committed, and admitted to, a serious offence causing a lot of damage and that by implication the seriousness of this offence would reflect on the others. She said that while Sharpe would plead guilty to offences of criminal damage, he had not acted in concert with others and so would not plead guilty to riot.

In the Crown Court his defence lawyer argued that Sharpe's statement had not been obtained by dictation but by question and answer and that it was not in his own words; the wording distorted what he had actually said he had done. The way the statement read made it sound as though Sharpe's actions had been very cohesive, deliberate and clear, to the extent that he had even gone to collect friends to join in the trouble. This was not the case. While he had done some destructive things he had not been part of a riot in law, he had had no over-riding unifying common purpose. His lawyer suggested that it was rather the police who acted in unison with a show of force in St Paul's.

The Judge took the view in his summing up, that because there was a riot in law, Sharpe's plain admission of participation was evidence of guilt.

Andrew Minter, also 16 at the time of the disturbance, is white, tall with dyed blond hair. His appearance is striking and he would be easily identifiable in a predominantly black crowd, so it is perhaps strange that there was in fact no police eyewitness evidence against him. He was arrested and interviewed by the police on 7 April and although he was a juvenile at the time he was interviewed initially alone, without a parent or guardian present. The warden of the hostel where he lived witnessed some of the later interview. The defence argued that the circumstances surrounding Minter's interview and the taking of his statement were unclear and that this evidence should not be relied upon as it might have been obtained under circumstances of loneliness and fear of police oppression. The defence suggested that a male officer had interviewed Minter alone prior to his being interviewed with a male and a female officer, but the police consistently denied this.

In his statement, Minter said that he had been walking home from town at 4.15 pm when he saw a crowd gathered in Grosvenor Road. He went back to his hostel and waited outside for the doors to open. While he was waiting he heard that there was trouble and went off to see for himself. He joined in; he told the police that he threw some stones and shouted 'get the police'. He defined these actions as 'nothing very bad', admitting some involvement in order to show the police interviewing him how limited it was. After shouting he returned to the hostel, had his tea and watched TV. Later on he looked out of the window and saw smoke rising, thinking a house must be on fire, he went outside to have a look. When he got onto the street he was chased by police and dogs and he had to take shelter in the hostel garden. Later he ventured out again, joined the crowd and again shouted at the police, but he did not throw any more stones and he left quickly to spend the rest of the evening in a pub with a friend.

The defence again argued that there was no riot in law and that even if there was, Minter was not part of it. Minter had shouted at the police briefly, but had then gone home for tea and to watch television. He could hardly be said to be sharing a common purpose to get rid of the police; he was not part of a concerted show of force; rather he drifted in and out of the crowd. The Judge took a different view and suggested that Minter's statement condemned him and because he admitted to being on the streets shouting at the police this was sufficient to prove a common purpose. The jury failed to agree on a verdict.

A Failed Strategy

At the end of seven weeks in the Crown Court, almost a year after the disturbance, and thousands of pounds later no one was convicted of riot. The police evidence was full of contradictions and conflicts, and there were irregularities in their statements and notes. While the DPP deemed it to be in the public interest to pursue this case, the Government deemed it unnecessary to hold a public inquiry. In the court of law it was not possible to seriously examine the charge that the police had, at least, contributed to causing the disturbance. Instead an apparently random selection of youths were processed in a court of law. They had to spend thirteen weeks in the Magistrates' and Crown Courts facing a serious charge. Some of them had committed acts such as shouting at the police and throwing a stone or bottle which hit nobody. Two had been involved in serious offences and caused a lot of damage but they had no ties with those standing in the dock with them.

The police evidence was confusing, and it transpired that evidence had been amended, amplified, and even altered over time, and much of it had not been written until the police were briefed, so in many cases it was not an independent eye witness account. In a few cases it appeared that evidence was deliberately changed, notebooks deliberately mislaid or forgotten in order to make the prosecution case stronger. The police evidence was the pivot on which this punitive charge was brought, yet when held up to scrutiny – and when listened to in all its detail in court – it barely sustained even lesser charges. At no time, during the trial or subsequently, have questions been raised about the quality of this evidence, why it was full of alterations and contradictions, or how far it was perhaps assembled with a view to glossing over police behaviour on the streets of St Paul's.

Yet it was on the basis of what seems to be appallingly flawed evidence that the DPP decided he could press these charges and win. The exercise failed for many reasons to be discussed in the next chapter, but it did succeed in focusing attention on 'the rioters' rather than either the police or the major issues concerning blacks in Britain.

6 Riding the Storm

'MEK THEM GWAN,
NOW WE CALM,
BUT A WE WHO REALLY
HAVE TO RIDE DE STORM'
– Linton Kwesi Johnson

We have been concerned in this book with collective racial violence and the state. In the opening chapter we rejected the proposition that collective racial violence could somehow be abstracted from social structure and treated as a 'problem' on its own. We rejected also those theories and understandings that attempted to represent collective violence variously as the result of disintegrative or alienating processes in society, as the direct by-product of wider and periodic social crisis, or as perpetrated by deviant or marginalised groups. Instead we attempted to describe collective racial violence as an element in the political activity of identifiable social groups seeking influence or control over the social, economic, and political mechanisms and institutions that determined their social location within society. It was in the nature of that social location, its conflicts and contradictions, that an understanding of the ideologies, goals and aspirations that informed the political activity of those social groups involved, was sought. This is the context within which collective racial violence acquires meaning and significance. But it is also the context within which the nature of the state's involvement may be more clearly perceived. First, in that the state incorporates, and *acts* upon, racial and class conflicts and contradictions in society, the question of how certain social groups come to occupy particular social locations cannot be understood without reference to the state. Secondly, it is the very stance of the state in relation to race and class contradictions, as objectified in the specific interventions and roles of individual state institutions and agencies, that collective racial violence is about. Finally, in that the state reserves for itself the monopoly of coercive power, it is uniquely compelled by collective social violence which is determined upon achieving political change. With these considerations, the binding theme running throughout this study is complete: the causes and significance of collective racial violence on the one hand, and the responses of the state on the other.

An understanding of the issues involved was first approached through an examination of the history of collective racial violence in Britain. From this it emerged that the criteria by which different types of collective racial violence are traditionally distinguished and explained, did not hold. The inter-communal racial violence of the pre-war era did not have any more right to the descriptive category 'race riot', than the police/black community violence of the 1970's and more recently. Racism was a central causal factor in both types; both also had to be understood in terms of class, and the state could not be excluded as a consideration in inter-communal racial violence simply because it was not the main object of attack. As argued in Chapter 1, more recent forms of collective violence had to be seen as evolving out of earlier forms, the explanatory link being the changing – though distinctive – subordination of black labour in different historic periods. Thus the white mobilised violence of the pre-war era was an outcome of the campaign by organised white wartime labour against shipowners to extend and reorganise racial structures and practices in the merchant navy. These structures and practices were not simply a matter of custom or tradition, but were embodied in different acts of Parliament. And it was from Parliament that the concession, in the form of the Special Restriction (Coloured Alien Seamen's) Order, 1925, was won. The legislative dimension, however, only partially indicated the roles of various state institutions in the wider social location of early black communities. These roles became more apparent when the part played by local government in the 'containment' of black settlement was examined. They were also evident in the less than impartial interventions of the police in the violence of 1919 and 1948, an aspect that culminated in violent black retaliation being directed not only at the attacking white crowds, but on occasions at the police themselves.

From these antecedents, it was firstly in the specificities of black subordination in the post-war era that we cited the emergence of black confrontation with the state as the dominant form of collective racial violence. That subordination was delineated initially by the different functions which the black population, as a distinct category of 'immigrant labour' was required to fulfil within the economy. Though these functions have modified with changing economic circumstances, they have not changed qualitatively. And, in conjunction with racial discrimination – in both its incidental and institutionalised forms – the result is that the black population has been unable to advance significantly beyond the social positions initially occupied at the onset of migration. These then were the circumstances shaping black political activism in the 60's and 70's. And taken together, the different political struggles represent an attempt to mobilise within the political regions of the state sufficient political forces against racism, in all the forms that it affects the black community.

These struggles it must be said have not been without positive, and in places, successful outcomes. In terms of legislation there is Section 11 of the 1966 Local Government Act; the 1976 Race Relations Act; and before the replacement of the Labour Government in 1979 an Ethnic Community Bill was under consideration. In less concrete terms, the notion of 'positive discrimination' has been placed on the political agenda, and the awareness of racism raised within the different institutions and apparatus of state. Such successes however must be seen in the context of the dominance of black immigration as *the* race issue within the state over the past two decades. Based on the assertion that 'black' immigration constituted a 'problem' and had to be stopped, the resulting legislation, and the arguments and political forces mobilised in their enactment, have to be seen as the primary means by which racism is transmitted from the political regions of the state into its various bureaucratic institutions. That racism has been increasingly reinforced by another assertion, also original to the immigration debate. This is that the presence of blacks 'causes' problems: social and environmental problems associated with 'immigrant concentrations' putting pressure on housing resources, the social services, the educational system, and in general accelerating the decline of inner-city areas; cultural problems resulting from the 'strangeness' of immigrants, and their lack of familiarity with the English language and culture; and last but not least, problems for the police. The kinds of policies and practices to which these perspectives have led, are not only a feature of continuing black subordination, but have brought the black population into conflict with the institutions of state. Thus in mobilising against racism in the 70's, the foremost concerns of black and other political activists have been the manifestations of racism within the state itself.

In the dominance exerted by the politics of black immigration over anti-discrimination and inner-city policies, it was the police and the courts that came increasingly to figure in the containment of black inner-city areas and black protest. Further, the coercive practices this entailed became more pronounced in the 70's given the greater impact of industrial recession, inflation, mass unemployment and public spending cut-backs on the black population – particularly black youth, and on the inner-city areas. Here is the immediate context within which collective resistance to the police takes shape. In this context events in Bristol on 2 April, 1980 were about as sudden and unexpected as any of the numerous but smaller incidents that occurred during the 1970's will allow.

We have concentrated thus far on the specificities of black subordination and black confrontation with the state. As we come to the central purpose of this concluding chapter, an assessment of the significance of the state's responses to the 'Bristol Riot' and the implications of these for the handling of the violence of 1981, it is necessary to take a wider view. The institutional changes that Bristol set in train may have resulted from a specific violent event involving predominantly a single social group. Nevertheless, these changes apply across the board, to society as a whole. This begs an important question: what has been the role of race in the wider political arena of the 70's and early 80's?

One influential argument is that the deepening economic crisis of the 70's has been marked by the gradual emergence of a 'soft law and order society', in the construction of which, race has had a pivotal role to play (Hall et al, 1978). With industrial recession, high inflation, and mass unemployment biting deeply into the economic gains made by the broad working classes, the first element in containing the power and protest of organised labour was the dismantling of the political consensus that operated in the 1950's and for much of the 60's. That consensus and the 'spontaneous' consent upon which it was based has been gradually replaced by what Hall et al in 'Policing the Crisis' called the politics of 'dissensus', by which is meant that consent is increasingly managed and coerced. Clearly, in the continuing attempt to bring the whole area of industrial relations into the orbit of the law and the courts, that coercion is most explicit. But trade union militancy and trade union power itself represent only one – all be it a central – aspect of the way in which the crisis is politically constructed and coercion justified. Other themes include terrorism in general, and Northern Ireland in particular (Boyle et al, 1980), public demonstrations, alternative life styles and associated political forms, crime, and blacks. It is through such themes that the crisis of the 70's is politically understood and represented. And it is through successive 'moral panics' manufactured around such themes that the state vindicates its need for an ever greater degree of direct control.

A number of features delineate what may be seen as a steady progression towards an increasingly 'authoritarian' state in the 70's. First, important new legislation was enacted. The Industrial Relations Act 1971 – repealed with the defeat of the Heath Government in 1974 – at once attacked trade union funds and threatened trade unionists with imprisonment for practices which had been standard throughout the 60's. Under the Prevention of Terrorism Act 1976, the basic and historic right of habeas corpus could be suspended. Secondly, old legislation, formerly moribund was revitalised and applied to contemporary situations. The 'sus' law (Section 4, 1824 Vagrancy Act) was frequently used to 'trawl' large areas of the city, and arrests were made simply on the say-so of police officers. In the area of public order, the 1936 Public Order Act was increasingly used to prevent demonstrations. Thirdly, the structure and organisation of the police, as well as police methods and practices, were changed radically from the middle 1960's. The police were reorganised into a smaller number of large forces and in 1966 the Special Patrol Group was created within the Metropolitan Police. These Groups are not attached to local police stations, may be quickly mobilised, often carry arms, and specialise in 'swamping' operations and crowd control. Outside London, other police forces either developed their own SPG's or an equivalent, and Police Support Units formerly intended for Civil Defence came more and more to fulfill SPG functions. Reorganisation also saw the emergence of 'reactive' or 'fire-brigade' policing which replaced the bobby on the beat; it further marked the onset of the era of the 'technological cop', symbolised by the increasing use of computers to gather and store large quantities of information, not all of which related directly either to crime or criminals. Hand in hand with the coercive methods implicit in these structural and operational changes, traditional civil rights have come under strain. Judges' Rules regarding rights on arrest and the collection of evidence continue to be frequently disregarded by the police. The role of the jury is no longer as sacrosanct as it once appeared to be. Finally, as police methods came less and less to depend on consent, and the gap between police and community widened, the whole process by which consent was actively organised became one of the primary functions of senior police spokesmen.

These developments and trends had their foundations in the economic crisis of the 70's. They were not *caused* by race, but in their political construction, race came to constitute a primary theme and further it articulated with other themes. With blacks as 'immigrants' and occupants of the 'explosive' inner-city, the external 'swamping' threat became linked with the internal public order threat; thus in March '82 Timothy Raison, in a speech defending the Government's record on crime was able to list 'the Nationality Act as an example of the Government's tough law and order policy' (*Searchlight*, January 1983, No. 91, p. 10). In almost all aspects of public order blacks figure prominently. The rising crime rates in many parts of the city are represented as black crime; instance the release of the 1982 crime figures by Scotland Yard, where the police gained vast publicity for their selective – and quite misleading – racial crime statistics. Black communities are said to be foremost amongst those which do not consent to policing. The rastafarian life styles of large sections of black youth are labelled deviant and criminalised. Black and race-related public demonstrations are prejudged as particularly prone to violence. In short, not only are blacks seen as a major threat to the British way of life, they are deemed to be part of what is wrong with British society. Thus represented, the coercive measures mobilised to deal with race, though having wider application, meet little opposition in terms of wider public protest.

From our examination of the various elements of the state's response to the 'Bristol Riot', what seems clear is that that response constituted a significant acceleration in the tempo towards state authoritarianism. We have argued that the crowd violence in Bristol only acquires meaning and significance when located within the context of wider resistance to black subordination in the 1970's. Certainly in response to the question asked in Chapter 2, 'what happened in Bristol?', there was little concerning initial events to distinguish Bristol from numerous other previous incidents. But, in so far as the initial crowd violence sucked in a significant section of the local community – black and white – Bristol indicated a new level in the order of violent collective resistance. It is clear from the state's reactions that Bristol represented a crisis for the state. But equally clearly it was not to be a crisis of race and racism in British society.

How the state went about formulating that crisis was first a product of the means through which it chose to inform itself about events in Bristol. No public or judicial inquiry had previously been undertaken into any major violent racial incident, and Bristol proved no exception. Nor, given the public pressure on the police after the crowd violence, and the bureaucratic constraints, did the Chief Constable's report prove an acceptable equivalent. Limited in scope and concerned primarily with the crowd violence and the police withdrawal, the Chief Constable's report was the first stage in the process of squeezing out social, political and economic dimensions. Certainly those dimensions were not forced onto the political agenda by the public debate in the media. And in the Home Secretary's policy statement to Parliament, they were decidedly absent – with the exception of accepting the limited initiatives of the local state. Within these parameters what essentially remained at the national level was violence that was meaningless and inexplicable. Links between the crowd violence and the current economic crisis were vigorously resisted by Government ministers, as were links with inner-city deprivation, disadvantage and decay. Stolidly, Government spokesmen even continued to insist that relations between the police and the local community had been good, so police methods, police/black relations, and consent did not form part of the official debate. The end result was a crisis reduced to its lowest common denominator – a crisis of law and public order.

The state did not move to diffuse or prevent the type of crowd violence that occurred in Bristol, but to repress it. Notwithstanding the protestations of Government ministers that the violence was inexplicable, it is difficult to accept that they were operating in the dark. Few could have been unaware of the causes and settings of the ghetto violence in the United States in the 1960's, or its escalation in response to repression. Similarly, with regard to the inner-city and race relations debates, few could not have been aware of the links commonly drawn between potential violence and urban decline and decay, racial discrimination and disadvantage. Thus, whatever else, the denial of any meaning or legitimacy to the violence, and the repressive law and order outcome, was not a product of ignorance or lack of familiarity with some strange new social phenomenon.

In essence the matter was handed over to the police and the courts. For the police the crucial issues became the 'spontaneous' nature of the crowd violence, amplified by the central fact of the police withdrawal from the scene. After high powered consultations, moves were set in train to re-examine and re-organise mutual-aid arrangements between adjoining forces, to improve police equipment, and police training in handling public disorder. The police had suffered a defeat. Quite simply, they did not intend to suffer another.

It was therefore from the law and the courts that the state's immediate and direct reply to the people of St Paul's came. Sixteen persons were arbitrarily selected from amongst those arrested – as it were, 'a proxy mob' – and the maximum charge, riot, brought against them. A charge of riot is not usually brought in cases of spontaneous public disorder, a situation which as Scarman suggested is normally dealt with by the 1936 Public Order Act. In this century the charge of riot has rarely been brought and usually only in cases where a group of people have got together in order to achieve a limited, clear and stated objective, e.g. to disrupt a dinner party or to break up a house to build a victory bonfire. The central issue relating to the charge, the existence of a common purpose, has been overt and jointly agreed in these cases. It has also been discrete. The charge of riot has not been brought where e.g. strikers or pickets have acted together for more general social and political reasons. So the bringing of this charge in Bristol was a precedent and one which raised a serious problem for the prosecution: what was the common purpose?

There was no stated or agreed crowd objective in St Paul's on 2 April 1980. And the Crown consistently denied that issues such as the social conditions or the military behaviour of the police had any relevance in the case. Because the Crown denied that the crowd had any real grievances or demands, these could not constitute the common purpose. The prosecution had, instead, to manufacture one. This they did, though it must be stressed that the common purpose put forward actually altered between the Magistrates' Court and the Crown Court; the common purpose finally settled on was 'a show of force against the police'. This raised a number of serious problems in practice because the common purpose must be different from the action, which in this case was also a show of force against the police. The Judge ruled that in Bristol the common purpose had come into existence merely seconds before the acts of force against the police, though presumably this could only be inferred. The Crown then had to carefully circumscribe that common purpose saying that it was a show of force only against those particular policemen, not against the police or policing as such. An attack on the police in general could have constituted a public purpose which would have demanded a treason trial.

The vast amount of time spent during the Bristol trial debating this issue of common purpose, and the tenuous twists of logic that were advocated were necessary because the prosecution was attempting to win the right to determine and define the common purpose, and so justify bringing this charge. Had this interpretation of the law of riot succeeded, then the possibility would have existed that any group of three or more persons who acted together against another or an object could be said to have a common purpose and be charged with riot – this will in fact be the case if the law is changed by legislation as has been recommended by the Law Commission. This would have resulted in a blurring of any distinction between the law of riot and other public order offences, and greatly extended the applicability of this previously circumscribed and rarely used law.

In the juncture between race in the 70's and race in the 80's, Bristol signified a crucial turning point. If previously, immigration legislation designed specifically to exclude blacks could be politically justified on the grounds that such facilitated the incorporation of the resident black population as equal and full citizens, that argument was now shattered. With Bristol, clearly those Acts of Parliament, structures and agencies formulated within the state to ameliorate the impact of discrimination and racism had failed. And the response of the state was not a serious re-examination of its stance on race, but to suppress the symptom of that failure – collective racial violence. In that suppression, authoritarian forces within the state gathered strength. In this process Bristol signified three important moments: the withdrawal of the police leading to institutional changes increasing the capacity of the police to deal with public disorder; the bringing and failure of the charge of riot; concerning which questions would undoubtedly be asked, and the denial – over and above law and order – of any wider and substantive significance to the crowd violence, with remedial responses entirely localised. We now turn to the implications of these moments for the way in which the crowd violence of 1981 was handled. But first, let us briefly review those events that came to be labelled by the media – 'The July Riots'.

The Summer of 1981

The summer of 1981 totally shattered any idea that the crowd violence in Bristol might be a 'one-off' or isolated event. Between March and August, events in Bristol were to be repeated in almost every major city in Britain. Rightfully, any re-statement of those events must begin not with the massive violence in Brixton on the weekend of 10–13 April, but with the protest march organised by the 'New Cross Massacre Action Committee', against police and court handling of the Deptford Fire in which thirteen black teenagers died. That march ended in violent confrontation with the police. And though in form most of the violence that summer was to conform to the basic community/police confrontation pattern, collective violence resulting from organised black protest against the refusal of the police and the courts to take racially motivated attacks seriously, formed a subsidiary but related theme. Following clashes with the police on the Deptford demonstration on 3 March, subsequent clashes were to occur over the same issue in Coventry in May, Thornton Heath, London in early June, and most notably in Southall on two separate occasions in July.

In Brixton April 1981, the worst official fears were confirmed. While attempts had been made to minimise the significance of the violence in Bristol by the rather unconvincing argument that Bristol was not representative of most black communities, no such excuses could be proffered in the case of Brixton. The violence began on Friday 10 April, continued for three days, and its intensity could not be compared with Bristol. Petrol bombs were used, many buildings burned, and nearly two hundred arrests made. The damage to property, estimated by some sources at £10 million, in no way signified the impact of this revolt on the body politic. Lord Scarman was called upon to perform the function of providing an official explanation, and this being a major break both in the state's response to Bristol and other preceding violent racial incidents, we shall refer to his report extensively in our concluding remarks. But Scarman's appointment did not prevent the flow of official explanations. Like Bristol, and for the same reasons, Brixton is declared to be not a 'race riot'. That it might have been caused by saturation policing was also denied. Instead the 'outside agitator' entered the stage. According to the Assistant Commissioner of Police, 'there were a number of people seen to be in an organising position with black youths' (*Guardian*, 13.4.81). Taken up by the press, the *Express* asked 'WHO LIT THE FUSE OF FURY?' (13.4.81). As will be seen, the suspicion that the violence was somehow 'stage-managed' by red conspirators became a ready official as well as media explanation that summer.

Over the following Easter weekend, 17–20 April, there were reports of clashes between blacks and the police in other parts of London, including Finsbury Park, and Ealing Common. These were relatively minor incidents, but the sense of a national crisis was increased by widespread violence between skinheads, punks and rockers at various seaside resorts including Brighton, Scarborough, and Margate, that same weekend.

The month of May was one of comparative calm. That however came to an end in Coventry when a march organised by the Asian community and anti-racist groups to protest against the incidence of violent racial attacks in the city, resulted in confrontation with the police themselves. The same issues were reportedly behind a serious incident in Thornton Heath early in June; there young blacks attacked a public house said to be habitually used by National Front supporters. That same night street violence again returned to parts of London.

By the end of June the violence had been largely restricted to London, and with the exception of Brixton, clashes with the police were not sustained. In the month of July, all this was to change. That the issue of violent racial attacks was the source of as much animosity against the police as against organised racist groups, and could lead to more generalised violence, was clearly evident from events in Southall on the afternoon and evening of 3 July. There, what started out as a battle between Asian youths and skinheads who had handed out racist leaflets and assaulted local Asian shopkeepers, developed into a major clash between the Asian community and the police. On the same night in the Toxteth area of Liverpool, a major battle developed between black and white youths on the one hand and the police on the other. It was this confrontation that dominated events over the next four successive nights. Abandoning all notions of 'minimum force', the police attempted to break up crowds by driving vehicles at them at high speed. And in the early hours of Sunday 5 July, CS gas was used to disperse crowds, for the first time in 'mainland' Britain. According to the Prime Minister, poor housing and unemployment had nothing to do with the violence in Liverpool. The explanation, she held, lay elsewhere, in 'NAKED GREED' (*Times*, 9.7.81). To this, a new explanatory theme was added, emanating most notably from the Chief Constable of Merseyside. In his estimation the violence could best be understood as a form of rampant hooliganism, caused by a breakdown of 'parental responsibility' (*Times*, 6.7.81). Seized upon by the Prime Minister, she appealed in a television broadcast for 'parents, grandparents, teachers, with a job or not, black and or white' to teach their children to 'obey the law' (*Mail*, 9.7.81).

Following Toxteth the street violence took on nationwide proportions. On 7 July there was looting and clashes with the police in Wood Green, London. On 8 July, Moss Side, Manchester was the scene of violence that continued over three days. There, after initial police attempts to contain the violence, tactics were changed and the police went in hard against participants. Subsequently the conspiracy theory attained new heights. According to the Chief Constable the crowd violence was preplanned, and well co-ordinated, with 'rioters' using CB radios and look-outs. With deadly seriousness he announced to the press that:

Before the riots, intelligence reports showed that people with London accents had been asking the way to Moss Side.
(*Times*, 10.7.81)

In response the *Mail* declared a national conspiracy – 'EXTREMISTS MASTER PLAN FOR CHAOS' (10.7.81), while the *Mirror* announced its famous 'HUNT FOR MASKED RIOT LEADERS' (11.7.81).

In the meantime there was renewed trouble in London, particularly Woolwich, Tooting, Dalston, and Fulham. On 10 July there was a second violent confrontation in Brixton. In fact, over that weekend the incidence of violence in London was too widespread to recount. Outside London, in Preston, Wolverhampton, Handsworth – Birmingham, Hull, Liverpool, Reading, Leicester, Huddersfield, Southampton, Nottingham, Derby and Leeds to name but a few, violent confrontations varying in scale and intensity occurred. Official spokesmen now frowned on grand conspiracy theories circulating in the press. In their estimation individual agitators 'latching-on' to individual crowds, seems much more plausible. But a new explanation fills the space left by grand conspiracy theory, and it also has an element of central orchestration. According to the Home Secretary, the weekend of violence was largely 'copy-cat hooliganism'. And the media was blamed for breaching the fine line between reporting events and amplifying them (Tumbor, 1982). Consistent with this a right-wing conservative MP called for the media to 'postpone until quieter times prolonged coverage of mayhem and arson' (*Times*, 13.7.81).

There had now been eleven days of continuous violent upheaval, but the violence was not at an end. On 15 July, following an early morning police raid on Brixton's Railton Road – the 'front line' – for the third time violence returned to the area. Nor had tensions in Liverpool subsided. Indicative of the intensity of earlier confrontations, there were scattered incidents on the night of 26 July, and two nights later the people of Toxteth and the police fought what can only be described as the most prolonged and uncompromising battle that summer.

Bristol, the State, and the Violence of '81
There is little to distinguish the origins and causes of the crowd violence in Bristol and those of the violence in '81. Where Bristol highlighted the nature of police raids in black communities, other immediate issues were highlighted elsewhere: 'swamping' or saturation policing in Brixton, the massive and aggressive policing of black political demonstrations in the instance of the Deptford March, the refusal of the police to accept racism as a motive for violent racial attack on blacks in Southall and Coventry, or simply the huge gap between police and community as in Toxteth – Liverpool. Even more than Bristol,

elements of the white community subject to the same inner-city conditions, to similar methods of policing, and impoverished by the current economic crisis, were a part of the '81 revolt. The violence did not occur simply because Bristol had already charted the way. However, it would be difficult to deny this as a contributory factor. Thus, even more a contributory factor was the absence of political signals and initiatives emerging from Bristol to the effect that black, inner-city and related grievances were being seriously considered. Further, where those signals did emerge, they were from the active and much publicised preparations of the police, and from the similarly publicised events in court. What then were the implications of the official perspectives and precedents set in Bristol for the different state responses to the violence of '81?

Police and Policing

One thing was almost certain, given the 'withdrawal' of the police in Bristol and the subsequent reorganisation of the police force with respect to its ability to handle 'spontaneous' public disturbances any future police/community confrontation would be more violent. Undoubtedly that reorganisation was at its most intense in conurbations like London, where 'mutual aid' consisted of riot trained Police Support Units and SPGs being centrally controlled and rapidly mobilised and deployed anywhere in the capital. When the violence in Brixton, immediately following operation 'Swamp '81', was directed exclusively at the police, any form of withdrawal or reduction of the police presence in the area as a way of diffusing violence was rejected by the police. In fact more police were brought in and the paramount concern was that the police would never again leave the streets. In the words of Sir David McNee, no doubt with the Bristol experience uppermost in his mind:

I have a message for the good people of Brixton. . . . We will uphold and enforce the law. Brixton is not a no-go area, nor will it be.
(*Guardian*, 13 April 1981)

As the violence escalated and spread beyond London, attitudes in the police force hardened. For Jim Jardine, the influential chairman of the Police Federation the issue was simple:

There is no need to beat about the bush. *This is a war we are waging* and it is one which the police and the forces of law and order have to win.
(Jim Jardine, *The Times*, 10 July 1981, our emphasis)

In this war seemingly nothing was to be ruled out. Certainly the ability of the police to win it was not to be constrained by either such traditonal police doctrines as 'minimum force' or concerns about the possible impact of an increasingly militarised police force on public attitudes and public consent. When on the morning of 6 July over twenty cannisters of CS gas were used to disperse crowds in Liverpool, this use was apparently against official standing policy. It was also in direct contravention of the makers' instructions, with cannisters designed to detonate against brick walls being fired directly at crowds (*New Statesman*, 17 July 1981). Other riot control tactics like driving police vehicles at high speeds directly at crowds were also imported from Northern Ireland. In Liverpool this resulted in one youth having his back broken and the death of David Moore; in Manchester injuries resulting from this tactic were said by a local doctor to be 'terrifying' (*Times*, 22 July 1981). By late summer not only was the extensive equipment of the police with protective clothing, more and new types of riot shields, helmets and armoured vehicles already well in hand, but CS gas, plastic bullets and water cannon were officially sanctioned by the Home Secretary, for use in the last resort (Hansard, 19 October, 1981). Scarman himself endorsed these measures in his report:

I recognise the importance, and necessity, of your decision that such equipment as water cannon, CS gas, and plastic bullets should be available in reserve to police forces: however, such equipment should not, I suggest, be used except in a grave emergency . . .
(Scarman, 1981a, p. 154)

Further he went on to recommend the rapid deployment of properly trained and equipped officers, increased riot training for junior and command level officers, and yet another 'review of tactics for handling public disorder' (p. 153).

The process of retraining and equipping the police did not end in the summer of 1981. Since then, some forces like Lancashire, have continued to build up their stocks of CS gas (*Guardian*, 11 September 1981). The Metropolitan police have acquired two water cannons on loan from West Germany, accompanied by German police officers for instruction in their use:

Regular police training on water cannon as an anti-riot measure began for the first time in Britain yesterday. Four West Germany policemen started a two week training programme . . . Meanwhile the Home Office has invited tenders for a prototype water cannon (*Daily Telegraph*, 18 May 1982).

Police officers from the Metropolitan police have gone variously to Hong Kong and to Northern Ireland as well as to Germany to familiarise themselves with riot control. Some 20,000 visored helmets, 8,000 shields and 6,000 special uniforms have been issued to the police. Finally, as confirmed by their appearance on the streets of Notting Hill in 1982 (*Guardian*, 21 May 1982) and by Sir David McNee even more specialist riot control squads have been formed:

during the year each police district set up special instant response units with 24 officers ready day and night. A reporting centre was set up in London to co-ordinate manpower for public disorders anywhere in the country. Every officer in the Metropolitan force learned to use riot shields.
(*Guardian*, 24 June 1982)

The police now have available to them a whole new array of defensive, protective clothing and offensive riot technology. But riot technology has not been the only feature of changing policing since the 'July riots'. Many forces have continued the process begun after Bristol of strengthening and expanding their PSU and SPG capacity. And if the saturation policing techniques, in which the SPG particularly specialises, were temporarily undermined by the repeal of 'sus', these will be adequately restored by the new Police and Criminal Evidence Bill (1982) which proposes greatly to extend the police powers of 'stop and search' throughout the country.

While following Bristol the issues of consent to policing and the nature of police methods and practices – both in general and in black communities – were not raised, after Brixton they could not be ignored. It was into these and other factors contributing to the crowd violence in 1981 that Scarman was appointed to inquire. Whatever leading Government spokesmen were publicly saying, Scarman's inquiry was a formal admission that there might be more to events than mindless violence, rampant hooliganism, a plague of copy cats, or red conspirators. Scarman was the means by which the state proposed to inform itself about the events; he was to identify causes, provide explanations and recommend remedies. This therefore was to be the form in which the state would talk to black communities in which crowd violence occurred.

While the riots compelled the attention of the state, communication with the black community was limited. Because of the quasi-legal nature of the hearings in Brixton, because Scarman sat alone, and because of fear of inadequate protection, participants in the violence did not give evidence to Scarman concerning what happened on the streets; for this account he relied on the police. He accepted their evidence apparently uncritically and in his report he found that the police had acted 'appropriately and sensibly' (p. 47) and that those who opposed them were wrong, 'their action was . . . criminal and not to be condoned' (p. 23). But the problems of relying only on police evidence have been analysed in detail in Chapter 2 and the same problems applied in Brixton, as the lawyer Ms Gareth Pierce reported:

(Scarman) put forward as factual, a report entitled: *The course of events*, which plausibly follows the account propounded by the police. He has unquestioningly accepted as truthful and accurate the evidence of some police officers whose accounts have since been rejected in court.
(*Guardian*, October 1981).

Scarman did talk to a much wider range of people about the underlying issues of what had caused the collapse of community consent to
policing, what had laid the foundations for and selected the targets of
the violence. Clearly his conclusions and recommendations would be
shaped crucially by how far he gave credence to this evidence; to what
extent was he prepared to accept the understandings and grievances
voiced by the community in Brixton? He in fact rejected much of the
evidence he was given concerning complaints about the basic policing
methods and racism within the police force. For example, a Brixton
Rastafarian Collective, for whom Scarman expressed admiration, submitted that:

the police were no longer protecting the area in a responsible manner. They
were in fact a force of occupation within the Brixton area.
(p. 9, their evidence)

The Lambeth Borough Council presented similar evidence showing:

that the condition of community/police relations in Lambeth is extremely
grave. This situation is created by the nature of the police force and basic
policing methods. At the moment the police are not controlled by the community or seen as part of it.
(Lambeth Borough Council, 1981, p. 87)

Evidence submitted by the Railton Road Youth and Community
Centre held that the black community was 'policed as though it were a
hostile territory requiring an army of occupation' (p. 10 of their report).
The same and similar themes were expressed by the Methodist Church
Board for Social Responsibility, the Bishop of Kingston, the London
Voluntary Services Council, John Tilley, MP, the Melting Pot Foundation, the National Council for Civil Liberties, and the Runnymede
Trust among others. While much of this evidence will doubtless be
dismissed by many as the rantings of blacks, interested parties and
extremists, the fact remains that there was a large body of consistent
evidence from diverse sources, most of which had predicted this kind of
violence well before even Bristol actually happened.

Yet Scarman found that while some errors had been made in policing, i.e. Swamp '81, essentially the police were tackling the problems of
policing Brixton adequately and he endorsed the very measures that
were the main source of complaint, including the use of the SPG, 'stop
and search' and saturation policing (p. 145). He also found that while
racial prejudice manifested itself 'occasionally in the behaviour of a few
officers on the streets' the overall 'direction and policies of the Metropolitan Police are not racist' (para. 8.20 Scarman, 1981). Indeed,
the report treated the whole issue of racism within the police force, and
police harassment as highly dubious – on the level of 'myth'. So the
violence in Brixton, he suggested, 'erupted from the spontaneous reactions of the crowds to *what they believed to be* police harassment' (ibid., p.

45). As a consequence the report was obliged to give much space to speculation as to how such rumour, suspicion and perceived police harassment ended in the massive and extremely violent 'Brixton Riot'. But as the report was not based on research but on evidence submitted from widely differing groups, these statements raise the question about why some evidence he heard was intrinsically acceptable and other evidence was rejected as 'rumour', 'myth' or 'belief'. In the end Scarman's conclusions on the reasons for the breakdown of community consent in Brixton were a masterpiece of officialise:

Whatever the reason for this loss of confidence, and whether the police were to blame for it or not, it produced the attitudes and beliefs which underlay the disturbances, providing the tinder to blaze into violence on the least provocation, *fancied or real*, offered by the police.
(Scarman, 1981a, p. 79, our emphasis)

'Fancied or real', the prevarication here is crucial, for the policy implications following from each are totally different.

Scarman's recommendations were inevitably contradictory, with coercive police measures unproblematically juxtaposed with measures designed to rescue consent. We have already referenced the report's support for the intensification of riot control training and the equipment of the police with CS gas, plastic bullets and water cannon, and the recommended continued role for 'saturation policing', 'stop and search operations', and the police units like the SPG (ibid., p. 145). Scarman rejected institutional racism and thus did not address himself to any of the issues raised by this. On the other side of the coin Scarman recommended five main proposals: the extension of initial police training with special attention to community relations; the introduction of an independent element in the complaints procedure; statutory liaison committees between police and community; that racial prejudice in individual officers should be made a disciplinary offence; and finally, he recommended a renewed emphasis on community policing.

In the aftermath of the violence the Home Secretary was apparently prepared to accept from Scarman recommendations on training which did not differ substantially from the findings of a Home Office 'Working Party on Police Training in Race Relations' whose report was made in 1971. The Home Secretary however firmly rejected the suggestion that racial prejudice should be made an offence within the force, and he has yet to decide on the issue of statutory liaison committees. The shift towards more community policing was accepted in principle, with its implementation being left to the judgement of individual Chief Constables. And while the introduction of an independent element in the complaints procedure has been accepted only for the most serious offences, professional police bodies have been firm in the view it will be expensive and likely to achieve little or nothing (Scarman Conference, Leicester, April 1982).

The impact of these measures will obviously depend on the extent to which they are finally adopted by Government. But even if they were all implemented in full, it is difficult to envisage any outcome other than the system of policing that led to Bristol and the 'July riots' being left basically intact. In rejecting that racism could be a factor in the policing of whole areas of the city, Scarman's findings in this respect hardly went further than the public admissions of senior officers that some of their officers might hold racially prejudiced views. It is therefore the proposal for statutory liaison committees and the renewed emphasis on community policing that must be seen as Scarman's most important contribution. Consequently it is these proposals that carry the burden of re-building consent.

Scarman's recommendation that liaison committees be statutory was partly a response to the fact that they are frequently bypassed if they are voluntary. In Bristol, it will be remembered, not only were those members of the Bristol Commission for Racial Equality concerned with police/community relations not told of the nature of the proposed raid on the Black and White cafe, but the senior police liaison officer was not consulted. The situation in Brixton, which Scarman studied was if anything worse, with the Lambeth Council for Community Relations withdrawing from the police liaison committee because it was continually bypassed by the police, and had little impact in changing police practices. But Scarman overlooked the fact that historically, rather than consulting or liaising, these committees not infrequently become sites of confrontation. They are either regarded by the police with suspicion, or used as part of the processes of managing consent within the community. Scarman recommended that they should be given 'real powers'; but he did not outline what these powers were to be or who should be co-opted onto the committees. Further, in his report, the issue of 'consultation' was used as an alternative to 'accountability', which for many of the groups giving evidence was the crux of their argument. On the central issue of accountability, i.e. giving the community some degree of control over the police and policing, the report had little to contribute, except to point out that such would not be one of the functions of the proposed statutory liaison committees. Finally, Scarman's understanding of community policing was not that it should come to comprise standard and basic police practice. Instead, community policing was seen as going hand in hand with the continuation of reactive or fire brigade policing. Given that these two approaches are mutually contradictory, the question already being asked is which will serve which. If, as seems to be emerging, community policing is to be the velvet glove that clothes the iron fist, then what might have been a genuine innovation will more than likely become the new guise in the 80's for the coercive police practices of the 70's.

The Law and the Courts

The first consequence of the experience in Bristol for the use of the law and the courts in 1981, was that the charge of riot could not be brought with any certainty. Nor was it. Within this constraint the use of the law and the courts took a different form, the call was for 'swift justice' with the overwhelming majority of those arrested being processed through the Magistrates' Courts on lesser public order and criminal charges. This also reflected the sheer logistics problem with which the popular violence of '81 presented the state. Quite literally, the police cells and the prisons were full to bursting. When therefore such headlines and reports were to be seen in the press as,

THATCHER URGES SPECIAL RIOT COURTS
(*Sunday Times*, 12 July 1981)
'Special courts are to be held at the Government's request to hand out swift justice and exemplary punishment to rioters and looters.'

RIOT OFFENDERS MAY GO INTO ARMY CAMPS
(*Times*, 14 July, 1981)

COURTS CRACK DOWN ON RIOT OFFENDERS
(*Guardian*, 14 July 1981)
'Courts all around the country responded to the Government's appeal to deal quickly with the rioters.'

Government spokesmen were not simply escalating the law and order option. Somewhere amongst the general hysteria, and the attempts at direct political intervention in the legal process, there was the pragmatic consideration that the prison and legal system was in danger of grinding to a halt.

This was the context shaping the form in which the courts were used. It was underpinned by the proposition that the ongoing violence could be contained if large numbers of participants were arrested, taken off the streets, and brought quickly before Magistrates rather than juries, where a summary good sharp shock could be administered. Where in Bristol the use of the courts came to be epitomised by the riot trial and its circumstances; in 1981 the courts were often involved in dispersing a rough and ready justice, sometimes unconstrained by due process according to many lawyers who were involved in these July and August trials. Many people were apparently arrested at random, often without knowing why, or what they were charged with. Many of them were held in custody for over forty eight hours. Access to solicitors was often refused in the police station; and many people under the age of 16 were

From milk crates to crash helmets and shields – the escalation of police riot control equipment

CORRUPT SOCIETY VIOLENT POLICE
CONSTANT HARRASMENT BRIXTON BRISTOL
LIVERPOOL—WHAT DO YOU EXPECT?

interviewed by the police without a parent or guardian being present, or even informed. People were brought to court often without their parents' knowledge, and in some cases without any legal representation. Leading solicitors in Nottingham, for example, observed that 'the police were determined to get a conviction and were not too over-worried about the way in which they obtained it; changing both the charges and the evidence in the course of time' (NCCL, 1982, p. 7). If a trial was adjourned bail was frequently refused. The shortcutting of legal procedures and the liberal disregard for the Judges' Rules bore many of the hallmarks of the kind of 'justice' handed out by Magistrates' Court after the Southall confrontation in 1979 (Lewis, 1980). The unease that these practices produced amongst solicitors found expression in an article in *The Times*:

The manner in which the courts initially dealt with some of the riot cases has led to some concern among a number of defence solicitors. Several have spoken of harsh sentences, a martial law atmosphere, defendants' rights denied and several cases in which their clients have been manhandled or 'roughed up' by the police . . . in Nottingham where over a hundred people were arrested, three solicitors produced a report which alleged a 'predetermined policy' by the courts and police which in some cases went against 'natural justice'. They complained of unreasonable haste . . . A solicitor in Manchester claimed there was a lot of confused police evidence and it appeared to him they had moved in, detaining everyone on the street and then tried to justify the arrest . . . in London solicitors spoke of their clients being found guilty on the minimum of evidence.
(*Times*, 23 November 1981).

The article concluded that 'Magistrates were both appalled at the level of violence . . . and determined to prevent a recurrence. As a result they initially handed out sentences in the spirit of the "Short Sharp Shock". However the courts tended to get more lenient for minor offences as the memory of the riots receded.' Even under normal circumstances black defendants, as a growing body of research has shown, do not fare well in Magistrates' Courts (McBarnett, 1982; Baldwin and McConville, 1979; McConville and Baldwin, 1981). Along with their white counterparts, both fared particularly badly in the post riot trials of 1981, with the courts being used more as a vehicle for the dispensation of punishment rather than justice.

These were the immediate consequences of the legal precedents set in Bristol. But the violence of 1981 revived and gave impetus to concerns to actually change the law. First, during the summer of '81 serious consideration was given to a very immediate change in the law with talk of reviving the Riot Act repealed in 1967. *McNee hints at backing for new riot law* (*Guardian*, 28 May 1981), *Government may bring in new Riot Act* (*Guardian*, 10 July 1981), *Tougher riot laws ahead* (*Daily Telegraph*, 10 July 1981). Though the idea never came to fruition, and it was later rejected by Lord Scarman, it was a popular idea at the height of the 1981 troubles. Scarman thought that the existing law was in fact adequate to deal with the situation on the street:

First the law does provide ample support of the power of arrest. Secondly, Section 5 of the *Public Order Act 1936* appears to work well enough in practice . . . Thirdly there are very real difficulties incorporating a public warning given in the din of turmoil as a necessary ingredient of the offence.
(Scarman, 1981, p. 121)

Second the events of 1981 revealed the deep concern that existed with regard to the way the common law on 'riotous assembly' had been interpreted in the Bristol trial. Scarman overruled the Bristol trial in his report and said that spontaneous street disorder can, after all, be a riot in law. He gave a definition of common purpose similar to that used by the prosecution in Bristol:

I see no reason why an expression of my opinion on the general behaviour of the disorderly crowds should pre-judge the trial of any individual accused of riot . . . for such a trial the question will be whether the accused himself participated in the riot . . . the disorder was not initially a riot. but it had become a riot by 6.36 pm . . . the critical moment was when the crowd turned and stoned the police. This was a violent crowd action in which the members of the crowd were mutually assisting each other in the execution of a common purpose, namely an attack on the police.
(Scarman, 1981, p. 42)

Scarman, by declaring that what happened in Brixton was a riot in law and stating that there was a common purpose, left only one question for the court to decide, whether or not the defendant himself was actually present and in some way involved. He removed from the prosecution the onus of proving the only stringent aspect of this very broad offence, the existence of a common purpose.

The impetus to reinterpret or change the law was taken further by the recommendations of the Law Commission in 1982 which suggested that the law be rewritten in a modern idiom and in such a way as to totally eliminate the concepts of mutual assistance or common purpose. While agreeing that riot is a 'crime of the utmost importance in the law of public order' (Williams, 1967, p. 239) and that it is a charge that can be used when the evidence required to prove more particular offences such as criminal damage or inflicting grievous bodily harm is absent, the 'faults' identified by the Commission were exactly those that had proved obstructive to the prosecution in Bristol. They referred to:

particular points where the law appears to be uncertain and where it has caused some misgivings. In the latter connection, we have in mind the particular elements of common purpose and the intent by the rioters to help each other in its execution, which has given rise to the criticism that the offence has become bound up with technical distinctions.
(Law Commission, 1982, p. 98)

Thus the Commission recommended that the complex concepts of common purpose and mutual help should be removed because they 'create unnecessary difficulties for the prosecution in many cases' (p. 113). This new charge of riot would carry a maximum of 14 years in prison, and could be used 'in circumstances, where although it is probable that such offences have occurred (e.g. criminal damage), there is *insufficient evidence* to prove their commission' (our emphasis, p. 115). The prosecution will be required only to prove that there were three or more people present, that three or more of them behaved violently in such a way as to frighten others who were, or who might have been present. The only necessary mental element would be that the accused 'knowingly' took part, and this knowing can be deduced from what the individual must have seen going on around him at the time that he shouted or threw a stone. Not only does the proposed new law on riotous assembly overcome the problems encountered by the Crown in Bristol, it is tailored precisely to meet the form that the disorders in Bristol and Brixton took by the loosening and lowering of the legal criteria for what constitutes a riot and riotous behaviour. The danger is firstly that all kinds of lesser public order situations may come to be defined as riot and secondly, as it is a charge intended to be used when there is insufficient evidence to say who did exactly what, a person may be found guilty and liable to a heavy prison sentence on no more than the accusation of a police officer.

One final and important aspect of the failure of the trial in Bristol was the extent to which the failure of the court to secure convictions was blamed on the jury system in general and black jurors in particular. Shortly after the Bristol trial had ended, the Conservative MP, Alan Clark, said in the House:

recent experience in Bristol – likely to be repeated in London following the Brixton riots – indicates that black juries, whether out of racial loyalty or fear of intimidation or a combination of both, are highly unlikely to convict black persons of offences connected with civil disturbances.
(*Guardian*, 19 May 1981).

This assertion and the attack on the jury system, it must be stressed, did not originate with the Bristol riot. Indeed the erosion of the status of juries forms part of the wider erosion of civil rights discernible from the late 1960's. In 1967 the need for a unanimous verdict by a jury was abolished. In 1977, in the Criminal Law Act, the right to trial by jury was abolished for a wide range of criminal offences. In addition, the right to reject a juror on sight was reduced for the defence from seven to three potential jurors. Yet the prosecution still retained the right to ask an unlimited number of people to stand by and jury vetting by the prosecution has increased in recent years (*State Research Bulletin*, 1979, Vol 3, No. 15). The lobby against the jury system has come from a variety of quarters, but undoubtedly the police have had a central role to play. Commenting on the new Criminal Law Act in 1977, a QC observed that

the downgrading of the jury began 11 years ago when Sir Robert Mark, then the Chief Constable of Leicester, was the vanguard of a campaign based on the return from Chief Constables of 120 police forces alleged to prove that the acquittal rate was far higher for juries than for Magistrates. Too many guilty men were getting away with it ran the argument.
(*Sunday Express*, 27 November 1977).

The same theme, phrased in this instance as 'too high a failure rate' was again voiced by Robert Mark after the 1976 Notting Hill Carnival trials (Thompson, 1980, p. 226). After Bristol, Robert Mark saw no need for such euphemisms. The police, he held,

draw (no) comfort from the justice system. Delays in trials, the inevitable uncertainty of controversial evidence, the vagaries of juries, the fact that the defendants are seen as token representatives of many not even prosecuted, all these encourage acquittal . . . no significant punishment has been imposed on a coloured person following conviction for a crime arising from riotous disorder. Notting Hill and Bristol point the way, Brixton will inevitably follow.
(*Sunday Times*, 19 April 1981)

Bristol was used to amplify the attack on the jury system and two months later a serious attack came from a High Court Judge. During July, Lord Denning delivered a broadside on the decision to acquit by the jury in Bristol. His speech received extensive newspaper coverage and his sentiments found support in many of their reports. Bristol, he said,

was a coloured area. A few of the good Bristol police force went in to enquire into some of the wrongful acts being committed there. They were set upon by coloured people living there. Twelve of the trouble makers were arrested and charged with riot – a riot it certainly was. They were tried by jury.
(*Daily Mail*, 10 July 1981)

He went on to say that by using their legitimate right to challenge, the defence lawyers were able

to get on the jury five coloured jurors. The jury so constituted acquitted eight of the accused defendants. Of the other four the jury could not agree, so they went free. The prosecution could proceed no further. The costs were £1 million. That was in my opinion an abuse of the right of challenge.
(*Times*, 10 July 1981).

He repeated these sentiments more forcibly almost a year later in his book 'What next in the law', but was later forced to retract his criticism. The book was withdrawn and he retired from the bench as a direct result (according to his wife). In blaming the acquittals on a jury which was less than fifty per cent black, Denning ignored both the nature of the legal arguments and the evidence put. Further, this attack ignored the fact that out of the sixteen charged in Bristol, nine were acquitted or dismissed by the Magistrates, the Judge or the DPP, so the jury was only involved in less than a third of the decisions.

While the Attorney General publicly dissociated himself from this view and the DPP endorsed the absolute legitimacy of the Bristol jury decision, this overt hostility was evident in Government circles following the 'July riots'. In an article dated 13 July, *The Times* reported that

many other Ministers, including the Prime Minister, believed that changes in the law (concerning riotous behaviour) are most needed to reassure the public. The most favoured change is to limit the present right to trial by jury . . . They have for some time been anxious that jury trials prevent justice. Juries, they believe, are becoming harder for prosecution council to convince.

Another 'Breach' in the Wall

What is by now clear is that, with its background in the 70's, the hardening in the coercive features and apparatus of the state has been decisive since Bristol. This observation cannot simply be said to be an inevitable result of the continuation and escalation of crowd violence after Bristol, or a consequence of the apparent ease with which the state is able to mobilise and justify law and order measures in relation to the black minority. It has also to be seen in the context of the extent to which the range of possible responses to the crowd violence has been restricted by certain characteristics in the recent ideological make-up of the political level of the state. The principal characteristic to which we refer is the notion that in order to overcome the crisis of inflation, mass unemployment, industrial decline and inner-city decay, society must discipline itself or be disciplined. In populist terms, this surfaces in appeals to 'the spirit of the war', or the need in these 'hard times' for a period of 'belt tightening'. More specifically, organised labour is asked to restrain its 'exhorbitant' wage demands, or have these restricted by statutory or other means; strikes, sympathy strikes, mass picketing and other devices by which 'the country is held to ransom,' must be reduced or be subject to legal regulation; the enormous welfare and public sector can no longer be afforded, so it must be restrained, rationalised, cut-back. While such themes find their clearest expression in the strategies and thinking of the present government, they were increasingly discernible in the workings of previous administrations in the 1970's. The policies to which they led only further emphasised the need for greater social discipline. Policies such as, industrial relations legislation, and public spending cut-backs resulting in a progressive constriction of the welfare function of the state, themselves became sites of confrontation.

The crowd violence in Bristol, we have argued, was primarily an expression of black resistance to and protest against racial subordination. But the nature of that subordination, as we have also argued, must be seen in the current social circumstances which have shaped it: thus initial incorporation as a distinctive category of 'immigrant' labour was compounded and modified by continued discrimination in employment, and the unequal impact of mass unemployment on the working black population – particularly black youth. Residential segregation in, and restriction to, the inner city became exacerbated by the inner city's continued decline, not only in respect of the environment but in terms of facilities, services and schools. Lastly, racism within the police force was compounded by changes in police methods and practices, changes shaped by the major consideration for the need to contain the inner city. In addition to racial subordination the violence in Bristol therefore challenged many of the themes and policy directions to which we have referred: could present levels of unemployment be allowed to remain and even rise? Could the decline in the inner city be allowed to continue? Could the welfare and other functions of the state concerned with social provision be progressively dismantled? Could present police methods and practices remain unchanged? Where these themes intersected, the primary challenge posed by the violence was to the core ideological assertion of the need for greater social discipline as the means of overcoming the crisis.

In the determination of the Government to hold that discipline and thus hold intact the ideological tenet upon which its broad policy approach rested, the range of possible responses to Bristol dramatically collapsed. In Chapter 4 we noted the signal moments in this process; the denial of racism and other social and economic factors as causes, the protestations of bafflement as to why the violence had occurred followed by the avoidance of any form of inquiry that might raise these issues. Broadly the underlying logic was that the black community could have no claim to being 'a special case'. They were not experiencing any hardship not also being experienced by other sections of the working classes in the current crisis. These other sections had not rioted. How then could the Government concede to blacks social resources that were being denied to the rest. To do so would be to undermine economic policies and deflect broad political strategies. Further, where one social group was allowed to succeed today, which would follow tomorrow? In official terms then, crowd violence became 'the' problem, not the social conditions and racial subordinations from which it sprang. And the solution' to 'the' problem was to be found in changes to the law of riot, and the reorganisation of the police to a higher state of readiness. Accordingly, wider social and economic responses were reduced to mere gesture. More precisely, if such factors had significance, they were peculiarly relevant only to the area in which the riot had occurred. In short, St Paul's came to represent a *breach* in the larger wall of social discipline. The wall was to be strengthened – the breach plugged.

Supposedly the nationwide violence of 1981 could not be responded to in these terms, but there is evidence to suggest that it was. First, however, let us consider those official responses in 1981 that broke with Bristol. Notwithstanding the constant flow of official rhetoric blaming the violence variously on hooliganism, parents, greed, and red conspirators – to name but a few – after the first massive instance of crowd violence in Brixton, the Government could no longer continue to pretend it was not interested in the more serious reasons behind the 'riots'. Scarman was appointed to make an inquiry, and he took his brief to include issues of race and racism, social conditions, community and policing. In July, as both the violence and official anxieties intensified, cracks began to appear in the official rhetoric. In a speech delivered at Warrington during a by-election campaign, Heseltine – the Minister for the Environment – suddenly found that inner-city decay was after all something to do with the disturbance (*Guardian*, 14 July, 1981). A few days later the full implications of this theme were to become clear in a statement by the Home Secretary in Parliament. In addition to the inner-city, race now had to be discussed, and the Home Secretary felt the situation serious enough to warrant a clear and positive assurance to the black community:

I think it is right, therefore, to repeat two assurances to the ethnic minority communities in Britain: first, the complete commitment of the Government to a society in which none is a second class citizen . . . second, my determination as Home Secretary to support the wish of the vast majority of citizens, black and white, to see the evils of extremist racialist activity isolated and eliminated. (*Times*, 17 July 1981)

The latter of these commitments was to lead directly to the Home Office initiating an inquiry into violent racist attacks. Later, the decision to scrap the 'sus' law may also be seen as a continuation of this theme. On the economic level a package costing some £10 million was announced to tackle youth unemployment. It is where the breaches were largest that political energies were concentrated: Scarman for Brixton, Heseltine to look at the inner city in Liverpool. But broad Government policies and ideologies remained intact. The emphasis formerly placed as Partnership Authorities (like Liverpool and Birmingham) under the Inner City Programme, which was reversed by Heseltine, did not again re-acquire importance after the violence stopped. Nor was the policy of curtailing Local Authority spending relaxed. Immigration control – albeit a question of whether or not a few hundred entered the country – continued and intensified. With unshakable determination the Government completed the rationalisation of previous immigration legislation, with the 1981 British Nationality Act. In addition, internal surveillance of blacks within the UK was increased with the introduction of charges for overseas visitors in the National Health Service which inevitably involves checking the immigration status of applicants for health care.

Indicative of the inability of the police to contain the kinds of social forces recently unleashed, as they lost the battle for the streets in Bristol, so did they lose the crucial battles in Brixton and Toxteth. In Brixton, for example, at the height of the violence, with over 4,000 officers deployed from all over the South East, all the police could do was to seal off the area while making occasional forays. In the absence of serious political initiatives and a repeat of the strategies following Bristol, the main emphasis was again on 'tooling up' the police for future confrontations. Future confrontations, then, will be more violent. We began this study with, at the turn of the century, small subordinated black communities resisting white violence mobilised against them. We end it with black communities still resisting racial subordination, but with new authoritarian forces gathering within the state, and the police being equipped with new means of coercion. The last word these days inevitably goes to some or other Chief Constable. We cite the words of John Alderson (*Sunday Telegraph*, 12 July 1981):

There has to be a better way than blind repression . . .

References

J. Alderson, 1979. *Policing Freedom*. London, MacDonald and Evans.

Annual Report of Metropolitan Police. See Home Office, 1948–81a.

J. Baldwin and M. McConville, 1979. *Jury Trials*. London, Oxford University Press.

G. Ben-Tovim et al, *eds*, 1980. *Racial Disadvantage in Liverpool – an area profile*. Evidence submitted to the Parliamentary Home Affairs Committee. Liverpool, Department of Sociology, University of Liverpool.

P.L. Berger and T. Luckmann, 1966. *The social construction of reality*, Middlesex, Penguin.

Bethnal Green and Stepney Trades Council, 1978. *Blood on the Streets*. London, Bethnal Green and Stepney Trades Council.

N. Blake, 1980. *The Police, the Law and the People*. London, Haldane Society of Socialist Lawyers.

D. Boesl and P.H. Rossi, *eds*, 1971. *Cities Under Siege: An Anatomy of the Ghetto*. New York, Basic Books.

H. Booth and D. Drew, 1980. 'Britain's Black Population' in Runnymede Trust and Radical Statistics Race Group.

N. Bosenquet and P.B. Doeringer, 1973. 'Is There a Dual Labour Market in Great Britain?', *Economic Journal*, Vol 83, June.

R. Boyle, T. Hadden and P. Hillyard, 1980. *Ten Years on in Northern Ireland: the Legal Control of Political Violence*. London, Cobden Trust.

Bristol Commission for Racial Equality, 1980. *Annual Report*. Bristol CRE.

D. Byrne, 1977. 'The 1930 "Arab Riot" in South Shields: a Race Riot That Never Was', *Race and Class*, Vol XVIII, No 3.

Campaign Against Racism and Fascism, 1982. 'Racism and Criminal Statistics', *Searchlight*, No 83.

Cardiff and District Citizen's Union, 1918. *Handbook on Cardiff Morals. Annual Report*. Cardiff, Cardiff and District Citizen's Union.

M. Castells, 1975. 'Immigrant workers and class struggles in advanced capitalism: the West European experience', *Politics and Society*, Vol 5, No. 1.

S. Castles and G. Kosack, 1973. *Immigrant Workers and Class Structure in Western Europe*. London, Oxford University Press for Institute of Race Relations.

Chief Constable's Report, 1980. See Secretary of State for the Home Department.

C.I.S., 1976. *Racism. Who Profits?* London, Counter Information Services.

S. Clarke, 'Easton (A Community Profile)'. Mimeo, Bristol.

S. Cohen and J. Young, *eds*, 1973. *The Manufacture of News: Social Problems, Deviance and the Mass Media*. London, Constable.

CRE/BBC, 1978, *Five Views of Multi-racial Britain*. London, CRE.

Crown Office, 1976. *Criminal Procedure in Scotland. Second Report*. Edinburgh, HMSO.

A. Dashwood, 1972. 'Juries in a Multi-racial Society', *Criminal Law Review*.

M.J. Daunton, 1978. 'Jack ashore; Unionisation of Seamen in Cardiff Before 1914', *Welsh History Review*, Vol 9, No 2.

C. Demuth, 1977. *Government Initiatives on Urban Deprivation*. London, Runnymede Trust.

C. Demuth, 1978. *'Sus' – A Report on the Vagrancy Act* 1824. London, Runnymede Trust.

J. Downing, 1980. *Now You do Know*. London, World Council of Churches/War on Want.

M. Duffield, 1981. 'Racism and Counter-Revolution in the Era of Imperialism: A Critique of the Political Economy of Migration'. Unpublished paper, SSRC Research Unit on Ethnic Relations.

A.J. Edwards and R. Batley, 1978. *The Politics of Positive Discrimination*. London, Tavistock.

R.C. Edwards, M. Reich and D.M. Gordon *eds.*, 1975. *Labor Market Segmentation*. Lexington, D.C. Heath.

N. Evans, 1980. 'The South Wales Race Riots of 1919', *Journal of the Society for the Study of Welsh Labour History*, Spring.

J.R. Feagin and H. Hahn, 1973. *Ghetto revolts: the politics of violence in American cities*. London, Collier-Macmillan.

I.K. Feierabend, R.L. Feierabend, and T.R. Gurr, *eds*, 1972, *Anger, Violence and Politics: Theories and Research*. New Jersey, Prentice-Hall.

N. Fielding, 1981. *The National Front*. London, Routledge and Kegan Paul.

R.M. Fogelson, 1971. *Violence as a protest: a study of riots and ghettos*. Garden City, N.Y., Doubleday and Company Inc.

R.M. Fogelson and R.B. Hill, 1968. *Who Riots? A Study of Participation in the 1967 Riots*, in Kerner Commission Report, Supplemental Studies.

P. Foot, 1965. *Immigration and Race in British Politics*. Middlesex, Penguin.

A. Gorz, 1970. 'Immigrant Labour', *New Left Review*, No. 61.

Governor's Commission on the Los Angeles Riots, 1965. *Violence in the City – An End or a Beginning?*

A.D. Grimshaw, *ed*, 1969. *Racial Violence in The United States* Chicago, Aldine.

H. Hahn and J.R. Feagin, 1973. 'Perspectives on collective violence: a critical review' in H. Hirsch and D.C. Perry, *eds*.

S. Hall, 1978. 'Racism and Reaction' in CRE/BBC.

S. Hall et al, 1978. *Policing the Crisis: Mugging, the State of Law and Order*. London, Macmillan.

P. Hartmann and C. Husband, 1973. 'The Mass Media and Racial Conflict', in Cohen and Young, *eds*.

P. Hartmann and C. Husband, 1974. *Racism and the Mass Media*. London, Davis-Poynter.

D. Hay, 1975. 'Property, authority and the criminal law' in D. Hay *et al.*

D. Hay, P. Linebaugh, J.G. Rule, E.P. Thompson and C. Winslow, 1975. *Albions fatal tree: crime and society in eighteenth century England*. London, Allen Lane.

J. Henriques, et al., 1980. 'Employment' in Runnymede Trust and Radical Statistics Race Group.

M.J. Hill and R.M. Issacheroff, 1971. *Community Action and Race Relations: A Study of Community Relations Committees in Britain*. London, Oxford University Press for the Institute of Race Relations.

H. Hirsh and D.C. Perry, *eds*, 1973. *Violence as Politics: a Series of Original Essays*. New York, Harper and Row.

E.J. Hobsbawn, 1968. *Labouring Men: Studies in the History of Labour*. London, Weidenfeld and Nicolson.

E.J. Hobsbawm, 1971. *Primitive Rebels: Studies in Archaic Forms of Social Movement in the 19th and 20th Centuries*, 3rd edition. Manchester, Manchester University Press.

Home Affairs Committee, 1981. *Racial Disadvantage. Fifth Session, 1980–81*. London, HMSO. HC 424.

Home Office, 1948–81. *Reports of Her Majesty's Chief Inspector of Constabulary*. London, HMSO.

Home Office, 1948–81a. *Reports of the Commissioner of Police of the Metropolis*. London, HMSO.

Home Secretary, 1980. *Statement on the Disturbances in Bristol, 2 April 1980*.

B.F. Hoselitz and W.E. Moore, *eds*, 1970. *Industrialisation and society*. Paris, Mouton for UNESCO.

D. Humphry, 1972. *Police Power and Black People*. London, Panther.

D. Humphry and G. John, 1971. *Because They're Black*. Middlesex, Penguin.

C. Husband, *ed*, 1975. *White Media and Black Britain*. London, Arrow.

Institute of Race Relations, 1979. *Police Against Black People*. Evidence submitted to the Royal Commission on Criminal Procedure. Race and Class Pamphlet No 6 London, Institute of Race Relations.

B. Jessop, 1978. 'Capitalism and democracy: the best possible political shell' in G. Littlejohn et al, *eds*.

Clement Jones, P. Hartland, H. Young and H. Evans, 1971. *Race and the Press*. London, Runnymede Trust.

I. Katznelson, 1970. 'The politics of racial buffering in Nottingham 1945–68', *Race*, Vol 11, No. 4.

M. Kettle and L. Hodges, 1982. *Uprising: The Police, the People and the Riots in Britain's Cities*. London, Pan.

The Keys. Journal of the League of Coloured People.

A. Kirby, 1975. 'Race Today, Gone Tomorrow' in C. Husband, *ed*.

A.W. Kirkaldy, 1914. *British Shipping, Its History, Organisation and Importance*. London, Kegan Paul.

The Law Commission, 1982. *Offences Against the Public Order*. Working Paper No 82. London, HMSO.

G. Le Bon, 1896. *The Crowd: a Study of the Popular Mind*. London: T. Fisher Unwin. (Reprinted 1977. Dunwoody, Georgia, Norman S. Berg).

K. Leech, 1980. *Brick Lane 1978: The Events and Their Significance*. Birmingham, AFFOR.

A. Lester and G. Bindman, 1972. *Race and the Law*. Middlesex, Penguin.

R. Lewis, 1980. *Real Trouble: A Study of the Southall Trials*. London, Runnymede Trust.

M. Lipsky and D.J. Olson, *eds*, 1977. '*Commission Politics*': *The Processing of Racial Crisis in America*. USA, Transaction Books.

G. Littlejohn, B. Smart, J. Wakefield and N. Yuval-Davis, *eds*, 1978. *Power and the State*. London, Croom Helm.

Liverpool Trades Council, 1980. *Merseyside Trade Union Inquiry into Allegations of Police Violence*. Liverpool, Liverpool Trades Council.

London Borough of Lambeth, 1981. *Final Report of the Working Party into the Community/Police Relations in Lambeth*. London, London Borough of Lambeth.

D. McBarnet, 1978. 'The police and the State: arrest, legality and the law' in G. Littlejohn et al, *eds*.

D. McBarnett, 1981. *Conviction*. London, Macmillan.

M. McConville and J. Baldwin, 1981. *Courts, Prosecution and Conviction*. Oxford, Clarendon Press.

N. McIntosh and D.J. Smith, 1974. *The Extent of Racial Discrimination*. London, P.E.P.

Sir R. Mark, 1978. *In the Office of Constable*. London, Collins.

R. May and R. Cohen, 1974. 'The Interaction Between Race and Colonialism: A Case Study of the Liverpool Race Riots of 1919', *Race and Class*, Vol XVI, No 2.

M. Meacher, 1974. 'The Politics of Positive Discrimination', in *Positive Discrimination and Inequality*, Fabian Research Series No. 314.

A. Meier and E. Rudwick, 1971. 'Black Violence in the Twentieth Century: A Study in Rhetoric and Retaliation' in D. Boesel and P.H. Rossie, *eds*.

Metropolitan Police, See Home Office, 1948–81a.

R. Miles and A. Phizacklea, 1977. *The TUC, Black Workers and New Commonwealth Immigration 1954–1973*, SSRC, Research Unit on Ethnic Relations, Working Paper No. 6.

R. Moore, 1975. *Racism and Black Resistance in Britain*. London, Pluto.

R. Moore and T. Wallace, 1974. *Slamming the Door – The Administration of Immigration Control*. London, Martin Robertson.

National Advisory Commission on Civil Disorders, 1968. (Kerner Commission), USA.

National Council for Civil Liberties (NCCL), 1980. *Southall 23 April 1979. The Report of the Unofficial Committee of Enquiry*. London, NCCL.

NCCL, 1980a, *The death of Blair Peach: the supplementary report of the unofficial committee of enquiry*. London, NCCL.

NCCL, 1981. *Civil Disorder and Civil Liberties. Evidence to the Scarman Enquiry*. London, NCCL.

NCCL, 1982. *Cause for Concern*. Nottingham, NCCL.

New Scotland Yard, 1982. 'Recorded Crime in London Rises by 8%' *Press Release*. London, Metropolitan Police.

M. Nikolinakos, 1975. 'Notes towards a general theory of migration in late capitalism', *Race and Class*, Vol. 17, No. 1.

North West Area Young Conservatives, 1974. *Sick Society. A Report on Community Relations in Liverpool*. Liverpool, Young Conservatives.

S. Patterson, 1969. *Immigration and Race Relations in Britain 1960–1967*. London, Oxford University Press and Institute of Race Relations.

C. Peach, 1968. *West Indian migration to Britain*. London, Oxford University Press for Institute of Race Relations.

N. Poulantzas, 1973. *Political power and social classes*. London, New Left Books.

H.E. Ransford, 1969. 'Isolation, Powerlessness and Violence' in A.D. Grimshaw, *ed*.

D. Ransom, 1981. *The Blair Peach Case: Licensed to Kill*. London, Friends of Blair Peach.

J. Rex and R. Moore, 1967. *Race, Community and Conflict: a study of Sparkbrook*. London, Oxford University Press.

J. Rex, 1978. 'Race and the Inner City' in BBC/CRE

A.H. Richmond, 1950. 'Economic Insecurity and Stereotypes as Factors in Colour Prejudice', *The Sociological Review*, Vol XLII, No. 8.

A.H. Richmond, 1954. *Colour Prejudice in Britain: A Study of West Indian Workers in Liverpool, 1941–1951*. London, Routledge and Kegan Paul.

P. Rock, 1973. 'News as an Eternal Recurrence' in S. Cohen and J. Young, *eds.*

E.J.B. Rose *et al*, 1969. *Colour and Citizenship: a Report on British Race Relations* London, Institute of Race Relations/Oxford University Press.

Royal Commission on Criminal Procedure, 1981. *Report*. London, HMSO. Cmnd 8092.

Royal Commission on the Police, 1960. *Interim Report*. London, HMSO, Cmnd 1222.

Royal Commission on the Police. 1962. *Final Report*. London, HMSO, Cmnd 1728.

Royal Commission on Population, 1949. Cmnd 7695.

Rubery, 1978. 'Structured Labour Markets, Worker Organisation and Low-pay', *Cambridge Journal of Economics*, Vol 2, No. 1.

G. Rude, 1970. *Paris and London in the eighteenth century*. London, Collins.

Runnymede Trust and Radical Statistics Race Group, 1980. *Britain's Black Population*. London, Heinemann.

The Right Honourable the Lord Scarman, 1981. *The Brixton Disorders 10–12 April 1981*. London, Pelican.

Schools Council Study, 1980. *Race and Teachers*. New Society, Vol 16.

Secretary of State for the Home Department, 1980. *Serious Disturbances in St Paul's Bristol*. Memorandum placed in the House of Commons Library following the report made to him by the Chief Constable of Avon and Somerset.

R. Segal, 1966. *The Race War*. London, Jonathan Cape.

Select Committee on Race Relations and Immigration, 1972. *Police/Immigrant Relations*. London, HMSO.

Select Committee on Race Relations and Immigration, 1977. *The West Indian Community*. London, HMSO.

C. Seymour-Ure, 1974. *The Political Impact of the Mass Media*, London, Constable.

A. Sivanandan, 1976. 'Race, Class and the State: The Black Experience in Britain', *Race and Class*, Vol XVII, No 4.

N. Smelser, 1962. *The Theory of Collective Behaviour*. London, Routledge.

N. Smelser, 1966. *Social Structure and mobility in economic development*. London. Routledge and Kegan Paul.

N. Smelser, 1970. 'Mechanisms of change and adjustment to change' in B. Hoselitz and W.E. Moore, *eds.*

D.J. Smith, 1974. *Racial Disadvantage in Employment* London. PEP Broadsheet.

D.J. Smith, 1976. *The Facts of Racial Disadvantage: A National Survey*. London, PEP Broadsheet.

D.J. Smith, 1977. *The Facts of Racial Disadvantage – a National Survey: a Summary*. London, Runnymede Trust.

D.J. Smith, and N. McIntosh, 1974. *The Extent of Racial Discrimination*. PEP Broadsheet.

State Research Bulletin, Independent Research Publication Ltd, London.

S. Taylor, 1982. *The National Front in English Politics*. London, Macmillan.

E.P. Thompson, 1971. 'The moral economy of the English crowd in the C18th', *Past and Present*, Vol 50.

E.P. Thompson, 1980. *Writing by Candlelight*. London, Merlin Press.

R.H. Thornton, 1959. *British Shipping*. Cambridge, Cambridge University Press.

C. Tilly, 1972. *Collective Violence in European Perspective*, in I.K. Feierabend et al.

C. Tilly, L. Tilly and R. Tilly, 1975. *The rebellious century 1830–1930*. London, Dent.

H. Tumbor, 1982. *Television and the Riots*, Broadcasting Research Unit.

E. Tupper, 1938. *Seamen's Torch*. London, Hutchinson.

A.I. Waskow, 1966. *From Race Riot to Sit-in, 1919 and the 1960s*. USA, Peter Smith.

White Paper, 1965. *Immigration from the Commonwealth*, London, HMSO, Cmnd 2739.

D.G.T. Williams, 1967. *Keeping the Peace*. London, Hutchinson.

Wise, 1907. *The Law Relating to Riots and Unlawful Assembly*.

H. Young, 1971. *The Treatment of race in the British Press*, in C. Jones et al.

Index